# RICHARD II

T. J. B. SPENCER, sometime Director of the Shakespeare Institute of the University of Birmingham, was the founding editor of the New Penguin Shakespeare, for which he edited both *Romeo and Juliet* and *Hamlet*.

STANLEY WELLS is Honorary President of the Shakespeare Birthplace Trust, Emeritus Professor of Shakespeare Studies at the University of Birmingham, and General Editor of the Oxford Shakespeare. His many books include *Shakespeare: For All Time*, *Shakespeare & Co.*, *Shakespeare, Sex, and Love* and *Great Shakespeare Actors*.

PAUL EDMONDSON is Head of Research at the Shakespeare Birthplace Trust and an Honorary Fellow of the Shakespeare Institute. His publications include *Shakespeare's Sonnets*; *A Year of Shakespeare: Re-living the World Shakespeare Festival*; *Shakespeare Beyond Doubt: Evidence, Argument, Controversy*; *The Shakespeare Circle: An Alternative Biography*; and *Shakespeare: Ideas in Profile*.

# WILLIAM SHAKESPEARE

# Richard II

*Edited with a Commentary by*
STANLEY WELLS
*and with an Introduction by*
PAUL EDMONDSON

PENGUIN BOOKS

PENGUIN CLASSICS

UK | USA | Canada | Ireland | Australia
India | New Zealand | South Africa

Penguin Books is part of the Penguin Random House group of companies
whose addresses can be found at global.penguinrandomhouse.com.

This edition first published in Penguin Books 1969
Reissued in the Penguin Shakespeare series 2008
Reissued in Penguin Classics 2015

001

Set in PostScript Monotype Fournier
Typeset by Palimpsest Book Production Limited, Falkirk, Stirlingshire
Printed in Great Britain by Clays Ltd, St Ives plc

ISBN: 978-0-141-39664-4

www.greenpenguin.co.uk

MIX
Paper from
responsible sources
FSC
www.fsc.org   FSC® C018179

Penguin Random House is committed to a
sustainable future for our business, our readers
and our planet. This book is made from Forest
Stewardship Council® certified paper.

# Contents

*General Introduction* vii
*The Chronology of*
  *Shakespeare's Works* xvii
*Introduction* xxi
*The Play in Performance* lix
*Further Reading* lxxix

RICHARD II 1

*An Account of the Text* 109
*Genealogical Table* 124
*Commentary* 125

# General Introduction

Every play by Shakespeare is unique. This is part of his greatness. A restless and indefatigable experimenter, he moved with a rare amalgamation of artistic integrity and dedicated professionalism from one kind of drama to another. Never shackled by convention, he offered his actors the alternation between serious and comic modes from play to play, and often also within the plays themselves, that the repertory system within which he worked demanded, and which provided an invaluable stimulus to his imagination. Introductions to individual works in this series attempt to define their individuality. But there are common factors that underpin Shakespeare's career.

Nothing in his heredity offers clues to the origins of his genius. His upbringing in Stratford-upon-Avon, where he was born in 1564, was unexceptional. His mother, born Mary Arden, came from a prosperous farming family. Her father chose her as his executor over her eight sisters and his four stepchildren when she was only in her late teens, which suggests that she was of more than average practical ability. Her husband John, a glover, apparently unable to write, was nevertheless a capable businessman and loyal townsfellow, who seems to have fallen on relatively hard times in later life. He would have been brought up as a Catholic, and may have retained

Catholic sympathies, but his son subscribed publicly to Anglicanism throughout his life.

The most important formative influence on Shakespeare was his school. As the son of an alderman who became bailiff (or mayor) in 1568, he had the right to attend the town's grammar school. Here he would have received an education grounded in classical rhetoric and oratory, studying authors such as Ovid, Cicero and Quintilian, and would have been required to read, speak, write and even think in Latin from his early years. This classical education permeates Shakespeare's work from the beginning to the end of his career. It is apparent in the self-conscious classicism of plays of the early 1590s such as the tragedy of *Titus Andronicus*, *The Comedy of Errors*, and the narrative poems *Venus and Adonis* (1592–3) and *The Rape of Lucrece* (1593–4), and is still evident in his latest plays, informing the dream visions of *Pericles* and *Cymbeline* and the masque in *The Tempest*, written between 1607 and 1611. It inflects his literary style throughout his career. In his earliest writings the verse, based on the ten-syllabled, five-beat iambic pentameter, is highly patterned. Rhetorical devices deriving from classical literature, such as alliteration and antithesis, extended similes and elaborate wordplay, abound. Often, as in *Love's Labour's Lost* and *A Midsummer Night's Dream*, he uses rhyming patterns associated with lyric poetry, each line self-contained in sense, the prose as well as the verse employing elaborate figures of speech. Writing at a time of linguistic ferment, Shakespeare frequently imports Latinisms into English, coining words such as abstemious, addiction, incarnadine and adjunct. He was also heavily influenced by the eloquent translations of the Bible in both the Bishops' and the Geneva versions. As his experience grows, his verse and prose become more supple, the patterning less apparent, more ready to accommodate the rhythms of ordinary speech, more colloquial in diction, as in the speeches of the Nurse in *Romeo and Juliet*, the characterful prose of Falstaff, and Hamlet's soliloquies. The effect is of increasing psychological realism, reaching its greatest heights in *Hamlet*, *Othello*, *King Lear*, *Macbeth* and *Antony and Cleopatra*. Gradually he discovered ways of adapting the regular beat of the pentameter to make it an infinitely flexible instrument for matching thought with feeling. Towards the end of his career, in plays such as *The Winter's Tale*, *Cymbeline* and *The Tempest*, he adopts a more highly mannered style, in keeping with the more overtly symbolical and emblematical mode in which he is writing.

So far as we know, Shakespeare lived in Stratford till after his marriage to Anne Hathaway, eight years his senior, in 1582. They had three children: a daughter, Susanna, born in 1583 within six months of their marriage, and twins, Hamnet and Judith, born in 1585. The next seven years of Shakespeare's life are virtually a blank. Theories that he may have been, for instance, a schoolmaster, or a lawyer, or a soldier, or a sailor, lack evidence to support them. The first reference to him in print, in Robert Greene's pamphlet *Greene's Groatsworth of Wit* of 1592, parodies a line from *Henry VI, Part III*, implying that Shakespeare was already an established playwright. It seems likely that at some unknown point after the birth of his twins he joined a theatre company and gained experience as both actor and writer in the provinces and London. The London theatres closed because of plague in 1593 and 1594; and during these years, perhaps recognizing the need for an alternative career, he wrote and published the narrative poems *Venus and Adonis* and *The Rape of Lucrece*. These are the only works we can be certain that Shakespeare himself was responsible for putting into print. Each bears the author's dedication to Henry Wriothesley, Earl of Southampton (1573–1624), the second in warmer terms than the first. Southampton, younger than Shakespeare by ten years, is the only person to whom he personally dedicated works. The Earl may have been a close friend, perhaps even the beautiful and adored young man whom Shakespeare celebrates in his *Sonnets*.

The resumption of playing after the plague years saw the founding of the Lord Chamberlain's Men, a company to which Shakespeare was to belong for the rest of his career, as actor, shareholder and playwright. No other dramatist of the period had so stable a relationship with a single company. Shakespeare knew the actors for whom he was writing and the conditions in which they performed. The permanent company was made up of around twelve to fourteen players, but one actor often played more than one role in a play and additional actors were hired as needed. Led by the tragedian Richard Burbage (1568–1619) and, initially, the comic actor Will Kemp (d. 1603), they rapidly achieved a high reputation, and when King James I succeeded Queen Elizabeth I in 1603 they were renamed as the King's Men. All the women's parts were played by boys; there is no evidence that any female role was ever played by a male actor over the age of about eighteen. Shakespeare had enough confidence in his boys to write for them long and demanding roles such as Rosalind (who, like other heroines of the romantic comedies, is disguised as a boy for much of the action) in *As You Like It*, Lady Macbeth and Cleopatra. But there are far more fathers than mothers, sons than daughters, in his plays, few if any of which require more than the company's normal complement of three or four boys.

The company played primarily in London's public playhouses – there were almost none that we know of in the rest of the country – initially in the Theatre, built in Shoreditch in 1576, and from 1599 in the Globe, on Bankside. These were wooden, more or less circular structures, open to the air, with a thrust stage surmounted by a canopy and jutting into the area where spectators who paid one penny stood, and surrounded by galleries where it was possible to be seated on payment of an additional penny. Though properties such as cauldrons, stocks, artificial trees or beds could indicate locality, there was no representational scenery. Sound effects such as flourishes of trumpets, music both martial and amorous, and accompaniments to songs were provided by the company's musicians. Actors entered through doors in the back wall of the stage. Above it was a balconied area that could represent the walls of a town (as in *King John*), or a castle (as in *Richard II*), and indeed a balcony (as in *Romeo and Juliet*). In 1609 the company also acquired the use of the Blackfriars, a smaller, indoor theatre to which admission was more expensive, and which permitted the use of more spectacular stage effects such as the descent of Jupiter on an eagle in *Cymbeline* and of goddesses in *The Tempest*. And they would frequently perform before the court in royal residences and, on their regular tours into the provinces, in non-theatrical spaces such as inns, guildhalls and the great halls of country houses.

Early in his career Shakespeare may have worked in collaboration, perhaps with Thomas Nashe (1567–c. 1601) in *Henry VI, Part I* and with George Peele (1556–96) in *Titus Andronicus*. And towards the end he collaborated with George Wilkins (*fl.* 1604–8) in *Pericles*, and with his younger colleagues Thomas Middleton (1580–1627), in *Timon of Athens*, and John Fletcher (1579–1625), in *Henry*

*VIII*, *The Two Noble Kinsmen* and the lost play *Cardenio*. Shakespeare's output dwindled in his last years, and he died in 1616 in Stratford, where he owned a fine house, New Place, and much land. His only son had died at the age of eleven, in 1596, and his last descendant died in 1670. New Place was destroyed in the eighteenth century but the other Stratford houses associated with his life are maintained and displayed to the public by the Shakespeare Birthplace Trust.

One of the most remarkable features of Shakespeare's plays is their intellectual and emotional scope. They span a great range from the lightest of comedies, such as *The Two Gentlemen of Verona* and *The Comedy of Errors*, to the profoundest of tragedies, such as *King Lear* and *Macbeth*. He maintained an output of around two plays a year, ringing the changes between comic and serious. All his comedies have serious elements: Shylock, in *The Merchant of Venice*, almost reaches tragic dimensions, and *Measure for Measure* is profoundly serious in its examination of moral problems. Equally, none of his tragedies is without humour: Hamlet is as witty as any of his comic heroes, *Macbeth* has its Porter, and *King Lear* its Fool. His greatest comic character, Falstaff, inhabits the history plays and *Henry V* ends with a marriage, while *Henry VI*, *Part III*, *Richard II* and *Richard III* culminate in the tragic deaths of their protagonists.

Although in performance Shakespeare's characters can give the impression of a superabundant reality, he is not a naturalistic dramatist. None of his plays is explicitly set in his own time. The action of few of them (except for the English histories) is set even partly in England (exceptions are *The Merry Wives of Windsor* and the Induction to *The Taming of the Shrew*). Italy is his favoured location. Most of his principal story-lines derive from printed writings; but the structuring and translation of these narratives into dramatic terms is Shakespeare's own, and he invents much additional material. Most of the plays contain elements of myth and legend, and many derive from ancient or more recent history or from romantic tales of ancient times and faraway places. All reflect his reading, often in close detail. Holinshed's *Chronicles* (1577, revised 1587), a great compendium of English, Scottish and Irish history, provided material for his English history plays. The *Lives of the Noble Grecians and Romans* by the Greek writer Plutarch, finely translated into English from the French by Sir Thomas North in 1579, provided much of the narrative material, and also a mass of verbal detail, for his plays about Roman history. Some plays are closely based on shorter individual works: *As You Like It*, for instance, on the novel *Rosalynde* (1590) by his near-contemporary Thomas Lodge (1558–1625), *The Winter's Tale* on *Pandosto* (1588) by his old rival Robert Greene (1558–92) and *Othello* on a story by the Italian Giraldi Cinthio (1504–73). And the language of his plays is permeated by the Bible, the Book of Common Prayer and the proverbial sayings of his day.

Shakespeare was popular with his contemporaries, but his commitment to the theatre and to the plays in performance is demonstrated by the fact that only about half of his plays appeared in print in his lifetime, in slim paperback volumes known as quartos, so called because they were made from printers' sheets folded twice to form four leaves (eight pages). None of them shows any sign that he was involved in their publication. For him, performance was the primary means of publication. The most frequently reprinted of his works were the non-dramatic poems – the erotic *Venus and Adonis* and the more moralistic *The Rape of Lucrece*. The *Sonnets*, which appeared in 1609, under his name but possibly without his consent, were less successful, perhaps because the vogue for sonnet sequences, which peaked in the 1590s, had passed by then. They were not reprinted until 1640, and then only in garbled form along with poems by other writers. Happily, in 1623, seven years after he died, his colleagues John Heminges (1556–1630) and Henry Condell (d. 1627) published his collected plays, including eighteen that had not previously appeared in print, in the first Folio, whose name derives from the fact that the printers' sheets were folded only once to produce two leaves (four pages). Some of the quarto editions are badly printed, and the fact that some plays exist in two, or even three, early versions creates problems for editors. These are discussed in the Account of the Text in each volume of this series.

Shakespeare's plays continued in the repertoire until the Puritans closed the theatres in 1642. When performances resumed after the Restoration of the monarchy in 1660, many of the plays were not to the taste of the times, especially because their mingling of genres and failure to meet the requirements of poetic justice offended against the dictates of neoclassicism. Some, such as *The Tempest* (changed by John Dryden and William Davenant in 1667 to suit contemporary taste), *King Lear* (to which Nahum Tate gave a happy ending in 1681) and *Richard III* (heavily adapted by Colley Cibber in 1700 as a vehicle for his own talents), were extensively rewritten; others fell into neglect. Slowly they regained their place in the repertoire, and they continued to be reprinted, but it was not until the great actor David Garrick (1717–79) organized a spectacular jubilee in Stratford in 1769 that Shakespeare began to be regarded as a transcendental genius. Garrick's idolatry prefigured the enthusiasm of critics such as Samuel Taylor Coleridge (1772–1834) and William Hazlitt (1778–1830). Gradually Shakespeare's reputation spread abroad, to Germany, America, France and to other European countries.

During the nineteenth century, though the plays were generally still performed in heavily adapted or abbreviated versions, a large body of scholarship and criticism began to amass. Partly as a result of a general swing in education away from the teaching of Greek and Roman texts and towards literature written in English, Shakespeare became the object of intensive study in schools and universities. In the theatre, important turning points were the work in England of two theatre directors, William Poel (1852–1934) and his disciple Harley Granville-Barker (1877–1946), who showed that the application of knowledge, some of it newly acquired, of early staging conditions to performance of the plays could render the original texts viable in terms of the modern theatre. During the twentieth century appreciation of Shakespeare's work, encouraged by the availability of audio, film and video versions of the plays, spread around the world to such an extent that he can now be claimed as a global author.

The influence of Shakespeare's works permeates the English language. Phrases from his plays and poems – 'a tower of strength', 'green-eyed jealousy', 'a foregone conclusion' – are on the lips of people who may never have read him. They have inspired composers of songs, orchestral music and operas; painters and sculptors; poets, novelists and film-makers. Allusions to him appear in pop songs, in advertisements and in television shows. Some of his characters – Romeo and Juliet, Falstaff, Shylock and Hamlet – have acquired mythic status. He is valued for his humanity, his psychological insight, his wit and humour, his lyricism, his mastery of language, his ability to excite, surprise, move and, in the widest sense of the word, entertain audiences. He is the greatest of poets, but he is essentially a dramatic poet. Though his plays have much to offer to readers, they exist fully only in performance. In these volumes we offer individual introductions, notes on language and on specific points of the text, suggestions for further reading and information about how each work has been edited. In addition we include accounts of the ways in which successive generations of interpreters and audiences have responded to challenges and rewards offered by the plays. The Penguin Shakespeare series aspires to remove obstacles to understanding and to make pleasurable the reading of the work of the man who has done more than most to make us understand what it is to be human.

Stanley Wells

# The Chronology of
# Shakespeare's Works

A few of Shakespeare's writings can be fairly precisely dated. An allusion to the Earl of Essex in the chorus to Act V of *Henry V*, for instance, could only have been written in 1599. But for many of the plays we have only vague information, such as the date of publication, which may have occurred long after composition, the date of a performance, which may not have been the first, or a list in Francis Meres's book *Palladis Tamia*, published in 1598, which tells us only that the plays listed there must have been written by that year. The chronology of the early plays is particularly difficult to establish. Not everyone would agree that the first part of *Henry VI* was written after the third, for instance, or *Romeo and Juliet* before *A Midsummer Night's Dream*. The following table is based on the 'Canon and Chronology' section in *William Shakespeare: A Textual Companion*, by Stanley Wells and Gary Taylor, with John Jowett and William Montgomery (1987), where more detailed information and discussion may be found.

| | |
|---|---|
| *The Two Gentlemen of Verona* | 1590–91 |
| *The Taming of the Shrew* | 1590–91 |
| *Henry VI, Part II* | 1591 |
| *Henry VI, Part III* | 1591 |

*Henry VI, Part I* (perhaps with Thomas Nashe)     1592
*Titus Andronicus* (perhaps with George Peele)     1592
*Richard III*                                      1592–3
*Venus and Adonis* (poem)                          1592–3
*The Rape of Lucrece* (poem)                        1593–4
*The Comedy of Errors*                             1594
*Love's Labour's Lost*                             1594–5
*Edward III* (authorship uncertain,     not later than 1595
    not included in this series)       (printed in 1596)
*Richard II*                                       1595
*Romeo and Juliet*                                 1595
*A Midsummer Night's Dream*                         1595
*King John*                                        1596
*The Merchant of Venice*                            1596–7
*Henry IV, Part I*                                 1596–7
*The Merry Wives of Windsor*                        1597–8
*Henry IV, Part II*                                1597–8
*Much Ado About Nothing*                            1598
*Henry V*                                          1598–9
*Julius Caesar*                                    1599
*As You Like It*                                   1599–1600
*Hamlet*                                           1600–1601
*Twelfth Night*                                    1600–1601
'The Phoenix and the Turtle' (poem)               by 1601
*Troilus and Cressida*                             1602
*The Sonnets* (poems)                  1593–1603 and later
*Measure for Measure*                              1603
*A Lover's Complaint* (poem)                        1603–4
*Sir Thomas More* (in part,
    not included in this series)                   1603–4
*Othello*                                          1603–4
*All's Well That Ends Well*                         1604–5
*Timon of Athens* (with Thomas Middleton)          1605
*King Lear*                                         1605–6

| | |
|---|---|
| *Macbeth* (revised by Middleton) | 1606 |
| *Antony and Cleopatra* | 1606 |
| *Pericles* (with George Wilkins) | 1607 |
| *Coriolanus* | 1608 |
| *The Winter's Tale* | 1609 |
| *Cymbeline* | 1610 |
| *The Tempest* | 1611 |
| *Henry VIII* (by Shakespeare and John Fletcher; known in its own time as *All is True*) | 1613 |
| *Cardenio* (by Shakespeare and Fletcher; lost) | 1613 |
| *The Two Noble Kinsmen* (by Shakespeare and Fletcher) | 1613–14 |

# Introduction

Throughout his dramatizations of English history, Shakespeare is fascinated by the personalities of the monarchs who wear the crown. After the violence he depicted in the *Henry VI* plays, and the almost overwhelming manipulation of the audience which he thoroughly and humorously deploys in *Richard III*, he made an altogether new departure in producing *Richard II* for the stage in or around 1595. Here, Shakespeare unravels the system of monarchy and depicts a tortured and morally ambivalent soul wearing a 'hollow crown' (III.2.160) in a more interiorized way than in *Henry VI, Part III*, and to greater tragic effect. There Queen Margaret of the House of Lancaster taunts and mocks another Richard, the Duke of York, with a *paper* crown before ordering him to be beheaded.

*Richard II* is the last of Shakespeare's English history plays to be cast in the form of a tragedy. It begins the succession of plays known usually as his second tetralogy (*Richard II*, *Henry IV, Parts I* and *II* and *Henry V*). They dramatize the events leading up to the start of the Wars of the Roses, which he had already finished writing about in a sequence of three plays on the reign of Henry VI, followed by *Richard III*. *Richard II* is the only one of Shakespeare's history plays (except the co-authored, more pageant-like *Henry VIII* or *All is True*) not to include a battle scene. Rather, it sets in train the events that will precipitate the great bloodshed at Shrewsbury (in *Henry IV, Part I* ), Agincourt (in *Henry V* ) and throughout the *Henry VI* plays. The main action of the play can be summed up in one sentence. Richard II's cousin, Henry Bolingbroke, is banished and returns with strong support, seizes the Crown and unwittingly authorizes Richard to be murdered in prison. The dramatic interest lies in the poetic and emotional transitions which delineate Richard's tragedy. Although no one could claim that *Richard II* is action-packed, the central conflict of the resignation of the Crown is situation enough to change irrevocably the lives of all the characters involved. This is a drama of inner and emotional conflict and, by the end of a successful production, the audience should feel that they too have been changed by what they have witnessed and have arrived at a very different place from where they started.

Richard II (1367–1400) was the last king who could claim direct lineage (through the first-born son) from William the Conqueror. Shakespeare's play presents an image of history not dissimilar to a great, multi-panelled, stained-glass window. 'Everybody in the play (even the horse in the last act) is in passionate relation to the central idea,' wrote John Masefield in 1911, rather like the individual fragments of stained-glass. And the window metaphor helpfully extends in order to illuminate the play's static and religious qualities. There are, on average, more lines per speech in *Richard II* than in any other Shakespeare play. The dramatic impact can be one of reflective stillness. Richard's tragedy includes a vision of himself as God's elected representative who must learn to live in a world which shatters that ideal before him.

Part of his breakdown is therefore to ask searching questions about the meaning of existence. In performance we see the part of the window in which he was depicted wearing the crown become outmoded and quaint. Its colours fade, it ceases to be life-enhancing and it is vandalized irrevocably.

At the heart of this play is the character of Richard himself; there can be no better reason for wanting to stage *Richard II* than there being an actor in the theatre company who has the vocal capability to make the words that Shakespeare puts into the mouth of his King Richard sing. But similar vocal demands will be made on the rest of the cast, too. This is the most operatic of Shakespeare's history plays in which the past is portrayed by an epic lyricism; full vocal and emotional intensity can be brought to almost every line. History and poetry are intertwined, speakers can luxuriate in what they have to say, and to shy away from the intrinsic quality of the language destroys Shakespeare's vision of the past as well as his theatrical dynamic.

Shakespeare's Richard II is initially a vain, self-indulgent and angry man, acting inconsistently on his own whims and then full of self-pity when the world does not conform to his own tyrannical will. As God's elected representative on earth, Richard II embodied the idea of the divine right of kings. The world should conform to his own will, and it can be a short step from this religious and political point of view to plain tyranny. But Shakespeare puts into Richard's mouth some of the most intoxicatingly beautiful language in the entire canon. As he makes his painfully cosseted journey – entirely in verse – towards his deposition, Richard experiences an almost overwhelming breakdown of self and the institution which he supremely represents. The tragedy is that

Richard perseveres with his own world view and persistently refuses to acknowledge an alternative. Shakespeare shows us what happens when Richard's enabling fiction shatters, when he can no longer sustain the dream he has of himself. Like Hamlet, Richard bares to us his own pain of being, unpacking his heart with words (though only once in soliloquy, in Act V, scene 5); we see him, like King Lear, making fatal decisions and struggling to find his way through a self and a kingdom which he has shattered; and like Caliban in *The Tempest*, Richard feels the pain of changing from ruler into subject and cries to dream again. 'Unkinged' and comfortless, 'love to Richard | Is a strange brooch in this all-hating world' (V.5.65–6). He is to be much pitied, but never relieved, and is set free only through being cruelly murdered in prison at the end of the play. Richard's ghost will haunt the conscience of Henry Bolingbroke, through *Henry IV, Parts I* and *II*, and Henry's son, Henry V, on the night before the battle of Agincourt when he prays:

> O not today, think not upon the fault
> My father made in compassing the crown!
> I Richard's body have interrèd new,
> And on it have bestowed more contrite tears
> Than from it issued forcèd drops of blood.
> Five hundred poor I have in yearly pay,
> Who twice a day their withered hands hold up
> Toward heaven, to pardon blood: and I have built
> Two chantries where the sad and solemn priests
> Sing still for Richard's soul. (*Henry V*, IV.1.286–95)

Richard II, like Julius Caesar at the battle of Philippi, is 'mighty yet' (*Julius Caesar*, V.3.94). Henry V's tortured bargain with God, and payment of the poor to pray, seem to work; he is victorious at Agincourt in spite of the unforgettable burden of his own father's guilt.

Just after Richard II has been deposed, the former king stares into a looking-glass, an episode not in any of Shakespeare's sources. Richard has just given away his Crown and needs to see if the divorce he has made between himself and his role has had any noticeable effect on his physical body. In the 2000 Royal Shakespeare Company production (directed by Steven Pimlott), Samuel West stared at this point into a vertically upright coffin which a few scenes later would become his own 'untimely bier' (V.6.52). It is a moment of untimely vanity in which Richard stares at the present, having relinquished his past and consequently erased his future. Shakespeare calls to mind his old friend and rival Christopher Marlowe's play *Doctor Faustus*, in which Faustus is allowed supernaturally to catch a glimpse of Helen of Troy before being condemned to everlasting damnation.

> Was this the face that launched a thousand ships
> And burnt the topless towers of Ilium?
> Sweet Helen, make me immortal with a kiss.
> Her lips sucks forth my soul. See where it flies!
> Come, Helen, come, give me my soul again.
> Here will I dwell, for heaven be in these lips,
> And all is dross that is not Helena.
>     (*Doctor Faustus*, 13.90–96)

Only a comparison with one of the most popular plays of his time, and with the most beautiful woman in history, will serve for Shakespeare to heighten this moment for his king who is no longer royal. Richard has just compared himself to a book, a book of life of which he himself is agent and in which he can read about all of his own sins. He then takes hold of the looking-glass and immediately the audience sees him reading himself:

> No deeper wrinkles yet? Hath sorrow struck
> So many blows upon this face of mine
> And made no deeper wounds? O, flattering glass,
> Like to my followers in prosperity,
> Thou dost beguile me. Was this face the face
> That every day under his household roof
> Did keep ten thousand men? Was this the face
> That like the sun did make beholders wink?
> Is this the face which faced so many follies,
> That was at last outfaced by Bolingbroke?
> A brittle glory shineth in this face.
> As brittle as the glory is the face.
>   (*he throws the glass down*)
> For there it is, cracked in an hundred shivers.
> Mark, silent King, the moral of this sport:
> How soon my sorrow hath destroyed my face.
>   (IV.1.276–90)

It is a supreme episode of gradual self-realization and utter self-indulgence, qualities of which Richard remains king, even when dethroned. From 'No deeper wrinkles', he moves towards an awareness of how brittle were his trappings of majesty. His now absent royal identity is united with the insubstantial illusion he is holding in his hand, which shows the world in reverse. Framed by the edge of the mirror, his face appears to him like a portrait, which he is able to destroy by shattering the glass.

His rhetorical questions emphasize the difference between the king's two bodies, the body politic and the body natural. The body politic never dies as long as the system of monarchy is upheld: the king is dead; long live the king. But here Richard finally realizes that his own body natural, Richard the man, is never again to be associated with that continuum of history, the body politic. When the glass shatters, so too do the final vestiges of Richard's royal persona.

Shakespeare provides a gift to the actor at this moment. The way in which he chooses to break the looking-glass will speak volumes about Richard's state of mind. Does he throw the glass to the floor in a rage, or let it fall incidentally, perhaps indifferently? If deliberately, does he proceed to stamp on it for the line 'there it is, cracked in an hundred shivers'? The choice the actor makes may vary, even during different performances of the same production, but whatever he chooses to do will impact on the audience differently at this crucial moment of severance and breaking of a self. The moment is perhaps comparable to Hamlet setting up for his mother Gertrude 'a glass, | Where [she] may see the inmost part of [herself]' and then proceeding to show her the image of two kings, Old Hamlet and Claudius (*Hamlet*, III.4.20–21). In the 1973 RSC production (directed by John Barton), the entire centre of the mirror was removed and Bolingbroke placed the circular frame over Richard's head, a hollow crown which slipped down around his neck and remained there until the end. The man and his crown became as insubstantial as the reflection in the mirror itself. In the Barton production the roles of Richard and Bolingbroke were alternated between Richard Pasco and Ian Richardson, so the cumulative effect of dual identities through the production's run – reflected, refracted, broken – added particular resonance to this moment. The episode with the mirror is Shakespeare's own poetic and dramatic idea, and it serves as a useful point of departure to consider the possible points of connection between the actual historical Richard and Shakespeare's own lyrical monarch. How is Shakespeare reflecting on history, and reflecting it back to his audience?

\*

The scene is the autumn of 1399. Richard II is deposed after having reigned twenty-two years. Fifty years before his coronation, his great-grandfather Edward II, too, had been deposed and murdered. Such royal tragedies clearly ran in the family. The events that led up to Richard's deposition accrued gradually over a period of time and it is crucial to understand how the chief figures in Richard II's history relate to Shakespeare's play.

Born at Bordeaux on the Feast of Epiphany, or Twelfth Night, in 1367, the second son of Joan of Kent and Edward the Black Prince, Richard spent the first four years of his life in France. He was only ten when he was crowned King of England. We can still see, as Shakespeare no doubt did, Richard's distinguished features in his portrait and on his tomb in Westminster Abbey (on which this book's cover is based): wavy auburn hair, heavy-lidded, slightly drooping eyes, with arched brows, a longish, thin nose, a finely bearded man of medium height. He seems strikingly handsome. A monk from Evesham Abbey records that Richard had a pale, rounded, feminine-looking complexion. At his tender age, Richard was thought unfit to rule and the power behind his throne lay for some years with his uncle John of Gaunt (meaning the Dutch city Ghent), Duke of Lancaster, the oldest surviving son of Edward III. Richard married Anne of Bohemia in 1382 and the marriage seems to have been happy. She died in 1394 and after Richard's death in 1400 they became the first English king and queen to share a tomb. Their marble effigies, commissioned by Richard in 1395, show them holding hands.

Richard survived two major deposition attempts during the course of his reign. The poll taxes levied on the people by Gaunt and his supporters were hugely unpopular and led to the so-called Peasants' Revolt of 1381. Later in the year, Richard and his Parliament were besieged in the Tower of London by Wat Tyler and his followers, who pledged loyalty to Richard but saw his councillors as traitors. Aged only fourteen, Richard skilfully managed to assuage their demands and avoid rebellion. He became unpopular in the mid-1380s because he tried to pursue a policy of peace with France. Thomas Woodstock, the Duke of Gloucester, was among those who wanted to pursue war, as Edward III, Richard's grandfather, had done. The Duke of Gloucester, Henry Bolingbroke (son of John of Gaunt) and Thomas Mowbray, Duke of Norfolk, belonged to a powerful faction of five called the Appellants (the other two were the Earls of Arundel and Warwick). In time this led to the arrest and the arraignment for treason of Richard's Lord Chancellor, members of his Council and his closest advisers. For two or three days towards the end of 1387, Richard was effectively deposed and deprived of his royal authority. After a great struggle, he was forced to preside over the so-called 'Merciless Parliament' (in 1388) which found his followers guilty of treason. At this point, the Duke of Gloucester might have become king, but Henry Bolingbroke, Richard's cousin, led a strong opposition against him.

Richard renewed his coronation oaths in 1388, and the Lords spiritual and temporal again promised their allegiance to him. In 1389, Richard, now twenty-two, called the Great Council of Westminster to explain that he was no longer going to allow his Crown to be controlled by others. The rest of his reign seems to have been dedicated to the reaffirming of his own spiritual and temporal authority as God's elected representative.

Richard's court delighted in feasting, tournaments, luxury of all kinds, and the arts: Geoffrey Chaucer (whose patron was John of Gaunt) was part of his household. Richard commissioned John Gower to write the *Confessio Amantis*. In Shakespeare's imagination, Gower would appear years later as the onstage storyteller of *Pericles*. Richard's lavish taste for clothes ran up a colossal bill of £38,000 for the royal wardrobe in 1397. Parliament demanded that he reduce his personal spending. He invented the handkerchief, a piece of historical trivia through which Mark Rylance generated much comedy in the 2003 Globe Theatre production (for example, dabbing his brow when emotionally overwrought). He married the six-year-old Isabella of Valois (the daughter of Charles VI of France) as his second wife in 1396. Richard was twenty-nine. History shows he was fond of her, that he got on well with children (though childless himself), and the marriage helped to keep the peace with France. Visiting Charles to complete the marriage negotiations, Richard changed his clothes three times, while the French king did not change at all, a sign of a high-minded sense of fashion and power dressing, as well as of a deep-seated neurosis and insecurity on Richard's part.

By 1397, he had succeeded in condemning two of the Appellants as traitors and winning over two more, Henry Bolingbroke and Thomas Mowbray. The Duke of Gloucester died in Calais, murdered, probably at the instigation of Richard. It is the quarrel between Bolingbroke and Mowbray over Gloucester's death that starts

Shakespeare's play. Their tournament at Coventry was due to be held on St Lambert's Day 1398. Shakespeare keeps from us the detail that while Mowbray did not actually kill Gloucester, he seems to have allowed the murderers access to him, and under Richard's orders. Shakespeare never explains to the audience the precise nature of Gloucester's death and leaves it up to them to decide how far, if at all, Richard might be implicated. On 29 September 1399, Richard resigned his throne to Henry Bolingbroke. The deposition, depicted by Shakespeare in Act IV, scene 1, took place in the magnificent, still surviving Westminster Hall, which Richard himself had ordered to be rebuilt just five years earlier. Richard was imprisoned in Pontefract (or Pomfret) Castle and later probably murdered. The chronicler Adam of Usk visited him in prison and records how Richard told him sad stories about the deaths of other kings. Richard, like Shakespeare himself, was clearly interested in history and how he could interpret it:

> For God's sake let us sit upon the ground
> And tell sad stories of the death of kings –
> How some have been deposed, some slain in war,
> Some haunted by the ghosts they have deposed,
> Some poisoned by their wives, some sleeping killed,
> All murdered. (III.2.155–60)

Sometime between 1395 and 1399 Richard commissioned the painting of the Wilton Diptych. You can usually see it on display in the Sainsbury Wing of the National Gallery, its permanent home, and you can view it on the gallery's website (see Further Reading). It was probably intended as a private altarpiece and presents Richard very much as a king enjoying his divine rights, kneeling in adoration of the Virgin and the Christ child, surrounded by angels, and in communion with St John the Baptist, St Edward the Confessor and St Edmund.

Art historians have long puzzled over the many fine nuances of this painting and the questions it raises. For instance, are Richard's hands empty, in anticipation of receiving the St George's flag the Virgin is about to give to him? Has he just given up the St George's flag to the protection of Christ, or is he receiving it as God's elected representative? Or is he at prayer, having a vision of the Madonna and eleven angels? If this is Richard at the time of his coronation, then the figure we see is only ten years old. Or, is it a depiction of the moment of Richard's death, just before he himself is translated into the twelfth angel? Richard wears his insignia of a white hart and so do all the angels: this divinely elected monarch keeps good company. The white hart also appears on the back of the altarpiece, surrounded by gold leaf, as are all the other figures we see depicted. The earliest record of the diptych after Richard's death is in the collection of Charles I in 1639, another king who was ultimately and brutally deposed. In the early eighteenth century it was bought by the Earl of Pembroke and taken to Wilton House (hence its name). In 1929 it was purchased for the National Gallery. The cultural perception of Richard II might be quite different if the altarpiece were to be (more properly) known as the 'Richard and All Angels Diptych'.

As an image, the Wilton Diptych relates closely to the poetic and dramatic characteristics of Shakespeare's play. It looks like a richly illustrated page from a medieval manuscript, transporting the modern viewer back in time to the world which created it. The painting's fine details – its angels' wings, flowers and Richard's robes – are captured in the richest of materials: gold leaf, beaten thinly out, is carefully applied to the oak panels. Ultramarine blue made from lapiṣ lazuli, which had to come all the way from Afghanistan, is used for the Virgin and the angels. Similarly, Shakespeare's play with all of its highly wrought rhetoric and rhyme possesses an archaic quality, densely patterned in its stateliness, as richly evocative of Richard's court for Shakespeare's original audiences as for us today. Through the artistry of the painting, as in the play, Richard is presented with the surety and the divinity of his own kingship. The highly decorated style of the Wilton Diptych is reflected in the play's language.

We probably will never know whether Shakespeare ever saw the Wilton Diptych, but moments in his play seem to recall this portrait of Richard II almost directly. On his return from Ireland in Act III, scene 2 (Richard went to fight the rebels there in 1394 and 1399, the first English king to do so in two hundred years), Richard reassures himself of his own divine protection, even in the face of the mounting popularity of Bolingbroke:

> Not all the water in the rough rude sea
> Can wash the balm off from an anointed king.
> The breath of worldly men cannot depose
> The deputy elected by the Lord.
> For every man that Bolingbroke hath pressed
> To lift shrewd steel against our golden crown,
> God for his Richard hath in heavenly pay
> A glorious angel. Then if angels fight,
> Weak men must fall; for heaven still guards the right.
>      (III.2.54–62)

Here is a vision of a host of angels rushing to Richard's protection in both play and altarpiece. The actor playing

Richard needs to see the angels coming to his aid at this point, and then (importantly) the audience will believe in his belief. Later, in Act V, the Duchess of York asks her son Aumerle:

> Who are the violets now
> That strew the green lap of the new-come spring?
>     (V.2.46–7)

Is she calling to mind the grass-covered, flowery meadow as depicted in the Wilton Diptych?

Most striking is John of Gaunt's great speech when he thinks himself 'a prophet new-inspired' (II.1.31) and delivers a hymn about a lost, ideal image of England:

> This royal throne of kings, this sceptred isle,
> This earth of majesty, this seat of Mars,
> This other Eden – demi-paradise –
> This fortress built by nature for herself
> Against infection and the hand of war,
> This happy breed of men, this little world,
> This precious stone set in the silver sea ... (II.1.40–46)

The top of the flag, the orb, was only rediscovered when the Wilton Diptych was cleaned in 1992. In the middle of it was found a coastline in miniature, a white castle (possibly invoking Richard's white hart emblem again) with two towers and a boat sailing across a 'silver sea'. The material used is silver leaf, but that has become tarnished black over six hundred years. So, Shakespeare's play can be linked quite compellingly to this religious and political treasure of Richard II's reign. Both the play and the altarpiece share qualities of the medieval world they are striving to depict, as well as using powerful images and ideas, captured in the most precious of materials, crafted and wrought by the richest of poetry.

Throughout *Richard II* Shakespeare employs many rhetorical figures, which he would have learned to use at the grammar school in Stratford. To name but a few devices, there are *accumulatio* (listing one detail after another: 'I have no name, no title – | No, not that name was given me at the font – | But 'tis usurped', IV.1.254–6), *divisio* (dividing a discussion into categories: 'Let's talk of graves, of worms, and epitaphs', III.2.145), *chiasmus* (a crossing over of a whole clause as if it were a reflection in a mirror: 'Think not the King did banish thee, | But thou the King', I.3.279–80) and *prosopopoeia* (the personification of abstract nouns such as Death, Time and Grief: 'Conceit is still derived | From some forefather grief', II.2.34–5). Such are some of the verbal colours which Shakespeare uses to paint his scene.

\*

When Shakespeare came to write *Richard II* around 1595, his main source was Raphael Holinshed's *Chronicles* (1577). His next major source was Samuel Daniel's long narrative poem *The First Four Books of the Civil Wars between the Houses of Lancaster and York*, which had just been published. He might also have read in manuscript the anonymous play about Thomas of Woodstock, Duke of Gloucester, written around 1591–5. Shakespeare's narrative begins at the same point as Edward Hall's snappily entitled 1548 work: *The Union of the Two Noble and Illustre Families of Lancaster and York, being long in continual dissension for the crown of this noble realm, with all the acts done in both the times of the princes, both of the one lineage and of the other, beginning at the time of King*

*Henry the Fourth, the first author of this division, and so successively proceeding to the reign of the high and prudent prince King Henry the Eight, the undubitate flower and very heir of both the said lineages.* Two French chronicles from the late fourteenth/early fifteenth century (only available in manuscript during Shakespeare's time) also influenced Shakespeare's creation: Jean Créton's *Histoire du Roi d'Angleterre Richard II* (which is in verse) and the anonymous *Chronique de la Traison et Mort de Richard Deux roi d'Angleterre*. *The Mirror for Magistrates* (1559), an anthology of historical casualties, was background with which Shakespeare was already familiar. The most obvious departures from, and additions to, his major sources include the greater focus he places on John of Gaunt, especially his visit to the Duchess of Gloucester (who also appears in the *Woodstock* play), the garden scene, Sir Piers of Exton presenting Henry IV with Richard's coffin, and all of the female roles.

After completing his two narrative poems *Venus and Adonis* and *The Rape of Lucrece*, published respectively in 1593 and 1594, Shakespeare made another conscious effort to produce a drama entirely in verse. He had done so before for the third and first parts of the Henry VI plays; he would do so only once more, for *King John*. Poetic drama of this kind is an uncompromising artistic choice and demands a highly stylized exchange of dialogue, a measured, controlled and stately way of speaking. In this context, *Richard II* becomes less about characterization, except for that of Richard and Bolingbroke, and more about history distilled through finely crafted poetry as well as eloquently expressed ideas and emotions.

*

It is crucial that characters representing the political factions and source of threat to Richard's Crown are clearly and successfully differentiated. As a history play, as well as a tragedy, its politics are the woof and warp of its dramatic texture, and the audience needs to know how the power struggles are bodied forth as the action unfolds. John of Gaunt, Bolingbroke, Northumberland, his son Harry Percy, the Lords Ross and Willoughby, and the neutral Duke of York, need to be set against the followers of Richard. There is his cousin Aumerle, used by Shakespeare as a significant emotional supporter of Richard (a prototype Horatio to Richard's Hamlet), whom in Act V we see struggling to survive under the new regime. The other supporters of Richard are Bushy, Bagot, Green, the Earl of Salisbury, Sir Stephen Scroop and the Bishop of Carlisle.

On this many peopled stage, Shakespeare does not avoid complexity in the way he suddenly introduces new characters only for short scenes. There is the haunting, chorus-like exchange between the anonymous Welsh Captain and Salisbury about the state of the commonwealth, 'The bay trees in our country are all withered, | And meteors fright the fixèd stars of heaven' (II.4.8–9); there are the gardeners in Act III, scene 4; there is the sudden appearance of Fitzwater, Surrey, the Abbot of Westminster and the Bishop of Carlisle in Act IV, scene 1. At the beginning of this scene, everyone on stage turns against Aumerle and Shakespeare shows us a glimpse of what Henry IV's new government might be like: plenty of people lost in plenty of arguments without really knowing why. There is the sudden appearance of the Duchess of York in Act V, scene 2 for a protracted and comic episode to counterbalance Richard's own tragic realization that follows. Sir Piers of Exton and another man appear for the first time in Act V, scene 4, a short episode which makes explicit Richard's inevitable murder; and there is the Groom, who comes to tell Richard about Henry Bolingbroke's coronation and how he rode through London on 'roan Barbary', Richard's favourite horse (V.5.67–94). In the 1973 RSC production, the Groom was doubled with Bolingbroke himself, a final flourish of the director's (John Barton) interest in reflection, self-splicing and role play. Each of these episodes allows Shakespeare to suspend the main narrative and to add particularities of detail to the complexion of his general commonwealth. In the case of the Welsh Captain, the gardeners and the Groom, Shakespeare is taking pains to show cultural diversity and gives these characters some of the most moving and most memorable lines.

Listen to an audio recording of *Richard II*, and you will hear almost homogeneous feelings of grief permeate all areas of the play, making it one of the greatest expressions of grief in the language. The word 'grief' is used or alluded to more in *Richard II* than in any other Shakespearian work, about thirty-six times. (Incidentally, the work which mentions grief with the second highest frequency is *The Rape of Lucrece*, which Shakespeare had completed and published just before working on *Richard II*.) In the theatre, grief is visually shared and an important part of Shakespeare's physical and emotional characterization.

The Duchess of Gloucester only appears in Act I, scene 2, to grieve the death of her husband with John of Gaunt and to remind us about the royal genealogy:

> Finds brotherhood in thee no sharper spur?
> Hath love in thy old blood no living fire?
> Edward's seven sons, whereof thyself art one,
> Were as seven vials of his sacred blood,
> Or seven fair branches springing from one root. (I.2.9–13)

John of Gaunt blames Richard for Gloucester's death, but allows for the possibility that Richard's cause might have been honourable. Although the Duchess of Gloucester is a small role (and there is every practical reason to double her with one of her niece Queen Isabel's ladies in waiting, as well as with her sister-in-law the Duchess of York, who only appears in Act V), Shakespeare shows a grief well observed through the way the Duchess of Gloucester talks to John of Gaunt. Towards the end of Act I, scene 2, Shakespeare gives his actor a speech full of implied silences and pauses over which she can choose to take as much time as she likes. The Duchess really has said all she has to, but not all she needs to. This is one of the most important qualities of the use of language in *Richard II*. She needs comfort and she needs to be listened to and so she begins, 'Yet one word more' (I.2.58). The promise of brevity is not usually kept by Shakespearian characters, and it is broken here: 'For sorrow ends not when it seemeth done' (I.2.61). Although Shakespeare is composing verse, he captures distress through broken language, implying both the exit of John of Gaunt and movement from the Duchess at the same time:

> Lo, this is all. – Nay, yet depart not so.
> Though this be all, do not so quickly go.
> I shall remember more. Bid him – ah, what? –
> With all good speed at Pleshey visit me. (I.2.63–6)

This halting in her speech paves the way towards Shakespeare's fuller expression of a grief-tormented mind in Hamlet's first soliloquy, five years later:

> That it should come to this –
> But two months dead, nay, not so much, not two!
> So excellent a king . . . (*Hamlet*, I.2.137–9)

The short scene with the Duchess of Gloucester provides the first of many sequences of grief. There follow: the parting of Thomas Mowbray to his life in exile (I.3.154–207), Bolingbroke's to the beginning of his six-year exile (I.3.213–309), the grief of John of Gaunt over 'This blessèd plot, this earth, this realm, this England' (II.1.31–68), the tears of Aumerle during Richard's long speech of surrender (III.3.160–70), and the many moments of grief that Richard himself experiences. Or as he himself laments:

> but still my griefs are mine.
> You may my glories and my state depose,
> But not my griefs. Still am I king of those.
> (IV.1.190–192)

The Duchess of Gloucester's last lines also prefigure the fate of Queen Isabel herself. Gloucester's palace at Pleshey has become like a desolate prison to her:

> But empty lodgings and unfurnished walls,
> Unpeopled offices, untrodden stones,
> . . . Desolate, desolate will I hence and die.
> The last leave of thee takes my weeping eye.
> (I.2.68–9, 73–4)

In Act V, scene 1, Queen Isabel must part painfully from her king and husband and meets him on his way to prison:

To Julius Caesar's ill-erected Tower,
To whose flint bosom my condemnèd lord
Is doomed a prisoner by proud Bolingbroke. (V.1.2–4)

She might have withstood her own grief a little longer,
were she not to be encouraged by Richard to give way
to it (V.1.16–25). Like the Duchess of Gloucester, she is
resigned to a life of lonely grief.

It is Queen Isabel whom Shakespeare uses most readily
to balance the grief of the Duchess of Gloucester. In Act
II, scene 2, the Queen tells her companions Bushy and
Bagot that she is possessed of a 'life-harming heaviness'
(II.2.3), but, like Antonio at the beginning of *The
Merchant of Venice*, she does not know why she is so sad.
She explains that she feels pregnant with grief, over-
whelmed by a terrible sense of presentiment:

> Yet again methinks
> Some unborn sorrow ripe in fortune's womb
> Is coming towards me, and my inward soul
> With nothing trembles. (II.2.9–12)

Shortly afterwards, her language becomes opaque and
fraught with impressionistic and imprecise meaning:

> 'Tis nothing less. Conceit is still derived
> From some forefather grief. Mine is not so,
> For nothing hath begot my something grief,
> Or something hath the nothing that I grieve –
> 'Tis in reversion that I do possess –
> But what it is that is not yet known what,
> I cannot name; 'tis nameless woe, I wot. (II.2.34–40)

Any actor having to remember these lines must be grateful to have that final rhyming couplet as her goal, and also grateful for the entrance of Green.

Three lots of bad news are brought on to the stage in quick succession. Bolingbroke has come back to England and rallied the support of the Earl of Northumberland and others; the Duke of York, Protector while Richard is in Ireland, feels unable to cope with the strain of current events; and an anonymous servingman enters to report the death of the Duchess of Gloucester. The Queen at least is able to connect these events with her own inter-nalized and malignant grief. Her relief at hearing Green's news is palpable. She describes having given birth to her grief, as if she herself was the point of origin for these dire events, after Green tells her that even all the house-hold servants have left Richard and joined ranks with Bolingbroke. It is indeed terrible news, and the actor playing Queen Isabel might discover that she can pause for as long as she likes after Green has delivered his news. There might be a moment of not knowing quite how the Queen is going to react, before she metaphorically gives birth:

> So, Green, thou art the midwife to my woe,
> And Bolingbroke my sorrow's dismal heir.
> Now hath my soul brought forth her prodigy,
> And I, a gasping new-delivered mother,
> Have woe to woe, sorrow to sorrow joined. (II.2.62–6)

These scenes of female grief are not in Shakespeare's source material, nor is the scene with the gardeners (III.4), where again the Queen expresses her grief. Shakespeare puts the state of the commonwealth into the mouths of the three gardeners whom Queen Isabel and her ladies in waiting overhear talking in the garden. These followers are shrewd commentators who turn the literal act of gardening into a potent political metaphor. In performance, it is meaningful to double John of Gaunt, who dies in Act II, scene 1, with one of the gardeners. England has become an unweeded garden, disordered and 'unruly'. It needs followers in the form of gardeners to care for it and restore its sense of place and order. So the Gardener gives orders to one of his men:

> Go thou, and like an executioner
> Cut off the heads of too fast-growing sprays
> That look too lofty in our commonwealth.
> All must be even in our government.
> You thus employed, I will go root away
> The noisome weeds which without profit suck
> The soil's fertility from wholesome flowers. (III.4.33–9)

Shakespeare here depicts the natural democracy of a garden and its gardener, an ultimate symbol of a divine order. On a deeper level, the garden scene serves to undercut the imposed authority of Henry Bolingbroke, who has broken and stolen the natural and divine order of monarchical succession for himself. Queen Isabel, who listens to the gardeners' conversation about the deposing of her husband, comes forward in anger and makes the parallel between the garden and a divine order explicit by comparing the Gardener to 'old Adam's likeness' (III.4.73). Yet it is as if the garden itself is of a symbolic order that is beyond any further kind of disruption. The Queen curses it, weeping, but the Gardener appears to remain unaffected:

> Poor Queen, so that thy state might be no worse
> I would my skill were subject to thy curse. (III.4.102–103)

Where her tears have fallen, he will plant 'a bank of rue, sour herb of grace' (III.4.105). Here the Queen's grief becomes something which is tilled back into the land of England and at the end of the scene the memory of the Queen's tears has been metamorphosed into nothing more than a symbolic herb. The gardeners presumably continue tending the land, rather like the ploughman in W. H. Auden's description of Brueghel's *The Fall of Icarus* in 'Musée des Beaux Arts': 'About suffering they were never wrong, | The Old Masters', and Icarus plunging to his death after flying too close to the sun was for the ploughman, 'not an important failure'.

Shakespeare's focus on the Queen's grief, which he depicts again as she waits to meet Richard on his way to the Tower (V.1.1–15), is matched only by that of her husband. If the Duchess of Gloucester shows how grieving can affect language and the kind of speech which then becomes necessary, if the Queen's grief is laden with the symbolism of childbirth – Richard, like Elizabeth I, produced no heir – then Richard's own grief serves to underpin the way in which he interprets the world and calls into question his own masculinity. On his return from Ireland, Richard imagines himself as the mother of his country, the essential physical and emotional nurturer:

> I weep for joy
> To stand upon my kingdom once again.
> Dear earth, I do salute thee with my hand,
> Though rebels wound thee with their horses' hoofs.
> As a long-parted mother with her child
> Plays fondly with her tears and smiles in meeting,
> So weeping, smiling, greet I thee, my earth,
> And do thee favours with my royal hands. (III.2.4–11)

Although history finally obscures Richard's sexuality, one of the charges levied at him in 1399 was sodomy. It is probable that he felt homosexual attraction to some of his courtiers. One of his closest devotees was Robert de Vere, the Earl of Oxford. The 1978 BBC version leaves the viewer in no doubt about the King's sexual attraction to his favourites: Bushy, Bagot and Green. Although Mark Rylance in the 2003 Globe Theatre production played Richard with boyish self-mockery – his hesitant delivery of the lines unravelling Richard's insecurities and providing not a little humour through the appearance of expedient improvisation – no attempt was made to relate the use of an all-male acting company to the play's possible homoerotic elements. As far as exploring gender, sexuality and power in *Richard II*, the Globe production represented a missed opportunity.

The only direct reference to Richard's sexuality in the play occurs when Bolingbroke orders the execution of Richard's favourites:

> You have misled a prince, a royal king,
> A happy gentleman in blood and lineaments,
> By you unhappied and disfigured clean.
> You have in manner with your sinful hours
> Made a divorce betwixt his Queen and him,
> Broke the possession of a royal bed,
> And stained the beauty of a fair queen's cheeks
> With tears drawn from her eyes by your foul wrongs.
>     (III.1.8–15)

Bolingbroke's words here hint strongly at a physical and sexual relationship between Richard and his friends. It will be up to a production to suggest how far this possible dimension of Richard's personality is explored and how far to leave it as part of Bolingbroke's aggressive and circumstantial accusation. There might have been a telling pause in an earlier scene, for example after Richard's own half-line, 'Ourself and Bushy' (I.4.23), perhaps indicating his particular favouritism of that follower in the presence of Aumerle, Bagot and Green, about thirty lines before Bushy himself enters. For a modern audience, hopefully unwilling to condemn anybody on the basis of their sexuality, Bolingbroke's allegations could lead to an overall impression of terrible injustice. Likewise, if a definite sexual or homoerotic relationship between Richard and his favourites has not been depicted, then the impression of Bolingbroke as a bully and a tyrant would intensify during this moment. Even so, productions do not usually seek very much sympathy for Richard on the grounds of his sexuality. Breaking 'the possession of a royal bed' would also signify quite differently if Queen Isabel were played as a nine-year-old girl, her historical age when the events of the play took place.

Shakespeare's Richard is prone to sudden mood swings; in this he seems to be an accurate reflection of his historical counterpart. Especially, Shakespeare depicts Richard self-indulgently fantasizing about his own despondency, someone who needs to articulate his feelings through self-dramatizing fiction. In Act I, scene 3 we see Richard's arbitrary interruption of Bolingbroke's and Mowbray's tournament. A performance will have to decide just how much pageantry and preliminary build-up there is to this event. The more ceremonial duty is on display, the greater and more contrary Richard's dismissal of it will seem. Fiona Shaw, who played Richard II in the 1995 Royal National Theatre production – 'I am a non-man playing somebody who

perceives himself to be a non-man' – portrayed a flicker
of erotic attraction between Richard and Bolingbroke.
The two engaged in a slow kiss on the lips just before
the tournament began in lines which clearly indicate
whose side Richard is on:

> Cousin of Hereford, as thy cause is right,
> So be thy fortune in this royal fight!
> Farewell, my blood – which if today thou shed,
> Lament we may, but not revenge thee dead. (I.3.55–8)

In Shaw's performance, this became a suggested reason
for Richard's intervention before the tournament begins.
Richard was in love with Bolingbroke and simply could
not bear the thought that he might be killed by Mowbray
– hence the difference in Richard's eventual scale of
punishment for the two men.

Queen Isabel is incredulous over and criticizes Richard's
passivity as he is being taken away to prison; Richard
offers comfort, at least for himself, in the form of another
self-indulgent fantasy, imagining his story being told by
female gossips around a hearth:

> In winter's tedious nights sit by the fire
> With good old folks, and let them tell thee tales
> Of woeful ages long ago betid;
> And ere thou bid goodnight, to quite their griefs
> Tell thou the lamentable tale of me,
> And send the hearers weeping to their beds . . . (V.1.40–45)

Giving Richard a propensity to self-dramatize enables
Shakespeare to use a rich palate of verbal colour for him
to do so. One of the most powerful self-comparisons
in which Richard seeks comfort is with Christ: 'He in

twelve | Found truth in all but one; I, in twelve
thousand, none' (IV.1.170–71). There is, too, Richard's
long meditation about the importance and comfort of
story-telling:

>              Of comfort no man speak.
>    Let's talk of graves, of worms, and epitaphs;
>    Make dust our paper, and with rainy eyes
>    Write sorrow on the bosom of the earth. (III.2.144–7)

At the end of this great speech, Shakespeare makes
wonderful use of monosyllables, a good example of
how musical his poetry can be. The moment bears
comparison with the beginning of the Adagio of Franz
Schubert's (1797–1828) great String Quintet in C Major
(D956). Richard becomes the sound of the short strokes
of a single mournful violin which is played above the
other instruments, and is grounded by the gentle pizzi-
cato of the solitary cello (Shakespeare's own iambic
pentameter):

>    I live with bread, like you; feel want,
>    Taste grief, need friends. Subjected thus,
>    How can you say to me I am a king? (III.2.175–7)

It is striking too how Shakespeare is also able to place
emphasis on that trisyllabic 'sub-jec-ted', which even
when read seems to stutter its way out of Richard's mouth.
But the mood of the moment might be positively
conveyed at the same time.

Later, Shakespeare shows that it is Richard's tendency
to unravel too much through the way he talks that
leads to his eventual deposition. In Act III, scene 3,
Northumberland returns from private conference with

Bolingbroke and Richard assumes that he has been asked to surrender. Theatrically sensitive and adept Richard may be, but here his actions seem to arise more out of his own deep-seated insecurity. Bolingbroke and Northumberland only have to stand by and listen as Richard does their work for them:

> What must the King do now? Must he submit?
> The King shall do it. Must he be deposed?
> The King shall be contented. Must he lose
> The name of king? A God's name, let it go. (III.3.143–6)

Through the process of unravelling himself in this way, Richard surprises himself and the audience by the way he describes his predicted transformation from king into subject. Shakespeare patterns the language with the rhetorical device *anaphora* (the repetition of the same words at the beginning of successive clauses), which, whether spoken slowly or even with seeming indifference, gives a repeated sense of Richard's security slipping away from him towards unknown conclusions:

> I'll give my jewels for a set of beads,
> My gorgeous palace for a hermitage,
> My gay apparel for an almsman's gown,
> My figured goblets for a dish of wood,
> My sceptre for a palmer's walking-staff,
> My subjects for a pair of carvèd saints ... (III.3.147–52)

The transition of thought that Shakespeare gives to the actor playing Richard in each one of these lines is similar in its extraordinary audacity to the moment in *Cymbeline* when Guiderius and Arvigarus sing that:

> Golden lads and girls all must,
> As chimney-sweepers, come to dust.
>            (*Cymbeline*, IV.2.262–3)

But, just as the violin in Schubert's Quintet is determined
and consistent in its gentle expression, here Richard might
be desirous of the fate he sees before him, giving up the
earthly world and becoming even more Christ-like by so
doing.

By Act V, scene 5, Richard's language of self-
expression has become much more metaphysical. His
long, sixty-six-line soliloquy (his only one) is a challenge
to even the greatest of actors. It represents a culmination
of our perceptions of Richard thus far: an acutely intelli-
gent mind, but one which is unable to see very much
beyond its own frames of reference, with a tendency to
over-complicate situations. Here, thought becomes
language and the language itself becomes action. A man
in solitary confinement tries to conjure up imagined action
around him, but realizes that he cannot because of his loneliness. His way of coping without his Crown is to try to
people his prison cell with a kingdom of thoughts, generated from the procreation of his female brain with his male
'father' soul. Richard is learning too late that the self
needs other people in order to survive. Self-reliance on his
kingly status has for him become synonymous with self-
indulgence. The language of his soliloquy testifies to
his over-complicating his understanding of himself. A
successful performance will allow the audience to follow
Richard's difficult ideas and transitions of thought, feeling
sympathy for him in his total loneliness. He still identifies
with Christ:

> For no thought is contented; the better sort,
> As thoughts of things divine, are intermixed
> With scruples, and do set the word itself
> Against the word; as thus: 'Come, little ones';
> And then again,
> 'It is as hard to come as for a camel
> To thread the postern of a small needle's eye.'
> (V.5.11–17)

Richard airs something he considers as a contradiction in the Gospels (and alludes to Matthew 19:14, 24, Mark 10:14, 25 and Luke 18:16, 25). If the Son of God, the Word made flesh (John 1:14), gives conflicting advice, then even a former king cannot be expected to cope with the dire circumstances in which he now finds himself. But the problem still lies in Richard's arrogance, and we hear him create his own philosophical stumbling block because of it. While the Gospels record that 'little ones' (children) are easily admitted into the Kingdom of God, Richard omits the significant detail that it is the *rich* who will find it as difficult to enter as 'for a camel | To thread the postern of a small needle's eye'. Shakespeare leads his Richard through a tortuous labyrinth of thought towards an oblivion of self:

> Sometimes am I king.
> Then treasons make me wish myself a beggar;
> And so I am. Then crushing penury
> Persuades me I was better when a king.
> Then am I kinged again; and by and by
> Think that I am unkinged by Bolingbroke,
> And straight am nothing. But whate'er I be,
> Nor I, nor any man that but man is,

With nothing shall be pleased till he be eased
With being nothing. (*The music plays*) Music do I hear.
   (V.5.32–41)

To modern ears, Richard seems to move beyond a specifically Christian interpretation of the self towards one
which gestures more towards a Buddhist understanding.
What is crucial is that Shakespeare shows one of his most
incorrigible egoists and narcissists realizing that human
happiness might actually begin at the point when the ego
is erased. Far from being incompatible with Christianity,
here is a formerly divine ruler experiencing a slowly
emerging and personal epiphany that 'being nothing' is
a consummation devoutly to be wished, losing his life in
order to save it (Matthew 16:25, Mark 8:35, Luke 9:24).
Momentarily, Richard's language surrenders to silence.
Perhaps he is catching a glimpse of oblivion as the offstage
music intervenes.

The soliloquy then moves on to show Richard's reaction to the music. Shakespeare shows one of his most
lyrical of dramatic and poetic voices proving itself to be
highly sensitive to the

         . . . music of men's lives;
   And here have I the daintiness of ear
   To check time broke in a disordered string,
   But for the concord of my state and time,
   Had not an ear to hear my true time broke.
   I wasted time, and now doth time waste me . . . (V.5.44–9)

The rest of the speech shows Shakespeare at his most
metaphysical. Richard's idea of himself is transformed
into a clock, one of the hands regularly wiping away his
tears, the bell of his heart groaning every hour. And so

his time passes in sadness, while Bolingbroke's moves forward in joy. Shakespeare glances back to Act II, scene 5 of *Henry VI, Part III*, when the King rests during the battle, to wish himself 'unkinged', to divide up time differently and decide how he would spend it. The soliloquy moves through a threat of madness; how close to despair we might see Richard at this point will depend on the production: 'This music mads me. Let it sound no more' (V.5.61). Finally, he recalls the literal situation. Richard reminds himself that someone else is making the music and he is able to think about the feelings and abilities of another person, apart from himself:

> Yet blessing on his heart that gives it me;
> For 'tis a sign of love, and love to Richard
> Is a strange brooch in this all-hating world. (V.5.64–6)

Although Richard returns to a position of abject self-pity, the audience has heard enough to know that his self-knowledge is now greater than it was at the beginning of the scene. The sudden entrance of an ordinary Groom and the irony of his greeting, 'Hail, royal prince!' should be keenly felt in performance. So abrupt and inappropriate is it, that Richard responds immediately on the half-line with 'Thanks, noble peer' (V.5.67). Like King Lear, who imagines he sees 'a soul in bliss' (IV.7.46) in his half-mad, half-recreated state, Richard's sense of self still shows itself to be sufficiently deluded and disconnected from the true state of affairs.

Richard's death is no less self-dramatization than the life we have seen him lead. In performance, he can seem especially heroic as he fights and kills several of his attackers. A king who has eschewed the name of action suddenly seizes a moment of heightened activity, which might be lavishly choreographed, and is seen fighting desperately for his life. Outnumbered he may be, but he is putting up an impressive defence. How far Richard might seek possible martyrdom will depend on the production. Shakespeare makes it clear that he is ready to mete out judgement and condemnation on his attackers, especially Exton: 'That hand shall burn in never-quenching fire | That staggers thus my person' (V.5.108–9). His final words anticipate his own soul's delivery into heaven, where an everlasting throne is waiting for him:

> Mount, mount, my soul. Thy seat is up on high,
> Whilst my gross flesh sinks downward here to die.
>     (V.5.111–12)

Shakespeare lived to see *Richard II* become very popular in print and performance. It was first printed in 1597 and five editions were published in quarto format by 1615. The first three of these omit the splendidly lachrymose and absurd deposition scene (IV.1), which did not appear in print until the fourth Quarto of 1608 with '*new additions of the Parliament Scene, and the deposing of King Richard*'. The earliest recorded performance was on 7 December 1595. Sir Edward Hoby invited Sir Robert Cecil, the Queen's private secretary, to supper and to see 'King Richard present himself to your view'. *Richard II* was still being performed at the Globe as late as 1631. In 1607, *Richard II* was performed on board Captain Keeling's ship, HMS *Dragon*, just off Sierra Leone. The crew were talented enough also to perform *Hamlet*; no doubt they had among them an actor with the right kind of sensibility to play the lyrical English monarch as well as his dramatic Shakespearian heir, the Prince of Denmark. If you can play one of these characters well, you can usually manage the other one, too. John Gielgud made both roles his own. Samuel West graduated from Richard II in 2000 to Hamlet in 2001 (both for the RSC, both directed by Steven Pimlott).

The vogue for the play in Shakespeare's day chimes with the fact that it is among the first of his works to receive literary critical attention. A manuscript by one William Scott, an MP, grandson of Sir Thomas Wyatt and associate of the Earl of Essex, resurfaced in a private country house collection in 2003. It is called 'The Model of Poesy' and is a long aesthetic discourse about poetic technique. Scott also wrote the epitaph for Elizabeth I's champion Sir Henry Lee, himself the dedicatee of Scott's dissertation. Scott compares Shakespeare to Chaucer:

Chaucer's Canterbury Tales (for aught I see) are to be counted with these [i.e. rustic poems, eclogues] and may be named of travellers or pilgrims, for the vulgar persons and for their manner is much after this. The gardener in like sort is with a passing good decorum brought on the stage in that well conceited tragedy of *Richard II*.

Later he goes on to allude to V.2.46–7:

Besides there is much sweetness in the witty conceits, apt sentences, proper allusions and applications to be dispersed in your poem, like so many goodly plots of lilies and violets strewed all over the new springing meadows.

And Scott refers directly to *Richard II* in describing a particular kind of literary grief:

Sometime the person shall be so plunged into the passion of sorrow that he will even forget his sorrow and seem to entertain his hardest fortune with dalliance and sport, as in the very well-penned Tragedy of Rich. the 2d is expressed in the King and the Queen whilst

> 'They play the wantons with their woes'

The correct quotation is 'Or shall we play the wantons with our woes' (III.3.164), but what is important here is that Scott is referring to Richard and Isabel. He is probably combining his theatrical memory of Act V, scene 1 with his own knowledge of the text. Finally, Scott corrects Shakespeare as originally printed. Scott copies out the lines from an early quarto text:

> That when the searching eye of heaven is hid
> Behind the globe that lights the lower world . . .
>     [III.2.37–8]

He goes on to comment: 'one would take it by the placing his words that he should mean that the globe of the earth enlighteneth the lower hemisphere.' He anticipates Sir Thomas Hanmer's 1743 emendation of 'that' to 'and' (38). This Penguin edition interestingly considers Hanmer's emendation as over-simplifying Richard's difficult syntax at this point, and instead inserts a comma (see note in the Commentary):

> That when the searching eye of heaven is hid
> Behind the globe, that lights the lower world . . .
>     (III.2.37–8)

Scott's observations not only provide the insights of a contemporary reader of Shakespeare, but also shed light on the popularity of *Richard II*.

Perhaps the most famous of all performances was given on the afternoon of Saturday, 7 February 1601. It was the eve of the Earl of Essex's ill-fated rebellion against Elizabeth I. The play was thought to be too politically sensitive by Elizabeth I, already sixty-three by the time Shakespeare wrote it, and who would not name her successor until just before she died. The deposition scene was not printed, so it is unlikely that it would have been performed. But on the day before the rebellion, Essex's supporters paid Shakespeare and his fellow-actors to perform *Richard II* at the Globe Theatre. During the subsequent interrogation, one of Shakespeare's colleagues, Augustine Phillips, stated that they had been offered '£2 more than their ordinary to play it'. Phillips's referring to it as 'an old play' has led some critics to suppose that it was not Shakespeare's play which was performed. But 'old' would be quite a justifiable description from a man who had acted in about fourteen new Shakespeare plays over six years. On behalf of the Lord Chamberlain's Men, Phillips might also have been trying to play down the political potency of *Richard II* itself. Besides, William Scott's association with Essex rather supports the notion that it was Shakespeare's play which was performed on this occasion.

The rebellion was a failure, even if the performance had been a success. Six months later, Elizabeth is reported to have said to William Lambarde, her Keeper of the Tower, 'I am Richard II, know ye not that? . . . He that will forget God will also forget his benefactors; this tragedy was played forty times in open streets and houses.'

In these two phrases are inscribed a confession of Elizabeth's own insecurities, the play's power to move audiences with its tragic presentation of a historical figure, and Shakespeare's own political potency and motivation as a playwright. If not for successful rebellion, *Richard II* can be made to speak equally for the Monarchical or Republican cause. Over four hundred years after the death of Elizabeth I, the British monarchy knows perhaps even more acutely than Richard what it means

> To'undeck the pompous body of a king;
> [Make] glory base, and sovereignty a slave;
> Proud majesty, a subject; state, a peasant. (IV.1.249–51)

The plucking out of the heart of monarchy's mystery by many a media-styled Bolingbroke through the second Elizabethan era makes *Richard II* very much a play for our times.

Paul Edmondson

# The Play in Performance

*Richard II* is not an action-packed drama. The overriding dynamic is its poetic presentation of history and human emotion. A touchstone for Shakespeare's still, stately world and the dramatic effect he achieves is provided by the Duchess of Gloucester, lamenting the murder of her husband, a son of Edward III. A close examination of this speech will serve as a way into the play in performance.

> Edward's seven sons, whereof thyself art one,
> Were as seven vials of his sacred blood,
> Or seven fair branches springing from one root.
> Some of those seven are dried by nature's course,
> Some of those branches by the destinies cut.
> But Thomas, my dear lord, my life, my Gloucester,
> One vial full of Edward's sacred blood,
> One flourishing branch of his most royal root,
> Is cracked, and all the precious liquor spilt;
> Is hacked down, and his summer leaves all faded,
> By envy's hand, and murder's bloody axe.
> Ah, Gaunt, his blood was thine! (I.2.11–22)

This is part of a twenty-eight-line speech which illustrates perfectly the play's imaginary and physical world.

The Duchess of Gloucester is painting an emblematic picture, a family tree from which a branch is lopped, her husband Thomas. Shakespeare allows plenty of time for this idea to develop. As well as seven branches, there are seven vials of 'sacred blood', 'sacred' because kingship was an office elected by God. The pictorial image of the family tree grows and resonates through this extract, 'flourishing' and reaching down into England's earth with its royal roots. The blood becomes a 'precious liquor spilt', as though it were wine used in the sacramental rite of Holy Communion. Summer leaves fade and the personifications of envy and murder arrive in the Duchess's imaginary world to wreak destruction. Finally, she turns the entire image on to the present moment with her sudden address to John of Gaunt, her brother-in-law. Fourteen more lines will follow from her before Gaunt speaks.

What about the verbal music of the Duchess's lines? In performance, the challenge of the play's rhetorical and musical patterning constitutes a great part of its dramatic pleasure for the audience. In this speech, repetition of the same words at the beginnings of lines (an example of the rhetorical figure *anaphora*) impresses upon us images and thoughts: 'Some', 'One' and 'Is' (14–20). These three pairs of lines are interrupted by 'But' at line 16. The aural and dramatic impact is intensified through this single line being surrounded by pairs of lines with identical beginnings. Here the repetition of 'my' at the beginning of syntactically climactic clauses (an example of the rhetorical figure *auxesis*) leads to the powerful climax of 'my Gloucester' at the end of the same line. The ends of the lines in this short extract are of equal importance. Working downwards from lines 11 to 18, our eyes (and in the theatre our ears) catch 'one', 'blood', 'root', 'course', 'cut', 'Gloucester', 'blood' and 'root'.

Again, Shakespeare is repeating important words, but this time at the ends of lines (an example of the rhetorical figure *epistrophe*). 'Blood' and 'root' are both monosyllabic, end in a hard consonant and put the actor's mouth into definite and expressive shapes with the reiterated plosive 'bl' as well as the pursing of the lips required to pronounce 'root'. To separate 'blood' and 'root' by the alliterative 'course' and 'cut', and the proper name 'Gloucester', serves to emphasize the severance of 'nature's course' from Gloucester himself, a severance conveyed as much through the musical value of the words as by their actual meanings. Shakespeare's use of rhetoric here combines with the sounds of words to depict irrevocable and brutal change. We move on to catch the different and contrasting 'spilt' and 'faded' at the ends of lines 19 and 20. The image of a 'bloody axe' is related to the immediacy of the Duchess's grief because the vowel sound of 'axe' is similar to that needed for the 'Ah' which follows it. This kind of repetition (an example of the rhetorical figure *anadiplosis*, where the same word is repeated at the end of one line and the beginning of the next) might even evoke the impression of two strokes of the axe, appalling for the Duchess of Gloucester to contemplate, as her husband is felled in her mind's eye. In Act III, scene 4 we will see actual gardeners enter to weed a metaphorically overgrown and unkempt garden of England.

Shakespeare is here turning history into richly described pictures, and this is what constitutes most of the imaginary world of *Richard II*. The Duchess of Gloucester scene can be omitted in performance, with little detriment to the overall plot. You would lose an early scene of mourning, which prefigures all those which are to follow, the effect of the murder on the Duke of

Gloucester's widow, and her accusation that Mowbray is to blame (I.2.47–53). You would also lose the effect that the Duchess of Gloucester's utterances have on John of Gaunt. He, too, will later make his own prophecy about the garden of England, and its decay: 'This royal throne of kings, this sceptred isle' (II.1.40–68). Rich in emblematic language and similar rhetoric, Gaunt's meditation of discontent at once depicts and undercuts an idealized state. It is interesting that in a production which did cut the Duchess of Gloucester (Sir Trevor Nunn's at the Old Vic in 2005), John of Gaunt's famous speech about England was performed as a series of political sound-bites at a media conference and relayed on large television screens. The realization still made the speech emblematic and visual, but allowed its lyrical qualities to shine.

It is not surprising that Sir John Gielgud felt strongly that in this play actors should be cast on account of their different vocal qualities, since long stretches of *Richard II* display similar kinds of rhetorical poetry. Nor is it surprising that for such a verbally brilliant and subtle play, a survey of notable Richards includes actors among the most sensitive to the demands of Shakespearian verse. Perhaps it is because there is an ever-present sense of lyrical regret for a lost world that permeates almost every line, that the role has tended to attract actors with a music-like quality in their vocal resonance.

Time and again critics have praised actors playing Richard for using their voices almost like musical instruments: Edmund Kean in 1815 (possibly the first great Richard since Shakespeare's own time), Charles Kean in 1857, and Sir Frank Benson from 1896 whose Richard, according to C. E. Montague's review, portrayed all the responsiveness and sensitivity of an artist. Together with

Hamlet, Gielgud made the role very much his own for the twentieth century. The 1960 Caedmon audio recording is still a pleasure to listen to and documents the immense success Gielgud had in a role he first performed in 1929, directed by Harcourt Williams (and again in 1937, in a production directed by Gielgud himself). Sir Michael Redgrave portrayed a weak and effeminate, though beautifully spoken, Richard for Anthony Quayle's tetralogy at Stratford in 1951 (the Festival of Britain year). Paul Scofield, with his unmistakably rich bass timbre, was directed by Gielgud in 1952 for Tennant Productions (in Stratford and London). Sir Ian McKellen was praised for the direct simplicity he brought to the verse-speaking for the Prospect Company's 1968 production, directed by Richard Cottrell. A year later, McKellen went on to alternate the role with Christopher Marlowe's Edward II. The self-evident homosexuality of the latter, however, did not inform his interpretation of Richard, which was focused on the family and portrayed genuine affection for Queen Isabel.

Ian Richardson and Richard Pasco famously alternated the roles of Richard and Bolingbroke in John Barton's 1973 Royal Shakespeare Company production. Their acting styles changed the central dynamic, depending on whose turn it was to play the King. Richardson brought a cool and rational sensibility to the role; Pasco was more romantic and impetuous. Depending on who played Richard, England's affairs under Bolingbroke were going to be managed very differently in the new regime. Sir Derek Jacobi's finely detailed and overtly homosexual portrayal can be seen in David Giles's 1978 BBC television version. Jeremy Irons (RSC, 1986, directed by Barry Kyle), Michael Pennington (English Shakespeare Company, 1987, directed by Michael Bogdanov) and Alex

Jennings (RSC, 1990, directed by Ron Daniels) all enjoyed success in the role, and all are actors who are especially noted for their vocal qualities.

Fiona Shaw brought a distinctive kind of interiorized neuroticism to her passionate interpretation for Deborah Warner's 1995 Royal National Theatre production (filmed for television in 1997). Shaw's Richard created even more space for the portrayal of the King's incorrigible self-indulgence; her own femininity automatically accentuated Richard's own, even though the production was not primarily concerned with Richard's sexuality. Samuel West brought a clipped intellectualism to bear on the role in Steven Pimlott's sparse production (RSC, 2000). But West's steely and frosty delivery of the poetry was moving none the less. Here was a man isolated by his own intelligence and irony. Mark Rylance's childlike Richard fooled his way through the role (though sometimes at the expense of the poetic resonance and pathos) at the Globe Theatre in 2003 (broadcast on BBC4, January 2004), and attempted to make our laughter part of the pity.

Kevin Spacey brought a carefully balanced sense of a corporate, businesslike identity to Richard in Sir Trevor Nunn's 2005 production for the Old Vic Theatre. By the end, his Richard had been replaced by a Bolingbroke (Ben Miles) keen to streamline his monarchical identity even further. Henry IV's concluding, kingly procession had distinctly fewer ceremonial trappings; his political game had a self-consciously lower profile, no doubt a response to Henry's own sense of guilt-ridden angst. But neither Spacey nor Miles was any less lyrical as a result of the production's anti-sentimentalist viewpoint.

From the first scene, Richard's personality and his power are bound inextricably to his language. He is silken tongued and in complete control. 'Which then our leisure would not let us hear' (I.1.5) is a languorously musical line. Later we hear from Richard's uncle, the Duke of York, that Richard's court surrounds him with 'Lascivious metres' (II.1.19). Richard is also self-consciously poetic for political effect. Just before the entrance of Bolingbroke and Mowbray we hear Richard's imagination anticipate the scene about to take place:

> Face to face,
> And frowning brow to brow, ourselves will hear
> The accuser and the accusèd freely speak.
> High-stomached are they both, and full of ire;
> In rage, deaf as the sea, hasty as fire. (I.1.15–19)

Many a Richard has made it clear to his audience just how much he relishes sitting on the throne and presiding over this disagreement. Richard's 'How high a pitch his resolution soars!' (I.1.109) was spoken by Jacobi (BBC, 1978) with delight; West (RSC, 2000) uttered the line with the full weight of an analytical intellect. It is an early indication of the nature of the relationship between Richard and Bolingbroke. As a moment of off-handed contrast with Bolingbroke's serious utterances it can easily generate laughter in performance, as well as serve to underline an audience's possible lack of sympathy for Richard. He can be as thoroughly dislikable as the actor may choose in the first two acts, the better to contrast with the depiction of his human sufferings from Act III onwards.

The more stage attention that is lavished on the preparation for the duel itself (I.3), the more outrageous Richard's interruption of it will seem. The scene also creates space to show how far Richard himself might be implicated in Gloucester's murder. McKellen (Prospect,

1968) left the audience in no doubt that his Richard was guilty as he took his throne at the tournament. The order of the first two scenes of that production was reversed, so that the audience was already suspicious of Mowbray. The text calls for a ceremonial entrance; the scene can seem pageant-like (I.3.6). Barton's production (RSC, 1973) even included chivalric-looking hobby-horses for Bolingbroke and Mowbray to ride, as though they really were about to joust. The stage may be especially reconfigured to create the tournament space, but the overall impression remains one of stillness, as the combatants are ceremoniously announced and prepare to fight.

Dramatic tension can intensify as the duel approaches, and the audience may even see the beginning of the combat before Richard interrupts. The throwing down of his warder (I.3.117) is the single most significant physical action that has occurred thus far. The amount of time that Richard remains offstage after the '*long flourish*' to consult his nobles about what should happen to the combatants (I.3.122) will give some indication as to whether his decision to interrupt the tournament was premeditated and his ensuing judgement predetermined, or whether he is acting more out of genuine expediency and fear for his cousin's life, as Shaw managed to convey (1997 film version of RNT, 1995).

A production will need to decide from which point (if any) the audience will be invited to feel an increasing sympathy for Richard. The Queen's scene of ominous grief (II.2), the return of the banished Bolingbroke and the emerging organization of the rebels against Richard (II.3) lead up to Richard's return from the Irish wars (III.2), when the stately behaviour of the King himself reminds us of the kind of world that is already passing. In Warner's production (1997 film version of RNT, 1995), the scene takes place on a brilliant white, otherworldly looking beach. The Bishop of Carlisle gives Richard Holy Communion, a cup symbolic of the King's gradually intensifying suffering. Interestingly, Act III, scene 2 also marks the beginning of Richard's own imaginary and gradual overthrow. The actor will need to show the audience how far he truly believes in – or even imagines seeing – the glorious angels that God will send to aid him in his fight against Bolingbroke (III.2.58–62). There are tears trickling down Shaw's cheeks for 'Too well, too well thou tellest a tale so ill' (III.2.121).

The scene parallels Act II, scene 2. There Queen Isabel received a succession of bad news and metaphorically gives birth to grief; here Richard is on the receiving end. Richard's way of managing the situation is to resign himself to it completely. Perhaps Sir Stephen Scroop gives Richard the idea for his lament about 'the death of kings' (III.2.156) with the line: 'And lie full low, graved in the *hollow ground*' (my italics) (III.2.140). Twenty lines later, Richard starts a lament of abject resignation in which he mentions the king's 'hollow crown' (III.2.160). Holding his own 'hollow crown' in his left hand, West (RSC, 2000) dropped a handful of dust through it with his right during this (III.2.144–77). It was as if seeing this ordinary dust slip through his fingers reminded West's Richard of his own ordinary, monosyllabic mortality:

> I live with bread, like you; feel want,
> Taste grief, need friends. (III.2.175–6)

Emphatic pity can be brought to that word 'need' (as Shaw performs it). McKellen was clear that his shattering and anguished delivery of 'need friends' was the turning point in the audience's sympathy for Richard. If we had

tears, we could prepare to shed them from hereon. The
audience might be invited to recall this beginning of
Richard's sufferings when he contemplates his tragic fate
even more intently in prison, just before his death, and
realizes that:

> . . . love to Richard
> Is a strange brooch in this all-hating world. (V.5.65–6)

It is during the next scene that the tide of sympathy
can begin to turn even more in Richard's favour. A
production will need to decide how far it wants to
show Richard as the author of his own undoing.
'Northumberland comes back from Bolingbroke'
(III.3.142) is a key moment because it is the reappear-
ance of Northumberland that provokes Richard's self-
unravelling:

> What must the King do now? Must he submit?
> The King shall do it. Must he be deposed?
> The King shall be contented. Must he lose
> The name of king? A God's name, let it go. (III.3.143–6)

Jacobi (BBC, 1978) said some of this speech privately to
Aumerle and his followers on the top of the battlements,
emphasizing 'now', as though his King had already done
more than could be expected. Rylance (Globe, 2003,
broadcast on BBC4 in January 2004) spoke the lines
publicly as no more than a necessary form of words that
he rushed through with as much seeming indifference as
possible. Both interpretations convey an inner sense of
pain but in very different ways. Some Richards might
seem desirous to let go of all their pomp (III.3.148–52),
the better to embrace a simple, more Christ-like life;

others may in the same lines express too much love for a world they do not want to leave behind. Rylance's Richard was like a spoiled child to whom nobody had ever refused anything. He rushed through these lines almost sarcastically, which meant that, surprisingly –

> And my large kingdom for a little grave,
> A little, little grave, an obscure grave (III.3.153–4)

– provoked laughter. Rylance paused after each 'little grave', creating the impression that he was improvising the lines for comic effect.

Shakespeare's artistry throughout the play also provides imagistic cues for performance. We begin with 'sacrificing Abel's' cries at the beginning (Bolingbroke, referring to the murder of the Duke of Gloucester, I.1.104) and end with Cain wandering 'thorough shades of night' (Bolingbroke, referring to Sir Piers of Exton's murder of Richard, V.6.43). We start with the murder of Gloucester and we end with the murder of Richard himself. Between this double reference to the Bible's first murder is the tragedy of Richard himself. He compares himself to Christ (either through references to Judas, III.2.132, Pontius Pilate, IV.1.238–9, or directly, IV.1.169–71, 240), which might inform the design of a production. Kyle's production (RSC, 1986) was designed by William Dudley to look like an illuminated medieval manuscript: a Book of Hours with cathedral-like fittings, which served to locate Richard's self-dramatizing in an ecclesiastical context. The rich excess of colours and textures conveyed the impression of a epic pageant, evoking all the powerful mythical and historical associations that inform *Richard II*'s imaginary world. In contrast, Barton's production (RSC, 1973) engaged with the play's muscular theatricality. The interpretation was as much about the process of theatre itself as about the tragedy of Richard. To play at being the king for Barton meant above all to heighten your awareness of mortality and to expose worldly power as mere pretence.

Richard also compares himself to Phaethon (III.3.178), the son of Apollo (also known as Phoebus):

> Down, down I come like glistering Phaethon,
> Wanting the manage of unruly jades.
> In the base-court – base-court, where kings grow base
> To come at traitors' calls, and do them grace.
> In the base-court. Come down – down court, down King,
> For night-owls shriek where mounting larks should sing.
>     (III.3.178–83)

In the story from Ovid's *Metamorphoses* Phaethon rides out on his father's, the sun-god's, chariot to make the sun rise. He dashes across the sky, forms the Milky Way and scorches the earth, but cannot control the horses. Zeus sends a thunderbolt which kills Phaethon. His sisters are turned into poplar trees.

Shakespeare's use of imagery here coincides with definite dramatic action. Richard, like Phaethon, descends, presumably from the upper playing space in the original theatre (and from 1599 in the Globe). Perhaps still aglow with a sense of his absolute royal power (though he knows it is a case of sunset rather than dawn) he may feel ready to scorch the earth, Bolingbroke and his followers, but, like Phaethon, he is also hurtling inevitably towards a tragic outcome, heading downwards in more ways than one. The moment marks the beginning of his emotional descent and eventual deposition. In the following scene, the whole stage, the state of England, is metamorphosed into a garden, and Queen Isabel's tears, we are told, mark the spot where a 'bank of rue' shall grow (III.4.105), if not a poplar tree. For the actor playing Richard, 'glistering Phaethon' can be a defining moment, marking the transition we see in Richard from a king to an ordinary and much to be pitied man. Barton's production (RSC, 1973) used the striking image of Richard's sun-like costume at precisely this moment; his arms opened out to reveal the full extent of generously pleated golden sleeves. Jacobi (BBC, 1978) is on fire with passionate anger and tragic resignation at this point. Just eleven lines later, Shakespeare's artistic vision again co-incides with a gift for the actor when we hear Richard's contrasting 'Up, cousin, up' (III.3.194), to Bolingbroke. Dramatically, the episode echoes Richard descending from his throne to embrace Bolingbroke just before the tournament at Coventry (I.3.54). Richard will not 'mount' again until he faces death (V.5.111–12).

In the deposition scene, the image of Bolingbroke being raised up and Richard being lowered (if not falling) down is given fuller expression. Physical movement required by the text resonates powerfully through the verbally active wordplay. The manner in which Richard enters Act IV, scene 1 will set the tone for the central occurrence: the giving up of his crown to Bolingbroke. West (RSC, 2000) self-mockingly entered whistling the British national anthem, 'God Save the King', cloaked in the English flag of St George. Shaw (1997 film version of RNT, 1995) entered almost imperceptibly, delivering Richard's first line – 'Alack, why am I sent for to a king' (IV.1.162) – as though in mid-sentence. Rylance (Globe, 2003) entered with a winning and gentleman-like humility, but raising a sarcastically induced laugh on the line: 'Yet I well remember | The favours of these men. Were they

not mine?' (IV.1.167–8). West called Bolingbroke over
towards the crown as one might playfully call a dog:
'Here, cousin' (IV.1.181, sounding like 'Here, boy'); Shaw
gave the impression of a game the two of them might
have played as children, patting and clapping her hands,
and then offering Bolingbroke the crown as though it
were merely his turn to wear it now.

Shakespeare seems careful to choreograph an emblematic moment of history: Richard and Bolingbroke each
hold the crown at the same time. There is a temporary
moment of equality as Richard speaks the following
words, and their respective fortunes are changed before
our eyes and ears:

> Here, cousin –
> On this side, my hand; and on that side, thine.
> Now is this golden crown like a deep well
> That owes two buckets, filling one another,
> The emptier ever dancing in the air,
> The other down, unseen, and full of water.
> That bucket down and full of tears am I,
> Drinking my griefs whilst you mount up on high.
> (IV.1.181–8)

Shaw chanted this last line, again recalling a childhood
game. Richard's powerful use of *antimetabole* (a rhetorical figure that symmetrically changes the order of words)
– 'Ay, no. No, ay' (IV.1.200) – allows the actor space for
physical gesture and emotional contrast in just four words.
Here is an expression of the political reshaping of English
monarchical succession in miniature, and it is equally
possible for the actors playing Richard to indulge themselves in pauses for thought, as to rush through the line
quickly in an attempt to rid themselves of an idea too

terrible to contemplate. Rylance presented the crown, took it back, and re-presented it. It was a painful moment of maturing for his Richard. The excess of Richard's verbal control throughout the rest of this scene usually builds up to an explosion of anger directed towards the Earl of Northumberland, who dares to interrupt Richard's self-dramatization (IV.1.221–53). For the audience, it can be satisfying to see Richard at least getting a little of his own back, even though it is too little, too late.

Among all this ever-mounting suffering, Shakespeare also allows space for humour. Some of it accrues around the presentation of Richard himself. There is opportunity for gentle sarcasm, achieved partly through the use of rhyming couplets and the reactions of those onstage to what Richard says. Take, for example, Richard's attempt to make a joke and gently mock the emotional intensity of Bolingbroke and Mowbray during their opening argument:

> Forget, forgive, conclude, and be agreed;
> Our doctors say this is no month to bleed.
>   (*To John of Gaunt*)
> Good uncle, let this end where it begun.
> We'll calm the Duke of Norfolk, you your son.
>   (I.1.156–9)

The portrayal of Richard's sheer nastiness is also bolstered by humour, especially in relation to John of Gaunt. On hearing that his uncle is dying, Richard outrageously plans to take his estate to help fund the war in Ireland. The humour lies not only in the audacity of Richard's intention, but also in the divinely elected and absolutist monarch's view of, and relationship to, God:

Now put it, God, in the physician's mind
To help him to his grave immediately!
The lining of his coffers shall make coats
To deck our soldiers for these Irish wars.
Come, gentlemen, let's all go visit him.
Pray God we may make haste and come too late!
        (I.4.59–64)

In the following scene, the dying Gaunt makes some
excessive puns on his own name (II.1.73–83) which, if
not intended by him to be amusing, are made so by
Richard's 'Can sick men play so nicely with their names?'
(II.1.84). A little later, Richard can shock the audience
into more laughter with his inappropriate approach to
the prayer he makes in response to the news of Gaunt's
death:

The ripest fruit first falls, and so doth he.
His time is spent, our pilgrimage must be.
So much for that. Now for our Irish wars. (II.1.153–5)

The slower the delivery of the first two of these lines,
the more emphasis a production may place on everyone
present on stage praying with Richard (as in the 1978
BBC production, for example) and the longer the pause
after 'be', the more intense the satirical effect. Just after
this comes the Duke of York's twenty-three-line objec-
tion to Richard's seizing of Gaunt's estate. Richard interrupts his uncle briefly in a half-line, which again may
generate laughter: 'Why, uncle, what's the matter?'
(II.1.186). All of these opportunities for humour in the
role of Richard are part of Shakespeare's way of showing
the King in ascendancy before his fall.

In a similar vein is the extended, comic episode with

the Duke and Duchess of York and their son Aumerle over two scenes (V. 2 and V. 3). Here, though, the humour accrues around the figure of Henry IV. It is the first real test of his kingship, and Shakespeare goes out of his way to make the pleading of the Duchess of York for her son's life comic. Humour here helps to establish the ascendancy of the newly created monarch. Henry IV himself observes:

> Our scene is altered from a serious thing,
> And now changed to 'The Beggar and the King'.
>   (V.3.78–9)

The space for comedy is partly achieved through the introduction of a new and female role very late in the play; the audience is suddenly presented with a new direction, a change of tone. Her role can be doubled with the Duchess of Gloucester (Paola Dionisotti played both for Warner in 1995, for example). As well as the race between the Duke, the Duchess and her son to reach the King, there is the comic business for the actor playing York to get into his riding boots (V.2.84–111). 'If you revive King Richard,' wrote the Shakespeare scholar George Steevens to the actor David Garrick in 1773, 'I beg that proper regard may be paid to old *puss in boots*, who arrives so hastily in the fifth act.' The Duke of York sets off before his son, but arrives after him. Once all three have arrived to plead on their knees before Henry IV (the mother and son for forgiveness, the father for filial condemnation), there is the Duchess of York's obsessive wordplay on 'pardon', and the Duke's mockery of her: 'Speak it in French, King: say "Pardonne-moi"' (V.3.111–129). The episode can suddenly become serious, though, within a single line, an effect achieved by David Troughton's

Henry IV (RSC, 2000), who allowed self-condemnation
to shine through his reply to the Duchess: 'I pardon him
[*pause to reflect*] as God shall pardon me' (V.3.130). Sir
Frank Benson (Shakespeare Memorial Theatre, 1901) and
Sir John Gielgud (Queen's Theatre, 1937) omitted the
Duchess of York scenes (though they were included in
1929 when Gielgud played Richard for Harcourt Williams
at the Old Vic). As Harley Granville-Barker had noted,
it is important to keep this episode intact since it serves
to contrast Richard's parting with Queen Isabel (V.1) and
bridges the gap between Richard's journey to prison and
his philosophical meditations in solitary confinement (V.5).

The closing moments will differ depending on whether
or not *Richard II* is being performed as the first part of
a tetralogy. A good example of a great tragic ending can
be cited from Barton's production (RSC, 1973). The
figure of Shakespeare, who had also appeared at the start,
entered to crown Henry IV. The King's court gathered
around him and he was invested in the coronation robes,
with his back to the audience. Two courtiers remained
beside him. Drums rolled. They pulled back their hoods
to reveal themselves as Richardson and Pasco, who
performed Bolingbroke and Richard. The kingly figure
between them was turned to reveal empty robes, a hollow
crown, in which death ever keeps his court.

A concluding example from Steven Pimlott's *Richard
II* (RSC, 2000) serves to show how the play might end
if staged as part one of a tetralogy. For Pimlott, *Richard
II* marked the start of the RSC's 'This England' season,
in which both of Shakespeare's tetralogies were to be
performed. Pimlott's production found it difficult to know
how to finish, and the ending changed several times before
press night. Eventually, the show decided to end with the
newly crowned king speaking the first line of *Henry IV*,

*Part I* ('So shaken as we are, so wan with care') while enthroned on top of Richard II's coffin. But there was another ending, too, during the production's week of previews. Seated in the same position, Henry looked towards the audience and cried out suddenly and terrifyingly. Here was all the guilt, anguish and total pain for an isolated and lonely king. It was like seeing a living tableau of Francis Bacon's painting *Study after Velasquez's portrait of Pope Innocent X*: the Pope grips the arm of his throne and screams. Poetry, history and politics finally gave way to expressionist despair. Blackout.

Paul Edmondson

# Further Reading

## EDITIONS

Major editions of *Richard II* include Andrew Gurr's New Cambridge edition (1984), Peter Ure's Arden edition (1956) and Charles R. Forker's Arden Third Series edition (2002). Forker's edition is particularly useful on the play's historical context, sources and language. The discussion of rhetorical figures included in this Penguin Introduction is indebted to Forker's study. All of these editions base their texts most closely on the 1597 Quarto. Forker believes that 'Q is apparently the text closest to Shakespeare's holograph and many scholars believe that it may even have been printed directly from it.' By necessity, editions usually look to the first Folio of 1623 for the great deposition scene (the fourth Quarto of 1608 printed a less satisfactory version), which was omitted from the play's earliest printing. Matthew Black's New Variorum edition (1955) includes useful material from previous commentaries.

## CRITICISM

Forker's *Richard II* in a series called 'Shakespeare: The Critical Tradition' (1998) reprints a generous selection of criticism from 1780 to 1918. There are theatre reviews (for example William Hazlitt's (1815) of Edmund Kean and C. E. Montague's (1899) of F. R. Benson), and observations on the play in general (for example Samuel Taylor Coleridge's important 1813 lecture and John Masefield's 1911 overview). A tightly structured overview of criticism is represented by Martin Coyle's commentary on the play's reception for the 'Icon Critical Guides' series (1998). A collection of essays from the last thirty years of the twentieth century is presented by Kirby Farrell in *Critical Essays on Shakespeare's 'Richard II'* (1999). James R. Simeon reconsiders the quality of the play's speech-acts through Bakhtinian theory in *Word Against Word: Shakespearean Utterance* (2002). An elegantly engaged overview of the play is represented by Margaret Healy's *William Shakespeare: 'Richard II'* in the 'Writers and their Work' series (1998).

## HISTORY AND POLITICS

The politics of *Richard II* have increasingly become a focus of criticism since around 1970. Michael Manheim's *The Weak King Dilemma in the Shakespearean History Play* (1973) discusses the play in the same context as Christopher Marlowe's *Edward II* and the anonymous *Woodstock* as a critique about 'the burden of monarchy'. H. M. Richmond's *Shakespeare's Political Plays* (1977) focuses on the play's political dynamics, rather than on the tragedy of Richard. For Leonard Tennenhouse in *Power on Display: The Politics of Shakespeare's Genres* (1979), the play dramatizes the effects of the 'failure to exercise force'. Alexander Leggatt's *Shakespeare's Political Drama: The History Plays and the Roman Plays* (1988) provides as good an overview as one could hope for of Shakespeare's political lens.

How are the play's politics understood? E. M. W. Tillyard's highly influential *Shakespeare's History Plays* (1944) and Lily B. Campbell's *Shakespeare's 'Histories': Mirrors of Elizabethan Policy* (1965) present what Campbell calls 'a dominant political pattern characteristic of the political philosophy of his age', in which events are providentially determined. Providentiality has been called strongly into question, most cogently by H. A. Kelly's *Divine Providence in the England of Shakespeare's Histories* (1978) and by Jonathan Hart in *Theater and World: The Problematics of Shakespeare's History* (1992): 'In the second tetralogy Shakespeare represents something akin to what in *The History of the World* Walter Raleigh calls the realm of secondary causes, a fallen world in which the search for meaning in the relation of cause and effect remains for ever uncertain.' Most critics would accept the politics of the play are of Shakespeare's time, rather than of Richard II's. Tillyard did not, and his influence can be felt in Graham Holderness's *Shakespeare Recycled: The Making of Historical Drama* (1992). Peter Saccio's *Shakespeare's English Kings: History, Chronicle, and Drama* (1977) examines the differences between medieval history as we now understand it and Shakespeare's versions of that history. Wolfgang Iser's *Staging Politics: The Lasting Impact of Shakespeare's Histories* (1993) presents *Richard II* in a context of Shakespeare reacting to 'historical actuality, not history itself', a deepening dislocation with a medieval past and the attempts to control an ever ambiguous future. Barbara Hodgdon's *The End Crowns All: Closure and Contradiction in Shakespeare's History* (1991) explores connections between Richard and the Earl of Essex. The manuscript of William Scott's 'The Model of Poesy' referred to in this Penguin Introduction can be consulted in the British Library.

The discussion in this Penguin introduction of the historical Richard, including the consideration of the Wilton Diptych in relation to Shakespeare's imagination, as well as Richard's identity, is indebted to Dillian Gordon's *Making and Meaning: The Wilton Diptych* (1993), and especially to Caroline M. Barron's essay 'Richard II: Image and Reality', included in that volume. The Wilton Diptych itself can be viewed in the National Gallery and on its website (www.nationalgallery.org.uk). Gwilym Dodd's collection of essays by a variety of historians, *The Reign of Richard II* (2000), provides fresh insights into Richard's reign. This volume also contains around thirty illustrations, including Richard's portrait and effigy in Westminster Abbey, his statue in York Minster, the interior of Westminster Hall, images of Richard's visit to the French court of Charles VI, and castles associated with his reign. John Julius Norwich offers a highly readable survey of the reigns of all of *Shakespeare's Kings* (1999) and asks where history ends and drama begins? Jean E. Howard and Phyllis Rackin present a refreshing, feminist account of Shakespeare's history plays in *Engendering a Nation* (1997).

## PERFORMANCE

The Cambridge and Arden Shakespeare Third Series editions both include good material on the play's performance history. Margaret Shewring's *King Richard II* for Manchester University Press's 'Shakespeare in Performance' series (1996) represents the fullest account of the play on stage and television. Shewring's helpfully illustrated book includes a discussion of an Italian and two French productions. A shorter, Canadian overview of performance history is provided by Malcolm Page's *Richard II: Text and Performance* (1987). Stanley Wells's much quoted and now classic essay on John Barton's landmark 1973 Royal Shakespeare Company production can be found in *Royal Shakespeare: Four Productions at Stratford-upon-Avon* (1976). Production material, including prompt books, photographs, programmes and reviews of all Stratford-upon-Avon productions of *Richard II* from 1879 can be consulted in the theatre archive of the RSC, held at the Shakespeare Centre Library, Stratford-upon-Avon (www.shakespeare.org.uk).

Anyone wishing to experience *Richard II* in performance but unable to get to a theatre production of it could see Sir Derek Jacobi in the title role in David Giles's stylish and well-delivered BBC television version (1978). The 1960 Caedmon audio recording, with Sir John Gielgud playing the King, is a joy to listen to. An audio recording made originally for BBC Radio 3 (2000) with Samuel West as Richard sounds more contemporary, but does not better the Gielgud recording.

Paul Edmondson and Michael Taylor

# KING RICHARD THE SECOND

# The Characters in the Play

KING RICHARD the Second
JOHN OF GAUNT, Duke of Lancaster, King Richard's uncle
Edmund of Langley, Duke of YORK, King Richard's uncle
Henry BOLINGBROKE, Duke of Hereford; John of Gaunt's son; afterwards KING HENRY the Fourth
Duke of AUMERLE, Earl of Rutland; the Duke of York's son

Thomas MOWBRAY, Duke of Norfolk
Earl of SALISBURY
Lord BERKELEY
BAGOT ⎫
BUSHY ⎬ followers of King Richard
GREEN ⎭
Henry Percy, Earl of NORTHUMBERLAND ⎫
Harry PERCY (Hotspur), the Earl of Northumberland's son ⎬ of Bolingbroke's party
Lord ROSS ⎪
Lord WILLOUGHBY ⎭
BISHOP OF CARLISLE
Sir Stephen SCROOP
Lord FITZWATER

Duke of SURREY
ABBOT OF WESTMINSTER
Sir Piers of EXTON
LORD MARSHAL
CAPTAIN of the Welsh army

QUEEN ISABEL, King Richard's wife
DUCHESS OF YORK
DUCHESS OF GLOUCESTER, widow of Thomas of Wood-
    stock, Duke of Gloucester (King Richard's uncle)
FIRST LADY
SECOND LADY

GARDENER
FIRST MAN
SECOND MAN
KEEPER of the prison at Pomfret
SERVINGMAN
GROOM to King Richard
FIRST HERALD
SECOND HERALD

Lords, officers, soldiers, and other attendants

*Enter King Richard and John of Gaunt, with other*
*nobles, including the Lord Marshal, and attendants*

KING RICHARD

Old John of Gaunt, time-honoured Lancaster,
Hast thou according to thy oath and band
Brought hither Henry Hereford, thy bold son,
Here to make good the boisterous late appeal –
Which then our leisure would not let us hear –
Against the Duke of Norfolk, Thomas Mowbray?

JOHN OF GAUNT

I have, my liege.

KING RICHARD

Tell me, moreover, hast thou sounded him
If he appeal the Duke on ancient malice,
Or worthily, as a good subject should,
On some known ground of treachery in him?

JOHN OF GAUNT

As near as I could sift him on that argument,
On some apparent danger seen in him
Aimed at your highness; no inveterate malice.

KING RICHARD

Then call them to our presence. *Exit Attendant*
                                  Face to face,
And frowning brow to brow, ourselves will hear

The accuser and the accusèd freely speak.
High-stomached are they both, and full of ire;
In rage, deaf as the sea, hasty as fire.
          *Enter Bolingbroke and Mowbray*

**BOLINGBROKE**

20    Many years of happy days befall
      My gracious sovereign, my most loving liege!

**MOWBRAY**

      Each day still better other's happiness
      Until the heavens, envying earth's good hap,
      Add an immortal title to your crown!

**KING RICHARD**

      We thank you both. Yet one but flatters us,
      As well appeareth by the cause you come,
      Namely, to appeal each other of high treason.
      Cousin of Hereford, what dost thou object
      Against the Duke of Norfolk, Thomas Mowbray?

**BOLINGBROKE**

30    First, heaven be the record to my speech!
      In the devotion of a subject's love,
      Tendering the precious safety of my prince,
      And free from other, misbegotten hate
      Come I appellant to this princely presence.
      Now, Thomas Mowbray, do I turn to thee;
      And mark my greeting well, for what I speak
      My body shall make good upon this earth
      Or my divine soul answer it in heaven.
      Thou art a traitor and a miscreant,
40    Too good to be so, and too bad to live,
      Since the more fair and crystal is the sky,
      The uglier seem the clouds that in it fly.
      Once more, the more to aggravate the note,
      With a foul traitor's name stuff I thy throat,
      And wish – so please my sovereign – ere I move

What my tongue speaks my right-drawn sword may
    prove.
MOWBRAY
    Let not my cold words here accuse my zeal.
    'Tis not the trial of a woman's war,
    The bitter clamour of two eager tongues,
    Can arbitrate this cause betwixt us twain.      50
    The blood is hot that must be cooled for this.
    Yet can I not of such tame patience boast
    As to be hushed, and naught at all to say.
    First, the fair reverence of your highness curbs me
    From giving reins and spurs to my free speech,
    Which else would post until it had returned
    These terms of treason doubled down his throat.
    Setting aside his high blood's royalty,
    And let him be no kinsman to my liege,
    I do defy him, and I spit at him,      60
    Call him a slanderous coward, and a villain;
    Which to maintain I would allow him odds,
    And meet him, were I tied to run afoot
    Even to the frozen ridges of the Alps,
    Or any other ground inhabitable
    Where ever Englishman durst set his foot.
    Meantime, let this defend my loyalty:
    By all my hopes most falsely doth he lie.
BOLINGBROKE (*throws down his gage*)
    Pale, trembling coward, there I throw my gage,
    Disclaiming here the kindred of the King,      70
    And lay aside my high blood's royalty,
    Which fear, not reverence, makes thee to except.
    If guilty dread have left thee so much strength
    As to take up mine honour's pawn, then stoop.
    By that, and all the rites of knighthood else,
    Will I make good against thee, arm to arm,

What I have spoke or thou canst worse devise.

MOWBRAY (*takes up the gage*)

    I take it up; and by that sword I swear
    Which gently laid my knighthood on my shoulder,
80    I'll answer thee in any fair degree
    Or chivalrous design of knightly trial;
    And when I mount, alive may I not light
    If I be traitor or unjustly fight!

KING RICHARD

    What doth our cousin lay to Mowbray's charge?
    It must be great that can inherit us
    So much as of a thought of ill in him.

BOLINGBROKE

    Look what I speak, my life shall prove it true:
    That Mowbray hath received eight thousand nobles
    In name of lendings for your highness' soldiers,
90    The which he hath detained for lewd employments,
    Like a false traitor and injurious villain.
    Besides I say, and will in battle prove
    Or here or elsewhere to the furthest verge
    That ever was surveyed by English eye,
    That all the treasons for these eighteen years
    Complotted and contrivèd in this land
    Fetch from false Mowbray, their first head and spring.
    Further I say, and further will maintain
    Upon his bad life to make all this good,
100    That he did plot the Duke of Gloucester's death,
    Suggest his soon-believing adversaries,
    And consequently, like a traitor coward,
    Sluiced out his innocent soul through streams of blood;
    Which blood, like sacrificing Abel's, cries
    Even from the tongueless caverns of the earth
    To me for justice and rough chastisement.
    And, by the glorious worth of my descent,

This arm shall do it, or this life be spent.

KING RICHARD

How high a pitch his resolution soars!
Thomas of Norfolk, what sayst thou to this?                110

MOWBRAY

O, let my sovereign turn away his face
And bid his ears a little while be deaf
Till I have told this slander of his blood
How God and good men hate so foul a liar!

KING RICHARD

Mowbray, impartial are our eyes and ears.
Were he my brother – nay, my kingdom's heir –
As he is but my father's brother's son,
Now by my sceptre's awe I make a vow
Such neighbour nearness to our sacred blood
Should nothing privilege him, nor partialize                120
The unstooping firmness of my upright soul.
He is our subject, Mowbray. So art thou.
Free speech and fearless I to thee allow.

MOWBRAY

Then, Bolingbroke, as low as to thy heart
Through the false passage of thy throat thou liest!
Three parts of that receipt I had for Calais
Disbursed I duly to his highness' soldiers.
The other part reserved I by consent
For that my sovereign liege was in my debt
Upon remainder of a dear account                            130
Since last I went to France to fetch his queen.
Now swallow down that lie! For Gloucester's death,
I slew him not, but to my own disgrace
Neglected my sworn duty in that case.
(*To John of Gaunt*)
For you, my noble lord of Lancaster,
The honourable father to my foe,

Once did I lay an ambush for your life,
A trespass that doth vex my grievèd soul.
But ere I last received the sacrament
140    I did confess it, and exactly begged
Your grace's pardon; and I hope I had it.
This is my fault. As for the rest appealed,
It issues from the rancour of a villain,
A recreant and most degenerate traitor,
Which in myself I boldly will defend,
And interchangeably hurl down my gage
Upon this overweening traitor's foot,
To prove myself a loyal gentleman
Even in the best blood chambered in his bosom.
     *He throws down his gage*
150    In haste whereof most heartily I pray
Your highness to assign our trial day.

KING RICHARD
Wrath-kindled gentlemen, be ruled by me:
Let's purge this choler without letting blood.
This we prescribe, though no physician;
Deep malice makes too deep incision.
Forget, forgive, conclude, and be agreed;
Our doctors say this is no month to bleed.
    (*To John of Gaunt*)
Good uncle, let this end where it begun.
We'll calm the Duke of Norfolk, you your son.

JOHN OF GAUNT
160    To be a make-peace shall become my age.
Throw down, my son, the Duke of Norfolk's gage.

KING RICHARD
And, Norfolk, throw down his.

JOHN OF GAUNT              When, Harry, when?
Obedience bids I should not bid again.

KING RICHARD
  Norfolk, throw down! We bid: there is no boot.
MOWBRAY (*kneels*)
  Myself I throw, dread sovereign, at thy foot.
  My life thou shalt command, but not my shame.
  The one my duty owes, but my fair name,
  Despite of death that lives upon my grave,
  To dark dishonour's use thou shalt not have.
  I am disgraced, impeached, and baffled here,                        170
  Pierced to the soul with slander's venomed spear,
  The which no balm can cure but his heart-blood
  Which breathed this poison.
KING RICHARD                          Rage must be withstood.
  Give me his gage. Lions make leopards tame.
MOWBRAY
  Yea, but not change his spots. Take but my shame
  And I resign my gage. My dear dear lord,
  The purest treasure mortal times afford
  Is spotless reputation. That away,
  Men are but gilded loam, or painted clay.
  A jewel in a ten-times barred-up chest                              180
  Is a bold spirit in a loyal breast.
  Mine honour is my life. Both grow in one.
  Take honour from me, and my life is done.
  Then, dear my liege, mine honour let me try.
  In that I live, and for that will I die.
KING RICHARD (*to Bolingbroke*)
  Cousin, throw up your gage. Do you begin.
BOLINGBROKE
  O God defend my soul from such deep sin!
  Shall I seem crest-fallen in my father's sight?
  Or with pale beggar-fear impeach my height
  Before this outdared dastard? Ere my tongue                         190
  Shall wound my honour with such feeble wrong,

Or sound so base a parle, my teeth shall tear
The slavish motive of recanting fear
And spit it bleeding in his high disgrace
Where shame doth harbour, even in Mowbray's face.

*Exit John of Gaunt*

KING RICHARD
We were not born to sue, but to command;
Which since we cannot do to make you friends,
Be ready as your lives shall answer it
At Coventry upon Saint Lambert's Day.
200   There shall your swords and lances arbitrate
The swelling difference of your settled hate.
Since we cannot atone you, we shall see
Justice design the victor's chivalry.
Lord Marshal, command our officers-at-arms
Be ready to direct these home alarms.          *Exeunt*


I.2      *Enter John of Gaunt with the Duchess of Gloucester*
JOHN OF GAUNT
Alas, the part I had in Woodstock's blood
Doth more solicit me than your exclaims
To stir against the butchers of his life.
But since correction lieth in those hands
Which made the fault that we cannot correct,
Put we our quarrel to the will of heaven
Who, when they see the hours ripe on earth,
Will rain hot vengeance on offenders' heads.
DUCHESS OF GLOUCESTER
Finds brotherhood in thee no sharper spur?
10    Hath love in thy old blood no living fire?
Edward's seven sons, whereof thyself art one,
Were as seven vials of his sacred blood,
Or seven fair branches springing from one root.

Some of those seven are dried by nature's course,
Some of those branches by the destinies cut.
But Thomas, my dear lord, my life, my Gloucester,
One vial full of Edward's sacred blood,
One flourishing branch of his most royal root,
Is cracked, and all the precious liquor spilt;
Is hacked down, and his summer leaves all faded,          20
By envy's hand, and murder's bloody axe.
Ah, Gaunt, his blood was thine! That bed, that womb,
That mettle, that self mould, that fashioned thee
Made him a man; and though thou livest and breathest
Yet art thou slain in him. Thou dost consent
In some large measure to thy father's death
In that thou seest thy wretched brother die,
Who was the model of thy father's life.
Call it not patience, Gaunt. It is despair.
In suffering thus thy brother to be slaughtered          30
Thou showest the naked pathway to thy life,
Teaching stern murder how to butcher thee.
That which in mean men we entitle patience
Is pale cold cowardice in noble breasts.
What shall I say? To safeguard thine own life
The best way is to venge my Gloucester's death.

JOHN OF GAUNT

God's is the quarrel; for God's substitute,
His deputy anointed in His sight,
Hath caused his death; the which if wrongfully,
Let heaven revenge, for I may never lift          40
An angry arm against His minister.

DUCHESS OF GLOUCESTER

Where then, alas, may I complain myself?

JOHN OF GAUNT

To God, the widow's champion and defence.

DUCHESS OF GLOUCESTER
   Why then, I will. Farewell, old Gaunt.
   Thou goest to Coventry, there to behold
   Our cousin Hereford and fell Mowbray fight.
   O, sit my husband's wrongs on Hereford's spear
   That it may enter butcher Mowbray's breast!
   Or if misfortune miss the first career,
50 Be Mowbray's sins so heavy in his bosom
   That they may break his foaming courser's back
   And throw the rider headlong in the lists,
   A caitiff recreant to my cousin Hereford!
   Farewell, old Gaunt! Thy sometimes brother's wife
   With her companion, grief, must end her life.

JOHN OF GAUNT
   Sister, farewell! I must to Coventry.
   As much good stay with thee as go with me!

DUCHESS OF GLOUCESTER
   Yet one word more. Grief boundeth where it falls,
   Not with the empty hollowness, but weight.
60 I take my leave before I have begun;
   For sorrow ends not when it seemeth done.
   Commend me to thy brother, Edmund York.
   Lo, this is all. – Nay, yet depart not so.
   Though this be all, do not so quickly go.
   I shall remember more. Bid him – ah, what? –
   With all good speed at Pleshey visit me.
   Alack, and what shall good old York there see
   But empty lodgings and unfurnished walls,
   Unpeopled offices, untrodden stones,
70 And what hear there for welcome but my groans?
   Therefore commend me. Let him not come there
   To seek out sorrow that dwells everywhere.
   Desolate, desolate will I hence and die.
   The last leave of thee takes my weeping eye.   *Exeunt*

*Enter the Lord Marshal and the Duke of Aumerle*          I.3

LORD MARSHAL
  My Lord Aumerle, is Harry Hereford armed?
AUMERLE
  Yea, at all points, and longs to enter in.
LORD MARSHAL
  The Duke of Norfolk, sprightfully and bold,
  Stays but the summons of the appellant's trumpet.
AUMERLE
  Why then, the champions are prepared, and stay
  For nothing but his majesty's approach.
    *The trumpets sound and the King enters with his*
    *nobles, including Gaunt, and Bushy, Bagot, and*
    *Green. When they are set, enter Mowbray, Duke of*
    *Norfolk, in arms, defendant; and a Herald*
KING RICHARD
  Marshal, demand of yonder champion
  The cause of his arrival here in arms.
  Ask him his name, and orderly proceed
  To swear him in the justice of his cause.                   10
LORD MARSHAL (*to Mowbray*)
  In God's name and the King's, say who thou art
  And why thou comest thus knightly-clad in arms,
  Against what man thou comest, and what thy quarrel.
  Speak truly on thy knighthood and thy oath,
  As so defend thee heaven and thy valour!
MOWBRAY
  My name is Thomas Mowbray, Duke of Norfolk,
  Who hither come engagèd by my oath, –
  Which God defend a knight should violate! –
  Both to defend my loyalty and truth
  To God, my King, and my succeeding issue                    20
  Against the Duke of Hereford that appeals me;
  And by the grace of God and this mine arm

To prove him, in defending of myself,
A traitor to my God, my King, and me.
And as I truly fight, defend me heaven!
  *The trumpets sound. Enter Bolingbroke, Duke of*
  *Hereford, appellant, in armour; and a Herald*

KING RICHARD
Marshal, ask yonder knight in arms
Both who he is, and why he cometh hither
Thus plated in habiliments of war;
And formally, according to our law,
30 Depose him in the justice of his cause.

LORD MARSHAL (*to Bolingbroke*)
What is thy name? And wherefore comest thou hither
Before King Richard in his royal lists?
Against whom comest thou? And what's thy quarrel?
Speak like a true knight, so defend thee heaven!

BOLINGBROKE
Harry of Hereford, Lancaster, and Derby
Am I, who ready here do stand in arms
To prove by God's grace and my body's valour
In lists on Thomas Mowbray, Duke of Norfolk,
That he is a traitor foul and dangerous
40 To God of heaven, King Richard, and to me;
And as I truly fight, defend me heaven!

LORD MARSHAL
On pain of death, no person be so bold
Or daring-hardy as to touch the lists
Except the Marshal and such officers
Appointed to direct these fair designs.

BOLINGBROKE
Lord Marshal, let me kiss my sovereign's hand
And bow my knee before his majesty;
For Mowbray and myself are like two men
That vow a long and weary pilgrimage.

Then let us take a ceremonious leave                          50
And loving farewell of our several friends.

LORD MARSHAL (*to King Richard*)
The appellant in all duty greets your highness
And craves to kiss your hand, and take his leave.

KING RICHARD
We will descend and fold him in our arms.
   *He leaves his throne*
Cousin of Hereford, as thy cause is right,
So be thy fortune in this royal fight!
Farewell, my blood – which if today thou shed,
Lament we may, but not revenge thee dead.

BOLINGBROKE
O, let no noble eye profane a tear
For me, if I be gored with Mowbray's spear!                   60
As confident as is the falcon's flight
Against a bird, do I with Mowbray fight.
(*To Lord Marshal*)
My loving lord, I take my leave of you;
(*to Aumerle*)
Of you, my noble cousin, Lord Aumerle;
Not sick, although I have to do with death,
But lusty, young, and cheerly drawing breath.
Lo, as at English feasts, so I regreet
The daintiest last, to make the end most sweet.
(*To John of Gaunt*)
O thou, the earthly author of my blood,
Whose youthful spirit in me regenerate                        70
Doth with a two-fold vigour lift me up
To reach at victory above my head,
Add proof unto mine armour with thy prayers,
And with thy blessings steel my lance's point
That it may enter Mowbray's waxen coat
And furbish new the name of John o' Gaunt

Even in the lusty haviour of his son!

JOHN OF GAUNT
God in thy good cause make thee prosperous!
Be swift like lightning in the execution,
80      And let thy blows, doubly redoubled,
Fall like amazing thunder on the casque
Of thy adverse pernicious enemy!
Rouse up thy youthful blood, be valiant, and live.

BOLINGBROKE
Mine innocence and Saint George to thrive!

MOWBRAY
However God or fortune cast my lot
There lives or dies true to King Richard's throne
A loyal, just, and upright gentleman.
Never did captive with a freer heart
Cast off his chains of bondage and embrace
90      His golden uncontrolled enfranchisement
More than my dancing soul doth celebrate
This feast of battle with mine adversary.
Most mighty liege, and my companion peers,
Take from my mouth the wish of happy years.
As gentle and as jocund as to jest
Go I to fight. Truth hath a quiet breast.

KING RICHARD
Farewell, my lord. Securely I espy
Virtue with valour couchèd in thine eye.
Order the trial, Marshal, and begin.

LORD MARSHAL
100     Harry of Hereford, Lancaster, and Derby,
Receive thy lance; and God defend the right.

BOLINGBROKE
Strong as a tower in hope, I cry 'Amen!'

LORD MARSHAL (*to an officer*)
Go bear this lance to Thomas, Duke of Norfolk.

FIRST HERALD

    Harry of Hereford, Lancaster, and Derby
    Stands here for God, his sovereign, and himself,
    On pain to be found false and recreant,
    To prove the Duke of Norfolk, Thomas Mowbray,
    A traitor to his God, his king, and him,
    And dares him to set forward to the fight.

SECOND HERALD

    Here standeth Thomas Mowbray, Duke of Norfolk,    110
    On pain to be found false and recreant,
    Both to defend himself and to approve
    Henry of Hereford, Lancaster, and Derby
    To God, his sovereign, and to him disloyal,
    Courageously and with a free desire
    Attending but the signal to begin.

LORD MARSHAL

    Sound, trumpets; and set forward, combatants!

      *A charge sounded. King Richard throws his warder*
      *into the lists*

    Stay! The King hath thrown his warder down.

KING RICHARD

    Let them lay by their helmets and their spears
    And both return back to their chairs again.    120
    (*To his counsellors*)
    Withdraw with us, and let the trumpets sound
    While we return these dukes what we decree.

      *A long flourish. King Richard consults his nobles,*
      *then addresses the combatants*

    Draw near,
    And list what with our council we have done.
    For that our kingdom's earth should not be soiled
    With that dear blood which it hath fosterèd,
    And for our eyes do hate the dire aspect
    Of civil wounds ploughed up with neighbours' sword,

And for we think the eagle-wingèd pride
130    Of sky-aspiring and ambitious thoughts
With rival-hating envy set on you
To wake our peace, which in our country's cradle
Draws the sweet infant-breath of gentle sleep,
Which so roused up with boisterous untuned drums,
With harsh-resounding trumpets' dreadful bray,
And grating shock of wrathful iron arms,
Might from our quiet confines fright fair peace
And make us wade even in our kindred's blood:
Therefore we banish you our territories.
140    You, cousin Hereford, upon pain of life
Till twice five summers have enriched our fields
Shall not regreet our fair dominions,
But tread the stranger paths of banishment.

BOLINGBROKE
Your will be done. This must my comfort be:
That sun that warms you here shall shine on me,
And those his golden beams to you here lent
Shall point on me, and gild my banishment.

KING RICHARD
Norfolk, for thee remains a heavier doom,
Which I with some unwillingness pronounce.
150    The sly slow hours shall not determinate
The dateless limit of thy dear exile.
The hopeless word of 'never to return'
Breathe I against thee upon pain of life.

MOWBRAY
A heavy sentence, my most sovereign liege,
And all unlooked-for from your highness' mouth.
A dearer merit, not so deep a maim
As to be cast forth in the common air
Have I deservèd at your highness' hands.
The language I have learnt these forty years,

My native English, now I must forgo,                    160
And now my tongue's use is to me no more
Than an unstringèd viol or a harp,
Or like a cunning instrument cased up –
Or being open, put into his hands
That knows no touch to tune the harmony.
Within my mouth you have engaoled my tongue,
Doubly portcullised with my teeth and lips,
And dull unfeeling barren ignorance
Is made my gaoler to attend on me.
I am too old to fawn upon a nurse,                      170
Too far in years to be a pupil now.
What is thy sentence then but speechless death,
Which robs my tongue from breathing native breath?

KING RICHARD
It boots thee not to be compassionate.
After our sentence plaining comes too late.

MOWBRAY
Then thus I turn me from my country's light,
To dwell in solemn shades of endless night.

KING RICHARD (to Bolingbroke and Mowbray)
Return again, and take an oath with thee.
Lay on our royal sword your banished hands.
Swear by the duty that you owe to God –                 180
Our part therein we banish with yourselves –
To keep the oath that we administer:
You never shall, so help you truth and God,
Embrace each other's love in banishment,
Nor never look upon each other's face,
Nor never write, regreet, nor reconcile
This lowering tempest of your home-bred hate,
Nor never by advisèd purpose meet
To plot, contrive, or complot any ill
'Gainst us, our state, our subjects, or our land.       190

**BOLINGBROKE**
I swear.
**MOWBRAY**
And I, to keep all this.
**BOLINGBROKE**
Norfolk, so far as to mine enemy:
By this time, had the King permitted us,
One of our souls had wandered in the air,
Banished this frail sepulchre of our flesh,
As now our flesh is banished from this land.
Confess thy treasons ere thou fly the realm.
Since thou hast far to go, bear not along
200   The clogging burden of a guilty soul.
**MOWBRAY**
No, Bolingbroke, if ever I were traitor
My name be blotted from the book of life,
And I from heaven banished as from hence!
But what thou art, God, thou, and I do know,
And all too soon, I fear, the King shall rue.
Farewell, my liege. Now no way can I stray;
Save back to England, all the world's my way.    *Exit*
**KING RICHARD** (*to John of Gaunt*)
Uncle, even in the glasses of thine eyes
I see thy grievèd heart. Thy sad aspect
210   Hath from the number of his banished years
Plucked four away. (*To Bolingbroke*) Six frozen winters
        spent,
Return with welcome home from banishment.
**BOLINGBROKE**
How long a time lies in one little word!
Four lagging winters and four wanton springs
End in a word – such is the breath of kings.
**JOHN OF GAUNT**
I thank my liege that in regard of me

He, shortens four years of my son's exile.
But little vantage shall I reap thereby;
For ere the six years that he hath to spend
Can change their moons, and bring their times about,     220
My oil-dried lamp and time-bewasted light
Shall be extinct with age and endless night.
My inch of taper will be burnt and done,
And blindfold death not let me see my son.

KING RICHARD
Why, uncle, thou hast many years to live.

JOHN OF GAUNT
But not a minute, King, that thou canst give.
Shorten my days thou canst with sullen sorrow,
And pluck nights from me, but not lend a morrow.
Thou canst help time to furrow me with age,
But stop no wrinkle in his pilgrimage.                    230
Thy word is current with him for my death,
But dead, thy kingdom cannot buy my breath.

KING RICHARD
Thy son is banished upon good advice
Whereto thy tongue a party-verdict gave.
Why at our justice seemest thou then to lour?

JOHN OF GAUNT
Things sweet to taste prove in digestion sour.
You urged me as a judge, but I had rather
You would have bid me argue like a father.
O, had it been a stranger, not my child,
To smooth his fault I should have been more mild.         240
A partial slander sought I to avoid,
And in the sentence my own life destroyed.
Alas, I looked when some of you should say
I was too strict, to make mine own away.
But you gave leave to my unwilling tongue
Against my will to do myself this wrong.

KING RICHARD

    Cousin, farewell – and, uncle, bid him so.

    Six years we banish him, and he shall go.

              *Flourish. Exit King Richard with his train*

AUMERLE

    Cousin, farewell! What presence must not know,

250    From where you do remain let paper show.

LORD MARSHAL

    My lord, no leave take I; for I will ride

    As far as land will let me by your side.

JOHN OF GAUNT

    O, to what purpose dost thou hoard thy words,

    That thou returnest no greeting to thy friends?

BOLINGBROKE

    I have too few to take my leave of you,

    When the tongue's office should be prodigal

    To breathe the abundant dolour of the heart.

JOHN OF GAUNT

    Thy grief is but thy absence for a time.

BOLINGBROKE

    Joy absent, grief is present for that time.

JOHN OF GAUNT

260    What is six winters? They are quickly gone.

BOLINGBROKE

    To men in joy; but grief makes one hour ten.

JOHN OF GAUNT

    Call it a travel that thou takest for pleasure.

BOLINGBROKE

    My heart will sigh when I miscall it so,

    Which finds it an enforcèd pilgrimage.

JOHN OF GAUNT

    The sullen passage of thy weary steps

    Esteem as foil wherein thou art to set

    The precious jewel of thy home return.

BOLINGBROKE

    Nay, rather every tedious stride I make
    Will but remember me what a deal of world
    I wander from the jewels that I love.               270
    Must I not serve a long apprenticehood
    To foreign passages, and in the end,
    Having my freedom, boast of nothing else
    But that I was a journeyman to grief?

JOHN OF GAUNT

    All places that the eye of heaven visits
    Are to a wise man ports and happy havens.
    Teach thy necessity to reason thus:
    There is no virtue like necessity.
    Think not the King did banish thee,
    But thou the King. Woe doth the heavier sit    280
    Where it perceives it is but faintly borne.
    Go, say I sent thee forth to purchase honour,
    And not the King exiled thee; or suppose
    Devouring pestilence hangs in our air
    And thou art flying to a fresher clime.
    Look what thy soul holds dear, imagine it
    To lie that way thou goest, not whence thou comest.
    Suppose the singing birds musicians,
    The grass whereon thou treadest the presence strewed,
    The flowers fair ladies, and thy steps no more    290
    Than a delightful measure or a dance;
    For gnarling sorrow hath less power to bite
    The man that mocks at it and sets it light.

BOLINGBROKE

    O, who can hold a fire in his hand
    By thinking on the frosty Caucasus,
    Or cloy the hungry edge of appetite
    By bare imagination of a feast,
    Or wallow naked in December snow

By thinking on fantastic summer's heat?
300    O no, the apprehension of the good
Gives but the greater feeling to the worse.
Fell sorrow's tooth doth never rankle more
Than when he bites, but lanceth not the sore.

JOHN OF GAUNT
Come, come, my son, I'll bring thee on thy way.
Had I thy youth and cause I would not stay.

BOLINGBROKE
Then, England's ground, farewell! Sweet soil, adieu,
My mother and my nurse that bears me yet!
Where'er I wander, boast of this I can:
Though banished, yet a trueborn Englishman! *Exeunt*


I.4        *Enter the King with Bagot and Green at one door,*
           *and the Lord Aumerle at another*

KING RICHARD
We did observe. Cousin Aumerle,
How far brought you high Hereford on his way?

AUMERLE
I brought high Hereford, if you call him so,
But to the next highway; and there I left him.

KING RICHARD
And say, what store of parting tears were shed?

AUMERLE
Faith, none for me, except the north-east wind,
Which then blew bitterly against our faces,
Awaked the sleeping rheum, and so by chance
Did grace our hollow parting with a tear.

KING RICHARD
10    What said our cousin when you parted with him?

AUMERLE
'Farewell' –

And, for my heart disdainèd that my tongue
Should so profane the word, that taught me craft
To counterfeit oppression of such grief
That words seemed buried in my sorrow's grave.
Marry, would the word 'farewell' have lengthened hours
And added years to his short banishment,
He should have had a volume of farewells;
But since it would not, he had none of me.

KING RICHARD
He is our cousin, cousin; but 'tis doubt,                    20
When time shall call him home from banishment,
Whether our kinsman come to see his friends.
Ourself and Bushy
Observed his courtship to the common people,
How he did seem to dive into their hearts
With humble and familiar courtesy;
What reverence he did throw away on slaves,
Wooing poor craftsmen with the craft of smiles
And patient underbearing of his fortune,
As 'twere to banish their affects with him.                 30
Off goes his bonnet to an oyster-wench.
A brace of draymen bid God speed him well,
And had the tribute of his supple knee,
With 'Thanks, my countrymen, my loving friends',
As were our England in reversion his,
And he our subjects' next degree in hope.

GREEN
Well, he is gone; and with him go these thoughts.
Now, for the rebels which stand out in Ireland,
Expedient manage must be made, my liege,
Ere further leisure yield them further means             40
For their advantage and your highness' loss.

KING RICHARD
We will ourself in person to this war;

And, for our coffers with too great a court
And liberal largess are grown somewhat light,
We are enforced to farm our royal realm,
The revenue whereof shall furnish us
For our affairs in hand. If that come short
Our substitutes at home shall have blank charters
Whereto, when they shall know what men are rich,
50    They shall subscribe them for large sums of gold
And send them after to supply our wants;
For we will make for Ireland presently.
   *Enter Bushy*
Bushy, what news?

BUSHY

Old John of Gaunt is grievous sick, my lord,
Suddenly taken, and hath sent post-haste
To entreat your majesty to visit him.

KING RICHARD

Where lies he?

BUSHY

At Ely House.

KING RICHARD

Now put it, God, in the physician's mind
60    To help him to his grave immediately!
The lining of his coffers shall make coats
To deck our soldiers for these Irish wars.
Come, gentlemen, let's all go visit him.
Pray God we may make haste and come too late!

ALL

Amen!                                              *Exeunt*

*

*Enter John of Gaunt sick, with the Duke of York, the*   **II.I**
*Earl of Northumberland, attendants, and others*

JOHN OF GAUNT

Will the King come, that I may breathe my last
In wholesome counsel to his unstaid youth?

YORK

Vex not yourself, nor strive not with your breath;
For all in vain comes counsel to his ear.

JOHN OF GAUNT

O, but they say the tongues of dying men
Enforce attention like deep harmony.
Where words are scarce they are seldom spent in vain,
For they breathe truth that breathe their words in pain.
He that no more must say is listened more
    Than they whom youth and ease have taught to glose.   10
More are men's ends marked than their lives before.
    The setting sun, and music at the close,
As the last taste of sweets, is sweetest last,
Writ in remembrance more than things long past.
Though Richard my life's counsel would not hear,
My death's sad tale may yet undeaf his ear.

YORK

No, it is stopped with other, flattering sounds,
As praises, of whose taste the wise are fond;
Lascivious metres, to whose venom sound
The open ear of youth doth always listen;                 20
Report of fashions in proud Italy,
Whose manners still our tardy-apish nation
Limps after in base imitation.
Where doth the world thrust forth a vanity —
So it be new there's no respect how vile —
That is not quickly buzzed into his ears?
Then all too late comes counsel to be heard
Where will doth mutiny with wit's regard.

Direct not him whose way himself will choose.

30  'Tis breath thou lackest, and that breath wilt thou lose.

JOHN OF GAUNT

Methinks I am a prophet new-inspired,
And thus, expiring, do foretell of him:
His rash fierce blaze of riot cannot last;
For violent fires soon burn out themselves.
Small showers last long, but sudden storms are short.
He tires betimes that spurs too fast betimes.
With eager feeding food doth choke the feeder.
Light vanity, insatiate cormorant,
Consuming means, soon preys upon itself.

40  This royal throne of kings, this sceptred isle,
This earth of majesty, this seat of Mars,
This other Eden – demi-paradise –
This fortress built by nature for herself
Against infection and the hand of war,
This happy breed of men, this little world,
This precious stone set in the silver sea,
Which serves it in the office of a wall,
Or as a moat defensive to a house
Against the envy of less happier lands;

50  This blessèd plot, this earth, this realm, this England,
This nurse, this teeming womb of royal kings,
Feared by their breed, and famous by their birth,
Renownèd for their deeds as far from home
For Christian service and true chivalry
As is the sepulchre in stubborn Jewry
Of the world's ransom, blessèd Mary's son;
This land of such dear souls, this dear dear land,
Dear for her reputation through the world,
Is now leased out – I die pronouncing it –

60  Like to a tenement or pelting farm.
England, bound in with the triumphant sea,

Whose rocky shore beats back the envious siege
Of watery Neptune, is now bound in with shame,
With inky blots and rotten parchment bonds.
That England that was wont to conquer others
Hath made a shameful conquest of itself.
Ah, would the scandal vanish with my life,
How happy then were my ensuing death!

*Enter King Richard, Queen Isabel, Aumerle, Bushy,*
*Green, Bagot, Ross, and Willoughby*

YORK

The King is come. Deal mildly with his youth;
For young hot colts being raged do rage the more.          70

QUEEN ISABEL

How fares our noble uncle Lancaster?

KING RICHARD

What comfort, man? How is't with agèd Gaunt?

JOHN OF GAUNT

O, how that name befits my composition!
Old Gaunt indeed, and gaunt in being old.
Within me grief hath kept a tedious fast;
And who abstains from meat that is not gaunt?
For sleeping England long time have I watched.
Watching breeds leanness; leanness is all gaunt.
The pleasure that some fathers feed upon
Is my strict fast – I mean my children's looks;          80
And therein fasting hast thou made me gaunt.
Gaunt am I for the grave, gaunt as a grave,
Whose hollow womb inherits naught but bones.

KING RICHARD

Can sick men play so nicely with their names?

JOHN OF GAUNT

No, misery makes sport to mock itself.
Since thou dost seek to kill my name in me,
I mock my name, great King, to flatter thee.

KING RICHARD
    Should dying men flatter with those that live?

JOHN OF GAUNT
    No, no. Men living flatter those that die.

KING RICHARD
90     Thou now a-dying sayst thou flatterest me.

JOHN OF GAUNT
    O, no. Thou diest, though I the sicker be.

KING RICHARD
    I am in health. I breathe, and see thee ill.

JOHN OF GAUNT
    Now he that made me knows I see thee ill;
    Ill in myself to see, and in thee seeing ill.
    Thy deathbed is no lesser than thy land,
    Wherein thou liest in reputation sick;
    And thou, too careless patient as thou art,
    Committest thy anointed body to the cure
    Of those 'physicians' that first wounded thee.
100    A thousand flatterers sit within thy crown,
    Whose compass is no bigger than thy head,
    And yet, encagèd in so small a verge,
    The waste is no whit lesser than thy land.
    O, had thy grandsire with a prophet's eye
    Seen how his son's son should destroy his sons,
    From forth thy reach he would have laid thy shame,
    Deposing thee before thou wert possessed,
    Which art possessed now to depose thyself.
    Why, cousin, wert thou regent of the world
110    It were a shame to let this land by lease.
    But for thy world enjoying but this land,
    Is it not more than shame to shame it so?
    Landlord of England art thou now, not king.
    Thy state of law is bondslave to the law,
    And thou –

KING RICHARD

               – a lunatic lean-witted fool,
Presuming on an ague's privilege,
Darest with thy frozen admonition
Make pale our cheek, chasing the royal blood
With fury from his native residence.
Now by my seat's right royal majesty,                    120
Wert thou not brother to great Edward's son,
This tongue that runs so roundly in thy head
Should run thy head from thy unreverent shoulders.

JOHN OF GAUNT

O, spare me not, my brother Edward's son,
For that I was his father Edward's son.
That blood already, like the pelican,
Hast thou tapped out and drunkenly caroused.
My brother Gloucester, plain well-meaning soul –
Whom fair befall in heaven 'mongst happy souls –
May be a precedent and witness good                      130
That thou respectest not spilling Edward's blood.
Join with the present sickness that I have,
And thy unkindness be like crookèd age,
To crop at once a too-long withered flower.
Live in thy shame, but die not shame with thee!
These words hereafter thy tormentors be!
Convey me to my bed, then to my grave.
Love they to live that love and honour have.

           *Exit with Northumberland and attendants*

KING RICHARD

And let them die that age and sullens have;
For both hast thou, and both become the grave.           140

YORK

I do beseech your majesty, impute his words
To wayward sickliness and age in him.
He loves you, on my life, and holds you dear

As Harry, Duke of Hereford, were he here.

KING RICHARD

Right, you say true. As Hereford's love, so his.
As theirs, so mine; and all be as it is.

*Enter Northumberland*

NORTHUMBERLAND

My liege, old Gaunt commends him to your majesty.

KING RICHARD

What says he?

NORTHUMBERLAND

Nay, nothing. All is said.
His tongue is now a stringless instrument.
150   Words, life, and all, old Lancaster hath spent.

YORK

Be York the next that must be bankrupt so!
Though death be poor, it ends a mortal woe.

KING RICHARD

The ripest fruit first falls, and so doth he.
His time is spent, our pilgrimage must be.
So much for that. Now for our Irish wars.
We must supplant those rough rug-headed kerns
Which live like venom where no venom else
But only they have privilege to live.
And for these great affairs do ask some charge,
160   Towards our assistance we do seize to us
The plate, coin, revenues, and moveables
Whereof our uncle Gaunt did stand possessed.

YORK

How long shall I be patient? Ah, how long
Shall tender duty make me suffer wrong?
Not Gloucester's death, nor Hereford's banishment,
Nor Gaunt's rebukes, nor England's private wrongs,
Nor the prevention of poor Bolingbroke
About his marriage, nor my own disgrace,

Have ever made me sour my patient cheek
Or bend one wrinkle on my sovereign's face.                    170
I am the last of noble Edward's sons,
Of whom thy father, Prince of Wales, was first.
In war was never lion raged more fierce,
In peace was never gentle lamb more mild
Than was that young and princely gentleman.
His face thou hast; for even so looked he
Accomplished with the number of thy hours;
But when he frowned it was against the French,
And not against his friends. His noble hand
Did win what he did spend, and spent not that            180
Which his triumphant father's hand had won.
His hands were guilty of no kindred blood,
But bloody with the enemies of his kin.
O, Richard! York is too far gone with grief,
Or else he never would compare between.

KING RICHARD
Why, uncle, what's the matter?

YORK                                         O, my liege,
Pardon me if you please. If not, I, pleased
Not to be pardoned, am content withal.
Seek you to seize and grip into your hands
The royalties and rights of banished Hereford?        190
Is not Gaunt dead? And doth not Hereford live?
Was not Gaunt just? And is not Harry true?
Did not the one deserve to have an heir?
Is not his heir a well-deserving son?
Take Hereford's rights away, and take from Time
His charters and his customary rights.
Let not tomorrow then ensue today.
Be not thyself; for how art thou a king
But by fair sequence and succession?
Now afore God – God forbid I say true –                 200

If you do wrongfully seize Hereford's rights,
Call in the letters patents that he hath
By his attorneys general to sue
His livery, and deny his offered homage,
You pluck a thousand dangers on your head,
You lose a thousand well-disposèd hearts,
And prick my tender patience to those thoughts
Which honour and allegiance cannot think.

KING RICHARD

Think what you will, we seize into our hands
His plate, his goods, his money, and his lands.

YORK

I'll not be by the while. My liege, farewell.
What will ensue hereof there's none can tell;
But by bad courses may be understood
That their events can never fall out good.          *Exit*

KING RICHARD

Go, Bushy, to the Earl of Wiltshire straight,
Bid him repair to us to Ely House
To see this business. Tomorrow next
We will for Ireland, and 'tis time I trow.
And we create in absence of ourself
Our uncle York Lord Governor of England;
For he is just, and always loved us well.
Come on, our Queen; tomorrow must we part.
Be merry; for our time of stay is short.
    *Flourish. Exeunt King Richard and Queen Isabel.*
    *Northumberland, Willoughby, and Ross remain*

NORTHUMBERLAND

Well, lords, the Duke of Lancaster is dead.

ROSS

And living too; for now his son is duke.

WILLOUGHBY

Barely in title, not in revenues.

NORTHUMBERLAND

  Richly in both if justice had her right.

ROSS

  My heart is great, but it must break with silence

  Ere't be disburdened with a liberal tongue.

NORTHUMBERLAND

  Nay, speak thy mind; and let him ne'er speak more    230

  That speaks thy words again to do thee harm.

WILLOUGHBY

  Tends that thou wouldst speak to the Duke of Hereford?

  If it be so, out with it boldly, man!

  Quick is mine ear to hear of good towards him.

ROSS

  No good at all that I can do for him,

  Unless you call it good to pity him,

  Bereft and gelded of his patrimony.

NORTHUMBERLAND

  Now, afore God, 'tis shame such wrongs are borne

  In him, a royal prince, and many more

  Of noble blood in this declining land.    240

  The King is not himself, but basely led

  By flatterers; and what they will inform

  Merely in hate 'gainst any of us all,

  That will the King severely prosecute

  'Gainst us, our lives, our children, and our heirs.

ROSS

  The commons hath he pilled with grievous taxes,

  And quite lost their hearts. The nobles hath he fined

  For ancient quarrels, and quite lost their hearts.

WILLOUGHBY

  And daily new exactions are devised,

  As blanks, benevolences, and I wot not what.    250

  But what o' God's name doth become of this?

NORTHUMBERLAND

Wars hath not wasted it; for warred he hath not,
But basely yielded upon compromise
That which his noble ancestors achieved with blows.
More hath he spent in peace than they in wars.

ROSS

The Earl of Wiltshire hath the realm in farm.

WILLOUGHBY

The King's grown bankrupt like a broken man.

NORTHUMBERLAND

Reproach and dissolution hangeth over him.

ROSS

He hath not money for these Irish wars –
His burdenous taxations notwithstanding –
But by the robbing of the banished Duke.

NORTHUMBERLAND

His noble kinsman! – most degenerate King!
But, lords, we hear this fearful tempest sing
Yet seek no shelter to avoid the storm.
We see the wind sit sore upon our sails
And yet we strike not, but securely perish.

ROSS

We see the very wrack that we must suffer,
And unavoided is the danger now
For suffering so the causes of our wrack.

NORTHUMBERLAND

Not so. Even through the hollow eyes of death
I spy life peering; but I dare not say
How near the tidings of our comfort is.

WILLOUGHBY

Nay, let us share thy thoughts, as thou dost ours.

ROSS

Be confident to speak, Northumberland.
We three are but thyself; and speaking so

Thy words are but as thoughts. Therefore be bold.
NORTHUMBERLAND
   Then thus: I have from Le Port Blanc,
   A bay in Brittaine, received intelligence
   That Harry Duke of Hereford, Rainold Lord Cobham,
   The son of Richard Earl of Arundel                    280
   That late broke from the Duke of Exeter,
   His brother, Archbishop late of Canterbury,
   Sir Thomas Erpingham, Sir John Ramston,
   Sir John Norbery, Sir Robert Waterton, and Francis
      Coint,
   All these well-furnished by the Duke of Brittaine
   With eight tall ships, three thousand men of war,
   Are making hither with all due expedience,
   And shortly mean to touch our northern shore.
   Perhaps they had ere this, but that they stay
   The first departing of the King for Ireland.        290
   If then we shall shake off our slavish yoke,
   Imp out our drooping country's broken wing,
   Redeem from broking pawn the blemished crown,
   Wipe off the dust that hides our sceptre's gilt,
   And make high majesty look like itself,
   Away with me in post to Ravenspurgh.
   But if you faint, as fearing to do so,
   Stay, and be secret; and myself will go.
ROSS
   To horse, to horse. Urge doubts to them that fear.
WILLOUGHBY
   Hold out my horse, and I will first be there.    *Exeunt*    300


    *Enter the Queen, Bushy, and Bagot*                    II.2
BUSHY
   Madam, your majesty is too much sad.

You promised when you parted with the King
To lay aside life-harming heaviness,
And entertain a cheerful disposition.

QUEEN ISABEL
To please the King I did. To please myself
I cannot do it. Yet I know no cause
Why I should welcome such a guest as grief
Save bidding farewell to so sweet a guest
As my sweet Richard. Yet again methinks
Some unborn sorrow ripe in fortune's womb
Is coming towards me, and my inward soul
With nothing trembles. At something it grieves
More than with parting from my lord the King.

BUSHY
Each substance of a grief hath twenty shadows
Which shows like grief itself, but is not so.
For sorrow's eye, glazèd with blinding tears,
Divides one thing entire to many objects,
Like perspectives which, rightly gazed upon,
Show nothing but confusion; eyed awry,
Distinguish form. So your sweet majesty,
Looking awry upon your lord's departure,
Find shapes of grief more than himself to wail,
Which looked on as it is, is naught but shadows
Of what it is not. Then, thrice-gracious Queen,
More than your lord's departure weep not – more is not
      seen,
Or if it be, 'tis with false sorrow's eye,
Which for things true weeps things imaginary.

QUEEN ISABEL
It may be so; but yet my inward soul
Persuades me it is otherwise. Howe'er it be
I cannot but be sad – so heavy-sad
As, though on thinking on no thought I think,

Makes me with heavy nothing faint and shrink.

BUSHY

'Tis nothing but conceit, my gracious lady.

QUEEN ISABEL

'Tis nothing less. Conceit is still derived
From some forefather grief. Mine is not so,
For nothing hath begot my something grief,
Or something hath the nothing that I grieve –
'Tis in reversion that I do possess –
But what it is that is not yet known what,
I cannot name; 'tis nameless woe, I wot.                    40

  *Enter Green*

GREEN

God save your majesty, and well met, gentlemen.
I hope the King is not yet shipped for Ireland.

QUEEN ISABEL

Why hopest thou so? 'Tis better hope he is,
For his designs crave haste, his haste good hope.
Then wherefore dost thou hope he is not shipped?

GREEN

That he, our hope, might have retired his power,
And driven into despair an enemy's hope,
Who strongly hath set footing in this land.
The banished Bolingbroke repeals himself,
And with uplifted arms is safe arrivéd                      50
At Ravenspurgh.

QUEEN ISABEL  Now God in heaven forbid!

GREEN

Ah, madam, 'tis too true! And, that is worse,
The Lord Northumberland, his son young Henry Percy,
The Lords of Ross, Beaumont, and Willoughby,
With all their powerful friends are fled to him.

BUSHY

Why have you not proclaimed Northumberland

And all the rest, revolted faction, traitors?

GREEN

We have; whereupon the Earl of Worcester
Hath broken his staff, resigned his stewardship,
60      And all the household servants fled with him
To Bolingbroke.

QUEEN ISABEL

So, Green, thou art the midwife to my woe,
And Bolingbroke my sorrow's dismal heir.
Now hath my soul brought forth her prodigy,
And I, a gasping new-delivered mother,
Have woe to woe, sorrow to sorrow joined.

BUSHY

Despair not, madam.

QUEEN ISABEL                      Who shall hinder me?
I will despair and be at enmity
With cozening hope. He is a flatterer,
70      A parasite, a keeper-back of death
Who gently would dissolve the bands of life
Which false hope lingers in extremity.
        *Enter York*

GREEN

Here comes the Duke of York.

QUEEN ISABEL

With signs of war about his agèd neck.
O, full of careful business are his looks!
Uncle, for God's sake speak comfortable words.

YORK

Should I do so I should belie my thoughts.
Comfort's in heaven, and we are on the earth,
Where nothing lives but crosses, cares, and grief.
80      Your husband, he is gone to save far off,
Whilst others come to make him lose at home.
Here am I left to underprop his land,

Who weak with age cannot support myself.
Now comes the sick hour that his surfeit made.
Now shall he try his friends that flattered him.

   *Enter a Servingman*

SERVINGMAN
My lord, your son was gone before I came.

YORK
He was? – why, so. Go all which way it will.
The nobles they are fled. The commons they are cold,
And will, I fear, revolt on Hereford's side.
Sirrah, get thee to Pleshey to my sister Gloucester.   90
Bid her send me presently a thousand pound –
Hold: take my ring.

SERVINGMAN
My lord, I had forgot to tell your lordship –
Today as I came by I callèd there –
But I shall grieve you to report the rest.

YORK
What is't, knave?

SERVINGMAN
An hour before I came the Duchess died.

YORK
God for his mercy, what a tide of woes
Comes rushing on this woeful land at once!
I know not what to do. I would to God –   100
So my untruth had not provoked him to it –
The King had cut off my head with my brother's.
What, are there no posts dispatched for Ireland?
How shall we do for money for these wars?
Come, sister – cousin, I would say – pray pardon me.
Go, fellow, get thee home, provide some carts,
And bring away the armour that is there.
Gentlemen, will you go muster men?
If I know how or which way to order these affairs

110   Thus disorderly thrust into my hands,
Never believe me. Both are my kinsmen.
T'one is my sovereign, whom both my oath
And duty bids defend. T'other again
Is my kinsman, whom the King hath wronged,
Whom conscience and my kindred bids to right.
Well, somewhat we must do. (*To the Queen*) Come,
    cousin,
I'll dispose of you. Gentlemen, go muster up your men,
And meet me presently at Berkeley.
I should to Pleshey, too,
120   But time will not permit. All is uneven,
And everything is left at six and seven.
                    *Exeunt York and the Queen*
    *Bushy, Bagot, and Green remain*

BUSHY
  The wind sits fair for news to go for Ireland,
But none returns. For us to levy power
Proportionable to the enemy
Is all unpossible.

GREEN
  Besides, our nearness to the King in love
Is near the hate of those love not the King.

BAGOT
  And that is the wavering commons; for their love
Lies in their purses, and whoso empties them
130   By so much fills their hearts with deadly hate.

BUSHY
  Wherein the King stands generally condemned.

BAGOT
  If judgement lie in them, then so do we,
Because we ever have been near the King.

GREEN
  Well, I will for refuge straight to Bristol Castle.

The Earl of Wiltshire is already there.

BUSHY

Thither will I with you; for little office
Will the hateful commons perform for us –
Except like curs to tear us all to pieces.
Will you go along with us?

BAGOT

No, I will to Ireland to his majesty.          140
Farewell. If heart's presages be not vain,
We three here part that ne'er shall meet again.

BUSHY

That's as York thrives to beat back Bolingbroke.

GREEN

Alas, poor Duke! The task he undertakes
Is numbering sands and drinking oceans dry.
Where one on his side fights, thousands will fly.

BAGOT

Farewell at once, for once, for all, and ever.

BUSHY

Well, we may meet again.

BAGOT                          I fear me, never.          *Exeunt*

*Enter Bolingbroke and Northumberland*          II.3

BOLINGBROKE

How far is it, my lord, to Berkeley now?

NORTHUMBERLAND

Believe me, noble lord,
I am a stranger here in Gloucestershire.
These high wild hills and rough uneven ways
Draws out our miles and makes them wearisome.
And yet your fair discourse hath been as sugar,
Making the hard way sweet and delectable.
But I bethink me what a weary way

From Ravenspurgh to Cotswold will be found
10   In Ross and Willoughby, wanting your company,
Which I protest hath very much beguiled
The tediousness and process of my travel.
But theirs is sweetened with the hope to have
The present benefit which I possess;
And hope to joy is little less in joy
Than hope enjoyed. By this the weary lords
Shall make their way seem short as mine hath done
By sight of what I have – your noble company.

BOLINGBROKE
Of much less value is my company
20   Than your good words. But who comes here?
   *Enter Harry Percy*
NORTHUMBERLAND
It is my son, young Harry Percy,
Sent from my brother Worcester whencesoever.
Harry, how fares your uncle?
PERCY
I had thought, my lord, to have learned his health of
      you.
NORTHUMBERLAND
Why, is he not with the Queen?
PERCY
No, my good lord, he hath forsook the court,
Broken his staff of office, and dispersed
The household of the King.
NORTHUMBERLAND          What was his reason?
He was not so resolved when last we spake together.
PERCY
30   Because your lordship was proclaimèd traitor.
But he, my lord, is gone to Ravenspurgh
To offer service to the Duke of Hereford,
And sent me over by Berkeley to discover

What power the Duke of York had levied there,
Then with directions to repair to Ravenspurgh.

NORTHUMBERLAND

Have you forgot the Duke of Hereford, boy?

PERCY

No, my good lord; for that is not forgot
Which ne'er I did remember. To my knowledge
I never in my life did look on him.

NORTHUMBERLAND

Then learn to know him now – this is the Duke.      40

PERCY

My gracious lord, I tender you my service,
Such as it is, being tender, raw, and young,
Which elder days shall ripen and confirm
To more approvèd service and desert.

BOLINGBROKE

I thank thee, gentle Percy; and be sure
I count myself in nothing else so happy
As in a soul remembering my good friends;
And as my fortune ripens with thy love
It shall be still thy true love's recompense.
My heart this covenant makes, my hand thus seals it.     50

NORTHUMBERLAND

How far is it to Berkeley, and what stir
Keeps good old York there with his men of war?

PERCY

There stands the castle by yon tuft of trees,
Manned with three hundred men as I have heard,
And in it are the Lords of York, Berkeley, and Seymour,
None else of name and noble estimate.

    *Enter Ross and Willoughby*

NORTHUMBERLAND

Here come the Lords of Ross and Willoughby,
Bloody with spurring, fiery red with haste.

**BOLINGBROKE**

Welcome, my lords. I wot your love pursues
60    A banished traitor. All my treasury
Is yet but unfelt thanks, which, more enriched,
Shall be your love and labour's recompense.

**ROSS**

Your presence makes us rich, most noble lord.

**WILLOUGHBY**

And far surmounts our labour to attain it.

**BOLINGBROKE**

Evermore thank's the exchequer of the poor,
Which till my infant fortune comes to years
Stands for my bounty. But who comes here?

*Enter Berkeley*

**NORTHUMBERLAND**

It is my Lord of Berkeley, as I guess.

**BERKELEY**

My Lord of Hereford, my message is to you.

**BOLINGBROKE**

70    My lord, my answer is to 'Lancaster'.
And I am come to seek that name in England,
And I must find that title in your tongue
Before I make reply to aught you say.

**BERKELEY**

Mistake me not, my lord. 'Tis not my meaning
To raze one title of your honour out.
To you, my lord, I come – what lord you will –
From the most gracious regent of this land,
The Duke of York, to know what pricks you on
To take advantage of the absent time
80    And fright our native peace with self-borne arms.

*Enter York*

**BOLINGBROKE**

I shall not need transport my words by you.

Here comes his grace in person. My noble uncle!
*He kneels*

YORK

Show me thy humble heart, and not thy knee,
Whose duty is deceivable and false.

BOLINGBROKE

My gracious uncle –

YORK

Tut, tut, grace me no grace, nor uncle me no uncle!
I am no traitor's uncle; and that word 'grace'
In an ungracious mouth is but profane.
Why have those banished and forbidden legs
Dared once to touch a dust of England's ground?          90
But then more 'why' – why have they dared to march
So many miles upon her peaceful bosom,
Frighting her pale-faced villages with war
And ostentation of despisèd arms?
Comest thou because the anointed King is hence?
Why, foolish boy, the King is left behind,
And in my loyal bosom lies his power.
Were I but now lord of such hot youth
As when brave Gaunt, thy father, and myself
Rescued the Black Prince – that young Mars of men –   100
From forth the ranks of many thousand French,
O then how quickly should this arm of mine,
Now prisoner to the palsy, chastise thee
And minister correction to thy fault!

BOLINGBROKE

My gracious uncle, let me know my fault.
On what condition stands it, and wherein?

YORK

Even in condition of the worst degree,
In gross rebellion and detested treason.
Thou art a banished man, and here art come

110    Before the expiration of thy time
       In braving arms against thy sovereign!
BOLINGBROKE
       As I was banished, I was banished Hereford;
       But as I come, I come for Lancaster.
       And, noble uncle, I beseech your grace
       Look on my wrongs with an indifferent eye.
       You are my father; for methinks in you
       I see old Gaunt alive. O then, my father,
       Will you permit that I shall stand condemned
       A wandering vagabond, my rights and royalties
120    Plucked from my arms perforce, and given away
       To upstart unthrifts? Wherefore was I born?
       If that my cousin King be King in England
       It must be granted I am Duke of Lancaster.
       You have a son, Aumerle, my noble cousin.
       Had you first died and he been thus trod down
       He should have found his uncle Gaunt a father
       To rouse his wrongs and chase them to the bay.
       I am denied to sue my livery here,
       And yet my letters patents give me leave.
130    My father's goods are all distrained and sold,
       And these, and all, are all amiss employed.
       What would you have me do? I am a subject,
       And I challenge law. Attorneys are denied me,
       And therefore personally I lay my claim
       To my inheritance of free descent.
NORTHUMBERLAND (*to York*)
       The noble Duke hath been too much abused.
ROSS
       It stands your grace upon to do him right.
WILLOUGHBY
       Base men by his endowments are made great.

YORK

    My lords of England, let me tell you this:

    I have had feeling of my cousin's wrongs,       140

    And laboured all I could to do him right.

    But in this kind to come, in braving arms,

    Be his own carver, and cut out his way

    To find out right with wrong – it may not be.

    And you that do abet him in this kind

    Cherish rebellion, and are rebels all.

NORTHUMBERLAND

    The noble Duke hath sworn his coming is

    But for his own, and for the right of that

    We all have strongly sworn to give him aid;

    And let him never see joy that breaks that oath.    150

YORK

    Well, well, I see the issue of these arms.

    I cannot mend it, I must needs confess,

    Because my power is weak and all ill-left.

    But if I could, by Him that gave me life,

    I would attach you all and make you stoop

    Unto the sovereign mercy of the King.

    But since I cannot, be it known unto you

    I do remain as neuter. So fare you well,

    Unless you please to enter in the castle

    And there repose you for this night.      160

BOLINGBROKE

    An offer, uncle, that we will accept;

    But we must win your grace to go with us

    To Bristol Castle, which they say is held

    By Bushy, Bagot, and their complices,

    The caterpillars of the commonwealth,

    Which I have sworn to weed and pluck away.

YORK

    It may be I will go with you, but yet I'll pause;

For I am loath to break our country's laws.
Nor friends, nor foes, to me welcome you are.
170  Things past redress are now with me past care.

*Exeunt*


II.4          *Enter Earl of Salisbury and a Welsh Captain*
CAPTAIN
My Lord of Salisbury, we have stayed ten days
And hardly kept our countrymen together,
And yet we hear no tidings from the King.
Therefore we will disperse ourselves. Farewell.
SALISBURY
Stay yet another day, thou trusty Welshman.
The King reposeth all his confidence in thee.
CAPTAIN
'Tis thought the King is dead. We will not stay.
The bay trees in our country are all withered,
And meteors fright the fixèd stars of heaven.
10  The pale-faced moon looks bloody on the earth,
And lean-looked prophets whisper fearful change.
Rich men look sad, and ruffians dance and leap –
The one in fear to lose what they enjoy,
The other to enjoy by rage and war.
These signs forerun the death or fall of kings.
Farewell. Our countrymen are gone and fled,
As well assured Richard their king is dead.          *Exit*
SALISBURY
Ah, Richard! With the eyes of heavy mind
I see thy glory like a shooting star
20  Fall to the base earth from the firmament.
Thy sun sets weeping in the lowly west,
Witnessing storms to come, woe, and unrest.

Thy friends are fled to wait upon thy foes,
And crossly to thy good all fortune goes.          *Exit*

\*

*Enter Bolingbroke, York, Northumberland, with*          III.1
*Bushy and Green, prisoners*

BOLINGBROKE
Bring forth these men.
Bushy and Green, I will not vex your souls,
Since presently your souls must part your bodies,
With too much urging your pernicious lives,
For 'twere no charity. Yet, to wash your blood
From off my hands, here in the view of men
I will unfold some causes of your deaths.
You have misled a prince, a royal king,
A happy gentleman in blood and lineaments,
By you unhappied and disfigured clean.          10
You have in manner with your sinful hours
Made a divorce betwixt his Queen and him,
Broke the possession of a royal bed,
And stained the beauty of a fair queen's cheeks
With tears drawn from her eyes by your foul wrongs.
Myself – a prince by fortune of my birth,
Near to the King in blood, and near in love
Till you did make him misinterpret me –
Have stooped my neck under your injuries,
And sighed my English breath in foreign clouds,          20
Eating the bitter bread of banishment
Whilst you have fed upon my signories,
Disparked my parks, and felled my forest woods,
From my own windows torn my household coat,
Razed out my imprese, leaving me no sign

Save men's opinions and my living blood
To show the world I am a gentleman.
This and much more, much more than twice all this,
Condemns you to the death. See them delivered over
30    To execution and the hand of death.

BUSHY

More welcome is the stroke of death to me
Than Bolingbroke to England. Lords, farewell.

GREEN

My comfort is that heaven will take our souls
And plague injustice with the pains of hell.

BOLINGBROKE

My Lord Northumberland, see them dispatched.

        *Exit Northumberland with Bushy and Green*

Uncle, you say the Queen is at your house.
For God's sake, fairly let her be intreated.
Tell her I send to her my kind commends.
Take special care my greetings be delivered.

YORK

40    A gentleman of mine I have dispatched
With letters of your love to her at large.

BOLINGBROKE

Thanks, gentle uncle. Come, lords, away,
To fight with Glendower and his complices.
A while to work, and after, holiday.              *Exeunt*


III.2        *Drums; flourish and colours. Enter King Richard,*
             *Aumerle, the Bishop of Carlisle, and soldiers*

KING RICHARD

Barkloughly Castle call they this at hand?

AUMERLE

Yea, my lord. How brooks your grace the air
After your late tossing on the breaking seas?

KING RICHARD
    Needs must I like it well. I weep for joy
    To stand upon my kingdom once again.
    Dear earth, I do salute thee with my hand,
    Though rebels wound thee with their horses' hoofs.
    As a long-parted mother with her child
    Plays fondly with her tears and smiles in meeting,
    So weeping, smiling, greet I thee, my earth,    10
    And do thee favours with my royal hands.
    Feed not thy sovereign's foe, my gentle earth,
    Nor with thy sweets comfort his ravenous sense,
    But let thy spiders that suck up thy venom,
    And heavy-gaited toads, lie in their way,
    Doing annoyance to the treacherous feet
    Which with usurping steps do trample thee.
    Yield stinging nettles to mine enemies;
    And when they from thy bosom pluck a flower
    Guard it, I pray thee, with a lurking adder,    20
    Whose double tongue may with a mortal touch
    Throw death upon thy sovereign's enemies.
    Mock not my senseless conjuration, lords.
    This earth shall have a feeling, and these stones
    Prove armèd soldiers ere her native king
    Shall falter under foul rebellion's arms.
BISHOP OF CARLISLE
    Fear not, my lord, that power that made you king
    Hath power to keep you king in spite of all.
    The means that heavens yield must be embraced
    And not neglected; else heaven would,    30
    And we will not – heaven's offer we refuse,
    The proffered means of succour and redress.
AUMERLE
    He means, my lord, that we are too remiss,
    Whilst Bolingbroke through our security

Grows strong and great in substance and in power.

KING RICHARD
Discomfortable cousin, knowest thou not
That when the searching eye of heaven is hid
Behind the globe, that lights the lower world,
Then thieves and robbers range abroad unseen
40      In murders and in outrage boldly here;
But when from under this terrestrial ball
He fires the proud tops of the eastern pines,
And darts his light through every guilty hole,
Then murders, treasons, and detested sins —
The cloak of night being plucked from off their backs —
Stand bare and naked, trembling at themselves?
So when this thief, this traitor Bolingbroke,
Who all this while hath revelled in the night
Whilst we were wandering with the Antipodes,
50      Shall see us rising in our throne, the east,
His treasons will sit blushing in his face,
Not able to endure the sight of day,
But self-affrighted, tremble at his sin.
Not all the water in the rough rude sea
Can wash the balm off from an anointed king.
The breath of worldly men cannot depose
The deputy elected by the Lord.
For every man that Bolingbroke hath pressed
To lift shrewd steel against our golden crown,
60      God for his Richard hath in heavenly pay
A glorious angel. Then if angels fight,
Weak men must fall; for heaven still guards the right.
        *Enter Salisbury*

KING RICHARD
Welcome, my lord. How far off lies your power?

SALISBURY
Nor nea'er nor farther off, my gracious lord,

Than this weak arm. Discomfort guides my tongue
And bids me speak of nothing but despair.
One day too late, I fear me, noble lord,
Hath clouded all thy happy days on earth.
O, call back yesterday – bid time return,
And thou shalt have twelve thousand fighting men.          70
Today, today, unhappy day too late,
O'erthrows thy joys, friends, fortune, and thy state;
For all the Welshmen, hearing thou wert dead,
Are gone to Bolingbroke – dispersed and fled.

AUMERLE
Comfort, my liege. Why looks your grace so pale?

KING RICHARD
But now the blood of twenty thousand men
    Did triumph in my face; and they are fled.
And till so much blood thither come again
    Have I not reason to look pale and dead?
All souls that will be safe fly from my side,                80
For time hath set a blot upon my pride.

AUMERLE
Comfort, my liege. Remember who you are.

KING RICHARD
I had forgot myself. Am I not King?
Awake, thou coward majesty; thou sleepest.
Is not the King's name twenty thousand names?
Arm, arm, my name! A puny subject strikes
At thy great glory. Look not to the ground,
Ye favourites of a King. Are we not high?
High be our thoughts. I know my uncle York
Hath power enough to serve our turn. But who comes          90
    here?
    *Enter Scroop*

SCROOP
More health and happiness betide my liege

Than can my care-tuned tongue deliver him.

KING RICHARD

Mine ear is open and my heart prepared.
The worst is worldly loss thou canst unfold.
Say, is my kingdom lost? Why, 'twas my care;
And what loss is it to be rid of care?
Strives Bolingbroke to be as great as we?
Greater he shall not be. If he serve God
We'll serve Him too, and be his fellow so.
Revolt our subjects? That we cannot mend.
They break their faith to God as well as us.
Cry woe, destruction, ruin, and decay.
The worst is death, and death will have his day.

SCROOP

Glad am I that your highness is so armed
To bear the tidings of calamity.
Like an unseasonable stormy day
Which makes the silver rivers drown their shores
As if the world were all dissolved to tears,
So high above his limits swells the rage
Of Bolingbroke, covering your fearful land
With hard bright steel, and hearts harder than steel.
Whitebeards have armed their thin and hairless scalps
Against thy majesty. Boys with women's voices
Strive to speak big and clap their female joints
In stiff unwieldy arms against thy crown.
Thy very beadsmen learn to bend their bows
Of double-fatal yew against thy state.
Yea, distaff-women manage rusty bills
Against thy seat. Both young and old rebel,
And all goes worse than I have power to tell.

KING RICHARD

Too well, too well thou tellest a tale so ill.
Where is the Earl of Wiltshire? Where is Bagot?

What is become of Bushy, where is Green,
That they have let the dangerous enemy
Measure our confines with such peaceful steps?
If we prevail, their heads shall pay for it.
I warrant they have made peace with Bolingbroke.

SCROOP

Peace have they made with him indeed, my lord.

KING RICHARD

O, villains, vipers, damned without redemption!
Dogs easily won to fawn on any man!                    130
Snakes in my heart-blood warmed, that sting my heart;
Three Judases, each one thrice worse than Judas –
Would they make peace? Terrible hell
Make war upon their spotted souls for this.

SCROOP

Sweet love, I see, changing his property,
Turns to the sourest and most deadly hate.
Again uncurse their souls. Their peace is made
With heads and not with hands. Those whom you curse
Have felt the worst of death's destroying wound,
And lie full low, graved in the hollow ground.          140

AUMERLE

Is Bushy, Green, and the Earl of Wiltshire dead?

SCROOP

Ay. All of them at Bristol lost their heads.

AUMERLE

Where is the Duke, my father, with his power?

KING RICHARD

No matter where. Of comfort no man speak.
Let's talk of graves, of worms, and epitaphs;
Make dust our paper, and with rainy eyes
Write sorrow on the bosom of the earth.
Let's choose executors and talk of wills –
And yet not so; for what can we bequeath

150     Save our deposèd bodies to the ground?
    Our lands, our lives, and all are Bolingbroke's,
    And nothing can we call our own but death
    And that small model of the barren earth
    Which serves as paste and cover to our bones.
    For God's sake let us sit upon the ground
    And tell sad stories of the death of kings –
    How some have been deposed, some slain in war,
    Some haunted by the ghosts they have deposed,
    Some poisoned by their wives, some sleeping killed,
160     All murdered. For within the hollow crown
    That rounds the mortal temples of a king
    Keeps death his court; and there the antic sits,
    Scoffing his state and grinning at his pomp,
    Allowing him a breath, a little scene,
    To monarchize, be feared, and kill with looks,
    Infusing him with self and vain conceit,
    As if this flesh which walls about our life
    Were brass impregnable; and humoured thus,
    Comes at the last, and with a little pin
170     Bores through his castle wall, and – farewell, king!
    Cover your heads, and mock not flesh and blood
    With solemn reverence. Throw away respect,
    Tradition, form, and ceremonious duty;
    For you have but mistook me all this while.
    I live with bread, like you; feel want,
    Taste grief, need friends. Subjected thus,
    How can you say to me I am a king?

BISHOP OF CARLISLE
    My lord, wise men ne'er sit and wail their woes,
    But presently prevent the ways to wail.
180     To fear the foe, since fear oppresseth strength,
    Gives in your weakness strength unto your foe,
    And so your follies fight against yourself.

Fear, and be slain. No worse can come to fight;
And fight and die is death destroying death,
Where fearing dying pays death servile breath.

AUMERLE

My father hath a power. Inquire of him,
And learn to make a body of a limb.

KING RICHARD

Thou chidest me well. Proud Bolingbroke, I come
To change blows with thee for our day of doom.
This ague-fit of fear is overblown.                    190
An easy task it is to win our own.
Say, Scroop, where lies our uncle with his power?
Speak sweetly, man, although thy looks be sour.

SCROOP

Men judge by the complexion of the sky
    The state and inclination of the day.
So may you by my dull and heavy eye
    My tongue hath but a heavier tale to say.
I play the torturer, by small and small
To lengthen out the worst that must be spoken.
Your uncle York is joined with Bolingbroke,               200
And all your northern castles yielded up,
And all your southern gentlemen in arms
Upon his party.

KING RICHARD        Thou hast said enough.
    (*To Aumerle*)
Beshrew thee, cousin, which didst lead me forth
Of that sweet way I was in to despair.
What say you now? What comfort have we now?
By heaven, I'll hate him everlastingly
That bids me be of comfort any more.
Go to Flint Castle. There I'll pine away.
A king, woe's slave, shall kingly woe obey.               210
That power I have, discharge, and let them go

To ear the land that hath some hope to grow;
For I have none. Let no man speak again
To alter this; for counsel is but vain.

AUMERLE
My liege, one word!

KING RICHARD          He does me double wrong
That wounds me with the flatteries of his tongue.
Discharge my followers. Let them hence away:
From Richard's night to Bolingbroke's fair day. *Exeunt*


III.3          *Enter with drum and colours Bolingbroke, York,*
               *Northumberland, attendants, and soldiers*

BOLINGBROKE
So that by this intelligence we learn
The Welshmen are dispersed, and Salisbury
Is gone to meet the King, who lately landed
With some few private friends upon this coast.

NORTHUMBERLAND
The news is very fair and good, my lord.
Richard not far from hence hath hid his head.

YORK
It would beseem the Lord Northumberland
To say 'King Richard'. Alack the heavy day
When such a sacred king should hide his head!

NORTHUMBERLAND
10   Your grace mistakes. Only to be brief
Left I his title out.

YORK                The time hath been,
Would you have been so brief with him, he would
Have been so brief with you to shorten you,
For taking so the head, your whole head's length.

BOLINGBROKE
Mistake not, uncle, further than you should.

YORK

    Take not, good cousin, further than you should,
    Lest you mistake the heavens are over our heads.

BOLINGBROKE

    I know it, uncle, and oppose not myself
    Against their will. But who comes here?
      *Enter Harry Percy*
    Welcome, Harry. What, will not this castle yield?    20

PERCY

    The castle royally is manned, my lord,
    Against thy entrance.

BOLINGBROKE

    Royally?
    Why, it contains no king.

PERCY                  Yes, my good lord,
    It doth contain a king. King Richard lies
    Within the limits of yon lime and stone,
    And with him are the Lord Aumerle, Lord Salisbury,
    Sir Stephen Scroop, besides a clergyman
    Of holy reverence; who, I cannot learn.

NORTHUMBERLAND

    O, belike it is the Bishop of Carlisle.    30

BOLINGBROKE

    Noble lord,
    Go to the rude ribs of that ancient castle,
    Through brazen trumpet send the breath of parley
    Into his ruined ears, and thus deliver:
    Henry Bolingbroke
    On both his knees doth kiss King Richard's hand,
    And sends allegiance and true faith of heart
    To his most royal person, hither come
    Even at his feet to lay my arms and power,
    Provided that my banishment repealed    40
    And lands restored again be freely granted.

If not, I'll use the advantage of my power
And lay the summer's dust with showers of blood
Rained from the wounds of slaughtered Englishmen;
The which how far off from the mind of Bolingbroke
It is such crimson tempest should bedrench
The fresh green lap of fair King Richard's land
My stooping duty tenderly shall show.
Go signify as much while here we march
50   Upon the grassy carpet of this plain.
Let's march without the noise of threatening drum,
That from this castle's tattered battlements
Our fair appointments may be well perused.
Methinks King Richard and myself should meet
With no less terror than the elements
Of fire and water when their thundering shock
At meeting tears the cloudy cheeks of heaven.
Be he the fire, I'll be the yielding water;
The rage be his, whilst on the earth I rain
60   My waters – on the earth, and not on him.
March on, and mark King Richard, how he looks.

> *The trumpets sound parley without, and answer*
> *within; then a flourish. King Richard appeareth on the*
> *walls with the Bishop of Carlisle, Aumerle, Scroop,*
> *and Salisbury*

BOLINGBROKE
See, see, King Richard doth himself appear,
As doth the blushing, discontented sun
From out the fiery portal of the east
When he perceives the envious clouds are bent
To dim his glory and to stain the track
Of his bright passage to the occident.

YORK
Yet looks he like a king. Behold, his eye,
As bright as is the eagle's, lightens forth

Controlling majesty. Alack, alack for woe                70
That any harm should stain so fair a show!

KING RICHARD

We are amazed; and thus long have we stood
To watch the fearful bending of thy knee
Because we thought ourself thy lawful king.
And if we be, how dare thy joints forget
To pay their awful duty to our presence?
If we be not, show us the hand of God
That hath dismissed us from our stewardship;
For well we know no hand of blood and bone
Can grip the sacred handle of our sceptre              80
Unless he do profane, steal, or usurp.
And though you think that all, as you have done,
Have torn their souls by turning them from us,
And we are barren and bereft of friends,
Yet know, my master, God omnipotent,
Is mustering in his clouds on our behalf
Armies of pestilence; and they shall strike
Your children yet unborn and unbegot,
That lift your vassal hands against my head
And threat the glory of my precious crown.             90
Tell Bolingbroke – for yon methinks he stands –
That every stride he makes upon my land
Is dangerous treason. He is come to open
The purple testament of bleeding war;
But ere the crown he looks for live in peace
Ten thousand bloody crowns of mothers' sons
Shall ill become the flower of England's face,
Change the complexion of her maid-pale peace
To scarlet indignation, and bedew
Her pastor's grass with faithful English blood.       100

NORTHUMBERLAND

The King of heaven forbid our lord the King

Should so with civil and uncivil arms
Be rushed upon. Thy thrice-noble cousin
Harry Bolingbroke doth humbly kiss thy hand;
And by the honourable tomb he swears
That stands upon your royal grandsire's bones,
And by the royalties of both your bloods,
Currents that spring from one most gracious head,
And by the buried hand of warlike Gaunt,
110  And by the worth and honour of himself,
Comprising all that may be sworn or said,
His coming hither hath no further scope
Than for his lineal royalties, and to beg
Enfranchisement immediate on his knees,
Which on thy royal party granted once
His glittering arms he will commend to rust,
His barbèd steeds to stables, and his heart
To faithful service of your majesty.
This swears he as he is a prince and just,
120  And as I am a gentleman I credit him.

KING RICHARD
Northumberland, say thus. The King returns
His noble cousin is right welcome hither,
And all the number of his fair demands
Shall be accomplished without contradiction.
With all the gracious utterance thou hast
Speak to his gentle hearing kind commends.
(*To Aumerle*)
We do debase ourselves, cousin, do we not,
To look so poorly and to speak so fair?
Shall we call back Northumberland and send
130  Defiance to the traitor, and so die?

AUMERLE
No, good my lord. Let's fight with gentle words
Till time lend friends, and friends their helpful swords.

KING RICHARD
    O God, O God, that e'er this tongue of mine,
    That laid the sentence of dread banishment
    On yon proud man, should take it off again
    With words of sooth! O that I were as great
    As is my grief, or lesser than my name,
    Or that I could forget what I have been,
    Or not remember what I must be now!
    Swellest thou, proud heart? I'll give thee scope to beat, 140
    Since foes have scope to beat both thee and me.

AUMERLE
    Northumberland comes back from Bolingbroke.

KING RICHARD
    What must the King do now? Must he submit?
    The King shall do it. Must he be deposed?
    The King shall be contented. Must he lose
    The name of king? A God's name, let it go.
    I'll give my jewels for a set of beads,
    My gorgeous palace for a hermitage,
    My gay apparel for an almsman's gown,
    My figured goblets for a dish of wood,                      150
    My sceptre for a palmer's walking-staff,
    My subjects for a pair of carvèd saints,
    And my large kingdom for a little grave,
    A little, little grave, an obscure grave;
    Or I'll be buried in the King's highway,
    Some way of common trade where subjects' feet
    May hourly trample on their sovereign's head,
    For on my heart they tread now whilst I live,
    And buried once, why not upon my head?
    Aumerle, thou weepest, my tender-hearted cousin.           160
    We'll make foul weather with despisèd tears.
    Our sighs and they shall lodge the summer corn
    And make a dearth in this revolting land.

Or shall we play the wantons with our woes,
And make some pretty match with shedding tears,
As thus to drop them still upon one place
Till they have fretted us a pair of graves
Within the earth, and therein laid there lies
Two kinsmen digged their graves with weeping eyes.
170     Would not this ill do well? Well, well, I see
I talk but idly, and you laugh at me.
Most mighty prince, my Lord Northumberland,
What says King Bolingbroke? Will his majesty
Give Richard leave to live till Richard die?
You make a leg, and Bolingbroke says 'Ay'.

NORTHUMBERLAND
My lord, in the base-court he doth attend
To speak with you, may it please you to come down.

KING RICHARD
Down, down I come like glistering Phaethon,
Wanting the manage of unruly jades.
180     In the base-court — base-court, where kings grow base
To come at traitors' calls, and do them grace.
In the base-court. Come down — down court, down
     King,
For night-owls shriek where mounting larks should sing.
                         *Exeunt from above*

BOLINGBROKE
What says his majesty?

NORTHUMBERLAND         Sorrow and grief of heart
Makes him speak fondly, like a frantic man.
Yet he is come.
     *Enter King Richard attended, below*

BOLINGBROKE
Stand all apart,
And show fair duty to his majesty.

*He kneels down*
My gracious lord!

KING RICHARD
Fair cousin, you debase your princely knee          190
To make the base earth proud with kissing it.
Me rather had my heart might feel your love
Than my unpleased eye see your courtesy.
Up, cousin, up. Your heart is up, I know,
Thus high at least, although your knee be low.

BOLINGBROKE
My gracious lord, I come but for mine own.

KING RICHARD
Your own is yours, and I am yours and all.

BOLINGBROKE
So far be mine, my most redoubted lord,
As my true service shall deserve your love.

KING RICHARD
Well you deserve. They well deserve to have          200
That know the strongest and surest way to get.
(*To York*)
Uncle, give me your hands. Nay, dry your eyes.
Tears show their love, but want their remedies.
(*To Bolingbroke*)
Cousin, I am too young to be your father
Though you are old enough to be my heir.
What you will have, I'll give, and willing too;
For do we must what force will have us do.
Set on towards London, cousin – is it so?

BOLINGBROKE
Yea, my good lord.

KING RICHARD          Then I must not say no.
                              *Flourish. Exeunt*

III.4        *Enter the Queen with two Ladies, her attendants*

QUEEN ISABEL
    What sport shall we devise here in this garden
    To drive away the heavy thought of care?
FIRST LADY
    Madam, we'll play at bowls.
QUEEN ISABEL
    'Twill make me think the world is full of rubs
    And that my fortune runs against the bias.
SECOND LADY
    Madam, we'll dance.
QUEEN ISABEL
    My legs can keep no measure in delight
    When my poor heart no measure keeps in grief.
    Therefore no dancing, girl. Some other sport.
FIRST LADY
10    Madam, we'll tell tales.
QUEEN ISABEL
    Of sorrow or of joy?
FIRST LADY                          Of either, madam.
QUEEN ISABEL
    Of neither, girl.
    For if of joy, being altogether wanting,
    It doth remember me the more of sorrow;
    Or if of grief, being altogether had,
    It adds more sorrow to my want of joy;
    For what I have I need not to repeat,
    And what I want it boots not to complain.
SECOND LADY
    Madam, I'll sing.
QUEEN ISABEL          'Tis well that thou hast cause;
20    But thou shouldst please me better wouldst thou weep.
SECOND LADY
    I could weep, madam, would it do you good.

QUEEN ISABEL
    And I could sing would weeping do me good,
    And never borrow any tear of thee.
        *Enter Gardeners, one the master, the other two his men*
    But stay, here come the gardeners.
    Let's step into the shadow of these trees.
    My wretchedness unto a row of pins
    They will talk of state; for everyone doth so
    Against a change. Woe is forerun with woe.
        *The Queen and her Ladies stand apart*
GARDENER (*to one man*)
    Go, bind thou up young dangling apricocks
    Which, like unruly children, make their sire                30
    Stoop with oppression of their prodigal weight.
    Give some supportance to the bending twigs.
    (*To the other*)
    Go thou, and like an executioner
    Cut off the heads of too fast-growing sprays
    That look too lofty in our commonwealth.
    All must be even in our government.
    You thus employed, I will go root away
    The noisome weeds which without profit suck
    The soil's fertility from wholesome flowers.
FIRST MAN
    Why should we, in the compass of a pale,                    40
    Keep law and form and due proportion,
    Showing as in a model our firm estate,
    When our sea-wallèd garden, the whole land,
    Is full of weeds, her fairest flowers choked up,
    Her fruit trees all unpruned, her hedges ruined,
    Her knots disordered, and her wholesome herbs
    Swarming with caterpillars?
GARDENER                          Hold thy peace.
    He that hath suffered this disordered spring

Hath now himself met with the fall of leaf.
50    The weeds which his broad-spreading leaves did shelter,
That seemed in eating him to hold him up,
Are plucked up, root and all, by Bolingbroke –
I mean the Earl of Wiltshire, Bushy, Green.

SECOND MAN
What, are they dead?

GARDENER                    They are; and Bolingbroke
Hath seized the wasteful King. O, what pity is it
That he had not so trimmed and dressed his land
As we this garden! We at time of year
Do wound the bark, the skin of our fruit trees,
Lest being overproud in sap and blood
60    With too much riches it confound itself.
Had he done so to great and growing men
They might have lived to bear, and he to taste
Their fruits of duty. Superfluous branches
We lop away that bearing boughs may live.
Had he done so, himself had borne the crown
Which waste of idle hours hath quite thrown down.

FIRST MAN
What, think you the King shall be deposed?

GARDENER
Depressed he is already, and deposed
'Tis doubt he will be. Letters came last night
70    To a dear friend of the good Duke of York's
That tell black tidings.

QUEEN ISABEL
O, I am pressed to death through want of speaking!
    *She comes forward*
Thou, old Adam's likeness, set to dress this garden,
How dares thy harsh rude tongue sound this unpleasing
        news?
What Eve, what serpent hath suggested thee

To make a second Fall of cursèd man?
Why dost thou say King Richard is deposed?
Darest thou, thou little better thing than earth,
Divine his downfall? Say, where, when, and how
Camest thou by this ill tidings? Speak, thou wretch!    80

GARDENER
Pardon me, madam. Little joy have I
To breathe this news. Yet what I say is true.
King Richard he is in the mighty hold
Of Bolingbroke. Their fortunes both are weighed.
In your lord's scale is nothing but himself
And some few vanities that make him light.
But in the balance of great Bolingbroke
Besides himself are all the English peers,
And with that odds he weighs King Richard down.
Post you to London and you will find it so.    90
I speak no more than everyone doth know.

QUEEN ISABEL
Nimble mischance, that art so light of foot,
Doth not thy embassage belong to me,
And am I last that knows it? O, thou thinkest
To serve me last that I may longest keep
Thy sorrow in my breast. Come, ladies, go
To meet at London London's king in woe.
What was I born to this – that my sad look
Should grace the triumph of great Bolingbroke?
Gardener, for telling me these news of woe,    100
Pray God the plants thou graftest may never grow.
                              *Exit Queen with her Ladies*

GARDENER
Poor Queen, so that thy state might be no worse
I would my skill were subject to thy curse.
Here did she fall a tear. Here in this place
I'll set a bank of rue, sour herb of grace.

Rue even for ruth here shortly shall be seen
In the remembrance of a weeping Queen.        *Exeunt*

\*

IV.I        *Enter Bolingbroke with the Lords Aumerle,*
           *Northumberland, Harry Percy, Fitzwater, Surrey,*
           *the Bishop of Carlisle, the Abbot of Westminster,*
           *another Lord, Herald, and officer, to Parliament*

BOLINGBROKE
Call forth Bagot.
           *Enter Bagot with officers*
Now, Bagot, freely speak thy mind
What thou dost know of noble Gloucester's death,
Who wrought it with the King, and who performed
The bloody office of his timeless end.

BAGOT
Then set before my face the Lord Aumerle.

BOLINGBROKE
Cousin, stand forth, and look upon that man.

BAGOT
My Lord Aumerle, I know your daring tongue
Scorns to unsay what once it hath delivered.
In that dead time when Gloucester's death was plotted
I heard you say 'Is not my arm of length,
That reacheth from the restful English court
As far as Calais to mine uncle's head?'
Amongst much other talk that very time
I heard you say that you had rather refuse
The offer of an hundred thousand crowns
Than Bolingbroke's return to England,
Adding withal how blest this land would be
In this your cousin's death.

AUMERLE                    Princes and noble lords,
What answer shall I make to this base man?                    20
Shall I so much dishonour my fair stars
On equal terms to give him chastisement?
Either I must, or have mine honour soiled
With the attainder of his slanderous lips.
    *He throws down his gage*
There is my gage, the manual seal of death,
That marks thee out for hell. I say thou liest,
And will maintain what thou hast said is false
In thy heart-blood, though being all too base
To stain the temper of my knightly sword.

BOLINGBROKE
Bagot, forbear. Thou shalt not take it up.                    30

AUMERLE
Excepting one, I would he were the best
In all this presence that hath moved me so.

FITZWATER
If that thy valour stand on sympathy
There is my gage, Aumerle, in gage to thine.
    *He throws down his gage*
By that fair sun which shows me where thou standest
I heard thee say, and vauntingly thou spakest it,
That thou wert cause of noble Gloucester's death.
If thou deniest it twenty times, thou liest,
And I will turn thy falsehood to thy heart,
Where it was forgèd, with my rapier's point.                    40

AUMERLE
Thou darest not, coward, live to see that day.

FITZWATER
Now by my soul, I would it were this hour.

AUMERLE
Fitzwater, thou art damned to hell for this.

PERCY
    Aumerle, thou liest. His honour is as true
    In this appeal as thou art all unjust;
    And that thou art so there I throw my gage
    To prove it on thee to the extremest point
    Of mortal breathing.
       *He throws down his gage*
                       Seize it if thou darest.

AUMERLE
    And if I do not may my hands rot off,
50    And never brandish more revengeful steel
    Over the glittering helmet of my foe.

ANOTHER LORD
    I task the earth to the like, forsworn Aumerle,
    And spur thee on with full as many lies
    As may be hollowed in thy treacherous ear
    From sun to sun.
       *He throws down his gage*
                  There is my honour's pawn.
    Engage it to the trial if thou darest.

AUMERLE
    Who sets me else? By heaven, I'll throw at all.
    I have a thousand spirits in one breast
    To answer twenty thousand such as you.

SURREY
60    My Lord Fitzwater, I do remember well
    The very time Aumerle and you did talk.

FITZWATER
    'Tis very true. You were in presence then,
    And you can witness with me this is true.

SURREY
    As false, by heaven, as heaven itself is true.

FITZWATER
    Surrey, thou liest.

SURREY                Dishonourable boy,
That lie shall lie so heavy on my sword
That it shall render vengeance and revenge
Till thou, the lie-giver, and that lie do lie
In earth as quiet as thy father's skull.
In proof whereof, there is my honour's pawn.                    70
    *He throws down his gage*
Engage it to the trial if thou darest.

FITZWATER
How fondly dost thou spur a forward horse!
If I dare eat, or drink, or breathe, or live,
I dare meet Surrey in a wilderness
And spit upon him whilst I say he lies,
And lies, and lies. There is my bond of faith
To tie thee to my strong correction.
As I intend to thrive in this new world
Aumerle is guilty of my true appeal.
Besides, I heard the banished Norfolk say                    80
That thou, Aumerle, didst send two of thy men
To execute the noble Duke at Calais.

AUMERLE
Some honest Christian trust me with a gage.
    *He throws down a gage*
That Norfolk lies here do I throw down this,
If he may be repealed to try his honour.

BOLINGBROKE
These differences shall all rest under gage
Till Norfolk be repealed. Repealed he shall be,
And, though mine enemy, restored again
To all his lands and signories. When he is returned
Against Aumerle we will enforce his trial.                    90

BISHOP OF CARLISLE
That honourable day shall never be seen.
Many a time hath banished Norfolk fought

For Jesu Christ in glorious Christian field,
Streaming the ensign of the Christian cross
Against black pagans, Turks, and Saracens,
And, toiled with works of war, retired himself
To Italy, and there at Venice gave
His body to that pleasant country's earth,
And his pure soul unto his captain, Christ,
100   Under whose colours he had fought so long.

BOLINGBROKE
Why, Bishop, is Norfolk dead?

BISHOP OF CARLISLE
As surely as I live, my lord.

BOLINGBROKE
Sweet peace conduct his sweet soul to the bosom
Of good old Abraham! Lords appellants,
Your differences shall all rest under gage
Till we assign you to your days of trial.
        *Enter York*

YORK
Great Duke of Lancaster, I come to thee
From plume-plucked Richard, who with willing soul
Adopts thee heir, and his high sceptre yields
110   To the possession of thy royal hand.
Ascend his throne, descending now from him,
And long live Henry, fourth of that name!

BOLINGBROKE
In God's name I'll ascend the regal throne.

BISHOP OF CARLISLE
Marry, God forbid!
Worst in this royal presence may I speak,
Yet best beseeming me to speak the truth:
Would God that any in this noble presence
Were enough noble to be upright judge
Of noble Richard. Then true noblesse would

Learn him forbearance from so foul a wrong.                    120
What subject can give sentence on his king? —
And who sits here that is not Richard's subject?
Thieves are not judged but they are by to hear
Although apparent guilt be seen in them;
And shall the figure of God's majesty,
His captain, steward, deputy elect,
Anointed, crownèd, planted many years,
Be judged by subject and inferior breath
And he himself not present? O, forfend it God
That in a Christian climate souls refined                     130
Should show so heinous, black, obscene a deed!
I speak to subjects, and a subject speaks,
Stirred up by God thus boldly for his king.
My Lord of Hereford here, whom you call king,
Is a foul traitor to proud Hereford's King;
And if you crown him, let me prophesy
The blood of English shall manure the ground,
And future ages groan for this foul act.
Peace shall go sleep with Turks and infidels,
And in this seat of peace tumultuous wars                     140
Shall kin with kin, and kind with kind, confound.
Disorder, horror, fear, and mutiny
Shall here inhabit, and this land be called
The field of Golgotha and dead men's skulls.
O, if you raise this house against this house
It will the woefullest division prove
That ever fell upon this cursèd earth.
Prevent it; resist it; let it not be so,
Lest child, child's children, cry against you woe.

NORTHUMBERLAND

Well have you argued, sir; and for your pains                 150
Of capital treason we arrest you here.
My Lord of Westminster, be it your charge

To keep him safely till his day of trial.
May it please you, lords, to grant the commons' suit?

**BOLINGBROKE**

Fetch hither Richard, that in common view
He may surrender. So we shall proceed
Without suspicion.

YORK                          I will be his conduct.          *Exit*

**BOLINGBROKE**

Lords, you that here are under our arrest,
Procure your sureties for your days of answer.
160   Little are we beholding to your love,
And little looked for at your helping hands.

    *Enter Richard and York*

**RICHARD**

Alack, why am I sent for to a king
Before I have shook off the regal thoughts
Wherewith I reigned? I hardly yet have learned
To insinuate, flatter, bow, and bend my knee.
Give sorrow leave awhile to tutor me
To this submission. Yet I well remember
The favours of these men. Were they not mine?
Did they not sometime cry 'All hail!' to me?
170   So Judas did to Christ. But He in twelve
Found truth in all but one; I, in twelve thousand, none.
God save the King! Will no man say Amen?
Am I both priest and clerk? Well then, Amen.
God save the King, although I be not he;
And yet Amen if Heaven do think him me.
To do what service am I sent for hither?

**YORK**

To do that office of thine own good will
Which tired majesty did make thee offer:
The resignation of thy state and crown
To Henry Bolingbroke.

RICHARD                    Give me the crown.                    180
Here, cousin – seize the crown. Here, cousin –
On this side, my hand; and on that side, thine.
Now is this golden crown like a deep well
That owes two buckets, filling one another,
The emptier ever dancing in the air,
The other down, unseen, and full of water.
That bucket down and full of tears am I,
Drinking my griefs whilst you mount up on high.

BOLINGBROKE
I thought you had been willing to resign.

RICHARD
My crown I am; but still my griefs are mine.                    190
You may my glories and my state depose,
But not my griefs. Still am I king of those.

BOLINGBROKE
Part of your cares you give me with your crown.

RICHARD
Your cares set up do not pluck my cares down.
My care is loss of care by old care done;
Your care is gain of care by new care won.
The cares I give, I have, though given away.
They 'tend the crown, yet still with me they stay.

BOLINGBROKE
Are you contented to resign the crown?

RICHARD
Ay, no. No, ay; for I must nothing be.                    200
Therefore no no, for I resign to thee.
Now mark me how I will undo myself.
I give this heavy weight from off my head,
And this unwieldy sceptre from my hand,
The pride of kingly sway from out my heart.
With mine own tears I wash away my balm,
With mine own hands I give away my crown,

With mine own tongue deny my sacred state,
With mine own breath release all duteous oaths.
210   All pomp and majesty I do forswear.
My manors, rents, revenues I forgo.
My acts, decrees, and statutes I deny.
God pardon all oaths that are broke to me;
God keep all vows unbroke are made to thee;
Make me, that nothing have, with nothing grieved,
And thou with all pleased, that hast all achieved.
Long mayst thou live in Richard's seat to sit,
And soon lie Richard in an earthy pit.
'God save King Henry,' unkinged Richard says,
220   'And send him many years of sunshine days.'
What more remains?

NORTHUMBERLAND      No more but that you read
These accusations and these grievous crimes
Committed by your person and your followers
Against the state and profit of this land,
That by confessing them the souls of men
May deem that you are worthily deposed.

RICHARD
Must I do so? And must I ravel out
My weaved-up follies? Gentle Northumberland,
If thy offences were upon record,
230   Would it not shame thee in so fair a troop
To read a lecture of them? If thou wouldst,
There shouldst thou find one heinous article,
Containing the deposing of a king
And cracking the strong warrant of an oath,
Marked with a blot, damned in the book of heaven.
Nay, all of you that stand and look upon me,
Whilst that my wretchedness doth bait myself,
Though some of you – with Pilate – wash your hands,
Showing an outward pity, yet you Pilates

Have here delivered me to my sour cross,                    240
And water cannot wash away your sin.

NORTHUMBERLAND

My lord, dispatch. Read o'er these articles.

RICHARD

Mine eyes are full of tears. I cannot see.
And yet salt water blinds them not so much
But they can see a sort of traitors here.
Nay, if I turn mine eyes upon myself
I find myself a traitor with the rest.
For I have given here my soul's consent
To'undeck the pompous body of a king;
Made glory base, and sovereignty a slave;          250
Proud majesty, a subject; state, a peasant.

NORTHUMBERLAND

My lord –

RICHARD

No lord of thine, thou haught, insulting man;
Nor no man's lord. I have no name, no title –
No, not that name was given me at the font –
But 'tis usurped. Alack the heavy day,
That I have worn so many winters out
And know not now what name to call myself!
O that I were a mockery king of snow,
Standing before the sun of Bolingbroke,          260
To melt myself away in water-drops!
Good king; great king – and yet not greatly good –
An if my word be sterling yet in England
Let it command a mirror hither straight
That it may show me what a face I have
Since it is bankrupt of his majesty.

BOLINGBROKE

Go some of you, and fetch a looking-glass.

*Exit attendant*

NORTHUMBERLAND
    Read o'er this paper while the glass doth come.
RICHARD
    Fiend, thou torments me ere I come to hell.
BOLINGBROKE
270     Urge it no more, my Lord Northumberland.
NORTHUMBERLAND
    The commons will not then be satisfied.
RICHARD
    They shall be satisfied. I'll read enough
    When I do see the very book indeed
    Where all my sins are writ; and that's myself.
        *Enter attendant with a glass*
    Give me that glass, and therein will I read.
    No deeper wrinkles yet? Hath sorrow struck
    So many blows upon this face of mine
    And made no deeper wounds? O, flattering glass,
    Like to my followers in prosperity,
280     Thou dost beguile me. Was this face the face
    That every day under his household roof
    Did keep ten thousand men? Was this the face
    That like the sun did make beholders wink?
    Is this the face which faced so many follies,
    That was at last outfaced by Bolingbroke?
    A brittle glory shineth in this face.
    As brittle as the glory is the face,
        (*he throws the glass down*)
    For there it is, cracked in an hundred shivers.
    Mark, silent King, the moral of this sport:
290     How soon my sorrow hath destroyed my face.
BOLINGBROKE
    The shadow of your sorrow hath destroyed
    The shadow of your face.
RICHARD                        Say that again!

'The shadow of my sorrow' – ha, let's see.
'Tis very true. My grief lies all within,
And these external manner of laments
Are merely shadows to the unseen grief
That swells with silence in the tortured soul.
There lies the substance; and I thank thee, King,
For thy great bounty, that not only givest
Me cause to wail, but teachest me the way                    300
How to lament the cause. I'll beg one boon,
And then be gone and trouble you no more.
Shall I obtain it?

BOLINGBROKE          Name it, fair cousin.

RICHARD
'Fair cousin'? I am greater than a king;
For when I was a king my flatterers
Were then but subjects; being now a subject
I have a king here to my flatterer.
Being so great, I have no need to beg.

BOLINGBROKE
Yet ask.

RICHARD
And shall I have?                                            310

BOLINGBROKE
You shall.

RICHARD
Then give me leave to go.

BOLINGBROKE
Whither?

RICHARD
Whither you will, so I were from your sights.

BOLINGBROKE
Go some of you, convey him to the Tower.

RICHARD
O, good, 'convey!' – Conveyors are you all,

That rise thus nimbly by a true king's fall.

BOLINGBROKE

On Wednesday next we solemnly proclaim
Our coronation. Lords, be ready, all.

*Exeunt all except the Abbot of Westminster,*
*the Bishop of Carlisle, Aumerle*

ABBOT OF WESTMINSTER

320    A woeful pageant have we here beheld.

BISHOP OF CARLISLE

The woe's to come. The children yet unborn
Shall feel this day as sharp to them as thorn.

AUMERLE

You holy clergymen, is there no plot
To rid the realm of this pernicious blot?

ABBOT OF WESTMINSTER

My lord,
Before I freely speak my mind herein
You shall not only take the Sacrament
To bury mine intents, but also to effect
Whatever I shall happen to devise.

330    I see your brows are full of discontent,
Your hearts of sorrow, and your eyes of tears.
Come home with me to supper, I will lay
A plot shall show us all a merry day.            *Exeunt*

*

V.I            *Enter the Queen with her attendants*

QUEEN ISABEL

This way the King will come. This is the way
To Julius Caesar's ill-erected Tower,
To whose flint bosom my condemnèd lord
Is doomed a prisoner by proud Bolingbroke.

Here let us rest, if this rebellious earth
Have any resting for her true King's Queen.
   *Enter Richard and guard*
But soft, but see, or rather do not see,
My fair rose wither. Yet look up, behold,
That you in pity may dissolve to dew
And wash him fresh again with true-love tears.                     10
Ah, thou the model where old Troy did stand!
Thou map of honour, thou King Richard's tomb,
And not King Richard! Thou most beauteous inn,
Why should hard-favoured grief be lodged in thee
When triumph is become an alehouse guest?

RICHARD

Join not with grief, fair woman, do not so,
To make my end too sudden. Learn, good soul,
To think our former state a happy dream,
From which awaked the truth of what we are
Shows us but this. I am sworn brother, sweet,                      20
To grim Necessity, and he and I
Will keep a league till death. Hie thee to France,
And cloister thee in some religious house.
Our holy lives must win a new world's crown
Which our profane hours here have thrown down.

QUEEN ISABEL

What, is my Richard both in shape and mind
Transformed and weakened? Hath Bolingbroke
Deposed thine intellect? Hath he been in thy heart?
The lion dying thrusteth forth his paw
And wounds the earth, if nothing else, with rage                   30
To be o'erpowered. And wilt thou pupil-like
Take the correction, mildly kiss the rod,
And fawn on rage with base humility,
Which art a lion and the king of beasts?

RICHARD

    A king of beasts indeed! If aught but beasts
    I had been still a happy king of men.
    Good sometimes queen, prepare thee hence for France.
    Think I am dead, and that even here thou takest
    As from my deathbed thy last living leave.
40    In winter's tedious nights sit by the fire
    With good old folks, and let them tell thee tales
    Of woeful ages long ago betid;
    And ere thou bid goodnight, to quite their griefs
    Tell thou the lamentable tale of me,
    And send the hearers weeping to their beds;
    For why the senseless brands will sympathize
    The heavy accent of thy moving tongue,
    And in compassion weep the fire out;
    And some will mourn in ashes, some coal-black,
50    For the deposing of a rightful king.

    *Enter Northumberland*

NORTHUMBERLAND

    My lord, the mind of Bolingbroke is changed.
    You must to Pomfret, not unto the Tower.
    And, madam, there is order ta'en for you:
    With all swift speed you must away to France.

RICHARD

    Northumberland, thou ladder wherewithal
    The mounting Bolingbroke ascends my throne,
    The time shall not be many hours of age
    More than it is ere foul sin, gathering head,
    Shall break into corruption. Thou shalt think,
60    Though he divide the realm and give thee half,
    It is too little, helping him to all.
    He shall think that thou, which knowest the way
    To plant unrightful kings, wilt know again,
    Being ne'er so little urged another way,

To pluck him headlong from the usurped throne.
The love of wicked men converts to fear,
That fear to hate, and hate turns one or both
To worthy danger and deservèd death.

NORTHUMBERLAND

My guilt be on my head, and there an end.
Take leave and part, for you must part forthwith.  70

RICHARD

Doubly divorced! Bad men, you violate
A two-fold marriage – 'twixt my crown and me,
And then betwixt me and my married wife.
(*To Queen Isabel*)
Let me unkiss the oath 'twixt thee and me;
And yet not so; for with a kiss 'twas made.
– Part us, Northumberland: I towards the north,
Where shivering cold and sickness pines the clime;
My wife to France, from whence set forth in pomp
She came adornèd hither like sweet May,
Sent back like Hallowmas or shortest of day.  80

QUEEN ISABEL

And must we be divided? Must we part?

RICHARD

Ay, hand from hand, my love, and heart from heart.

QUEEN ISABEL (*to Northumberland*)

Banish us both, and send the King with me.

RICHARD

That were some love, but little policy.

QUEEN ISABEL

Then whither he goes, thither let me go.

RICHARD

So two together weeping make one woe.
Weep thou for me in France, I for thee here.
Better far off than, near, be ne'er the nea'er.
Go count thy way with sighs, I mine with groans.

QUEEN ISABEL

90      So longest way shall have the longest moans.

RICHARD

Twice for one step I'll groan, the way being short,
And piece the way out with a heavy heart.
Come, come – in wooing sorrow let's be brief,
Since wedding it, there is such length in grief.
One kiss shall stop our mouths, and dumbly part.
Thus give I mine, and thus take I thy heart.

     *They kiss*

QUEEN ISABEL

Give me mine own again. 'Twere no good part
To take on me to keep and kill thy heart.

     *They kiss*

So, now I have mine own again, be gone,

100      That I may strive to kill it with a groan.

RICHARD

We make woe wanton with this fond delay.
Once more, adieu. The rest let sorrow say.     *Exeunt*


**V.2**      *Enter Duke of York and the Duchess*

DUCHESS OF YORK

My lord, you told me you would tell the rest,
When weeping made you break the story off,
Of our two cousins' coming into London.

YORK

Where did I leave?

DUCHESS OF YORK    At that sad stop, my lord,
Where rude misgoverned hands from windows' tops
Threw dust and rubbish on King Richard's head.

YORK

Then, as I said, the Duke, great Bolingbroke,
Mounted upon a hot and fiery steed

Which his aspiring rider seemed to know,
With slow but stately pace kept on his course,          10
Whilst all tongues cried 'God save thee, Bolingbroke!'
You would have thought the very windows spake,
So many greedy looks of young and old
Through casements darted their desiring eyes
Upon his visage, and that all the walls
With painted imagery had said at once
'Jesu preserve thee, welcome Bolingbroke',
Whilst he, from the one side to the other turning,
Bare-headed, lower than his proud steed's neck
Bespake them thus: 'I thank you, countrymen.'          20
And thus still doing, thus he passed along.

DUCHESS OF YORK
Alack, poor Richard! Where rode he the whilst?

YORK
As in a theatre the eyes of men,
After a well graced actor leaves the stage,
Are idly bent on him that enters next,
Thinking his prattle to be tedious:
Even so, or with much more contempt, men's eyes
Did scowl on gentle Richard. No man cried 'God save
    him!'
No joyful tongue gave him his welcome home;
But dust was thrown upon his sacred head,               30
Which with such gentle sorrow he shook off,
His face still combating with tears and smiles,
The badges of his grief and patience,
That had not God for some strong purpose steeled
The hearts of men, they must perforce have melted,
And barbarism itself have pitied him.
But heaven hath a hand in these events,
To whose high will we bound our calm contents.
To Bolingbroke are we sworn subjects now,

40    Whose state and honour I for aye allow.
        *Enter Aumerle*
DUCHESS OF YORK
    Here comes my son Aumerle.
YORK                            Aumerle that was;
    But that is lost for being Richard's friend;
    And, madam, you must call him Rutland now.
    I am in Parliament pledge for his truth
    And lasting fealty to the new-made King.
DUCHESS OF YORK
    Welcome, my son! Who are the violets now
    That strew the green lap of the new-come spring?
AUMERLE
    Madam, I know not, nor I greatly care not.
    God knows I had as lief be none as one.
YORK
50    Well, bear you well in this new spring of time,
    Lest you be cropped before you come to prime.
    What news from Oxford? Do these justs and triumphs
        hold?
AUMERLE
    For aught I know, my lord, they do.
YORK
    You will be there, I know.
AUMERLE
    If God prevent not, I purpose so.
YORK
    What seal is that that hangs without thy bosom?
    Yea, lookest thou pale? Let me see the writing.
AUMERLE
    My lord, 'tis nothing.
YORK                        No matter, then, who see it.
    I will be satisfied. Let me see the writing.

AUMERLE

    I do beseech your grace to pardon me.        60

    It is a matter of small consequence

    Which for some reasons I would not have seen.

YORK

    Which for some reasons, sir, I mean to see.

    I fear – I fear!

DUCHESS OF YORK

               What should you fear?

    'Tis nothing but some bond that he is entered into

    For gay apparel 'gainst the triumph day.

YORK

    Bound to himself? What doth he with a bond

    That he is bound to? Wife, thou art a fool.

    Boy, let me see the writing.

AUMERLE

    I do beseech you, pardon me. I may not show it.    70

YORK

    I will be satisfied. Let me see it, I say.

       *He plucks it out of his bosom, and reads it*

YORK

    Treason! Foul treason! Villain! Traitor! Slave!

DUCHESS OF YORK

    What is the matter, my lord?

YORK

    Ho, who is within there? Saddle my horse.

    God for his mercy! What treachery is here!

DUCHESS OF YORK

    Why, what is it, my lord?

YORK

    Give me my boots, I say. Saddle my horse.

    Now, by mine honour, by my life, by my troth,

    I will appeach the villain.

DUCHESS OF YORK
80    What is the matter?
YORK                    Peace, foolish woman.
DUCHESS OF YORK
    I will not peace. What is the matter, Aumerle?
AUMERLE
    Good mother, be content. It is no more
    Than my poor life must answer.
DUCHESS OF YORK                    Thy life answer?
YORK
    Bring me my boots. I will unto the King.
        *His man enters with his boots*
DUCHESS OF YORK
    Strike him, Aumerle! Poor boy, thou art amazed.
    (*To York's man*)
    Hence, villain! Never more come in my sight!
YORK
    Give me my boots, I say!
        *York's man gives him the boots and goes out*
DUCHESS OF YORK
    Why, York, what wilt thou do?
    Wilt thou not hide the trespass of thine own?
90   Have we more sons? Or are we like to have?
    Is not my teeming-date drunk up with time?
    And wilt thou pluck my fair son from mine age?
    And rob me of a happy mother's name?
    Is he not like thee? Is he not thine own?
YORK
    Thou fond, mad woman,
    Wilt thou conceal this dark conspiracy?
    A dozen of them here have ta'en the Sacrament
    And interchangeably set down their hands
    To kill the King at Oxford.
DUCHESS OF YORK                    He shall be none.

We'll keep him here. Then what is that to him?          100
YORK

   Away, fond woman. Were he twenty times my son
   I would appeach him.
DUCHESS OF YORK

   Hadst thou groaned for him as I have done
   Thou wouldst be more pitiful.
   But now I know thy mind. Thou dost suspect
   That I have been disloyal to thy bed,
   And that he is a bastard, not thy son.
   Sweet York, sweet husband, be not of that mind.
   He is as like thee as a man may be;
   Not like to me, or any of my kin,                  110
   And yet I love him.
YORK                          Make way, unruly woman.     *Exit*
DUCHESS OF YORK

   After, Aumerle. Mount thee upon his horse.
   Spur, post, and get before him to the King,
   And beg thy pardon ere he do accuse thee.
   I'll not be long behind – though I be old,
   I doubt not but to ride as fast as York;
   And never will I rise up from the ground
   Till Bolingbroke have pardoned thee. Away, be gone!
                               *Exeunt*


*Enter Bolingbroke, now King Henry, with Harry*     V.3
*Percy and other lords*
KING HENRY

   Can no man tell me of my unthrifty son?
   'Tis full three months since I did see him last.
   If any plague hang over us, 'tis he.
   I would to God, my lords, he might be found.
   Inquire at London 'mongst the taverns there;

For there, they say, he daily doth frequent
With unrestrainèd loose companions,
Even such, they say, as stand in narrow lanes
And beat our watch, and rob our passengers,
10   Which he – young wanton, and effeminate boy –
Takes on the point of honour to support
So dissolute a crew.

PERCY
My lord, some two days since I saw the Prince,
And told him of those triumphs held at Oxford.

KING HENRY
And what said the gallant?

PERCY
His answer was he would unto the stews,
And from the commonest creature pluck a glove,
And wear it as a favour; and with that
He would unhorse the lustiest challenger.

KING HENRY
20   As dissolute as desperate. Yet through both
I see some sparks of better hope, which elder years
May happily bring forth. But who comes here?
    *Enter Aumerle, amazed*

AUMERLE
Where is the King?

KING HENRY
What means our cousin, that he stares and looks so
    wildly?

AUMERLE
God save your grace. I do beseech your majesty
To have some conference with your grace alone.

KING HENRY
Withdraw yourselves, and leave us here alone.
        *Exeunt Harry Percy and the other lords*
What is the matter with our cousin now?

AUMERLE

> For ever may my knees grow to the earth,
> My tongue cleave to my roof within my mouth,                    30
> Unless a pardon ere I rise or speak.

KING HENRY

> Intended or committed was this fault?
> If on the first, how heinous e'er it be
> To win thy after-love I pardon thee.

AUMERLE

> Then give me leave that I may turn the key
> That no man enter till my tale be done.

KING HENRY

> Have thy desire.

> > *Aumerle locks the door. The Duke of York knocks at*
> > *the door and crieth*

YORK (*within*)

> My liege, beware, look to thyself,
> Thou hast a traitor in thy presence there.

KING HENRY (*to Aumerle*)

> Villain, I'll make thee safe!                                    40

AUMERLE

> Stay thy revengeful hand, thou hast no cause to fear.

YORK

> Open the door, secure foolhardy King.
> Shall I for love speak treason to thy face?
> Open the door, or I will break it open.

> > *King Henry opens the door. Enter York*

KING HENRY

> What is the matter, uncle? Speak, recover breath,
> Tell us how near is danger,
> That we may arm us to encounter it.

YORK

> Peruse this writing here, and thou shalt know
> The treason that my haste forbids me show.

AUMERLE

50    Remember, as thou readest, thy promise passed.
      I do repent me. Read not my name there.
      My heart is not confederate with my hand.

YORK

      It was, villain, ere thy hand did set it down.
      I tore it from the traitor's bosom, King.
      Fear, and not love, begets his penitence.
      Forget to pity him lest thy pity prove
      A serpent that will sting thee to the heart.

KING HENRY

      O, heinous, strong, and bold conspiracy!
      O loyal father of a treacherous son,

60    Thou sheer immaculate and silver fountain
      From whence this stream through muddy passages
      Hath held his current and defiled himself –
      Thy overflow of good converts to bad,
      And thy abundant goodness shall excuse
      This deadly blot in thy digressing son.

YORK

      So shall my virtue be his vice's bawd
      An he shall spend mine honour with his shame,
      As thriftless sons their scraping fathers' gold.
      Mine honour lives when his dishonour dies,

70    Or my shamed life in his dishonour lies.
      Thou killest me in his life – giving him breath,
      The traitor lives, the true man's put to death.

DUCHESS OF YORK (*within*)

      What ho, my liege, for God's sake let me in!

KING HENRY

      What shrill-voiced suppliant makes this eager cry?

DUCHESS OF YORK

      A woman, and thy aunt, great King. 'Tis I.
      Speak with me, pity me, open the door!

A beggar begs that never begged before.

KING HENRY

Our scene is altered from a serious thing,
And now changed to 'The Beggar and the King'.
My dangerous cousin, let your mother in.                    80
I know she is come to pray for your foul sin.
*Aumerle admits the Duchess. She kneels*

YORK

If thou do pardon, whosoever pray,
More sins for this forgiveness prosper may.
This festered joint cut off, the rest rest sound;
This let alone will all the rest confound.

DUCHESS OF YORK

O King, believe not this hard-hearted man.
Love loving not itself, none other can.

YORK

Thou frantic woman, what dost thou make here?
Shall thy old dugs once more a traitor rear?

DUCHESS OF YORK

Sweet York, be patient. Hear me, gentle liege.          90

KING HENRY

Rise up, good aunt!

DUCHESS OF YORK    Not yet, I thee beseech.
For ever will I walk upon my knees,
And never see day that the happy sees
Till thou give joy, until thou bid me joy
By pardoning Rutland, my transgressing boy.

AUMERLE

Unto my mother's prayers I bend my knee.
*He kneels*

YORK

Against them both my true joints bended be.
*He kneels*
Ill mayst thou thrive if thou grant any grace.

DUCHESS OF YORK
    Pleads he in earnest? Look upon his face.
100    His eyes do drop no tears, his prayers are in jest;
    His words come from his mouth, ours from our breast.
    He prays but faintly, and would be denied;
    We pray with heart and soul, and all beside.
    His weary joints would gladly rise, I know;
    Our knees still kneel till to the ground they grow.
    His prayers are full of false hypocrisy,
    Ours of true zeal and deep integrity.
    Our prayers do outpray his: then let them have
    That mercy which true prayer ought to have.

KING HENRY
110    Good aunt, stand up!

DUCHESS OF YORK    Nay, do not say 'Stand up!'
    Say 'Pardon' first, and afterwards, 'Stand up!'
    An if I were thy nurse thy tongue to teach,
    'Pardon' should be the first word of thy speech.
    I never longed to hear a word till now.
    Say 'Pardon', King. Let pity teach thee how.
    The word is short, but not so short as sweet.
    No word like 'Pardon' for kings' mouths so meet.

YORK
    Speak it in French, King: say 'Pardonne-moi.'

DUCHESS OF YORK
    Dost thou teach pardon pardon to destroy?
120    Ah, my sour husband, my hard-hearted lord!
    That sets the word itself against the word.
    Speak 'Pardon' as 'tis current in our land;
    The chopping French we do not understand.
    Thine eye begins to speak. Set thy tongue there;
    Or in thy piteous heart plant thou thine ear,
    That hearing how our plaints and prayers do pierce,
    Pity may move thee pardon to rehearse.

KING HENRY

Good aunt, stand up.

DUCHESS OF YORK       I do not sue to stand.

Pardon is all the suit I have in hand.

KING HENRY

I pardon him as God shall pardon me.                    130

DUCHESS OF YORK

O, happy vantage of a kneeling knee!

Yet am I sick for fear. Speak it again.

Twice saying pardon doth not pardon twain,

But makes one pardon strong.

KING HENRY                              With all my heart

I pardon him.

DUCHESS OF YORK

A god on earth thou art!

*York, Duchess of York, and Aumerle stand*

KING HENRY

But for our trusty brother-in-law and the Abbot,

With all the rest of that consorted crew,

Destruction straight shall dog them at the heels.

Good uncle, help to order several powers

To Oxford, or where'er these traitors are.                    140

They shall not live within this world, I swear,

But I will have them if I once know where.

Uncle, farewell; and cousin, adieu.

Your mother well hath prayed; and prove you true.

DUCHESS OF YORK

Come, my old son. I pray God make thee new. *Exeunt*


*Enter Sir Piers of Exton and a Man*                    V.4

EXTON

Didst thou not mark the King, what words he spake?

'Have I no friend will rid me of this living fear?'

Was it not so?

MAN                    These were his very words.

EXTON

'Have I no friend?' quoth he. He spake it twice,
And urged it twice together, did he not?

MAN

He did.

EXTON

And speaking it, he wishtly looked on me,
As who should say 'I would thou wert the man
That would divorce this terror from my heart' –
10  Meaning the King at Pomfret. Come, let's go.
I am the King's friend, and will rid his foe.      *Exeunt*


V.5        *Enter Richard alone*

RICHARD

I have been studying how I may compare
This prison where I live unto the world;
And for because the world is populous,
And here is not a creature but myself,
I cannot do it. Yet I'll hammer it out.
My brain I'll prove the female to my soul,
My soul the father, and these two beget
A generation of still-breeding thoughts,
And these same thoughts people this little world,
10  In humours like the people of this world.
For no thought is contented; the better sort,
As thoughts of things divine, are intermixed
With scruples, and do set the word itself
Against the word; as thus: 'Come, little ones';
And then again,
'It is as hard to come as for a camel
To thread the postern of a small needle's eye.'

Thoughts tending to ambition, they do plot
Unlikely wonders – how these vain weak nails
May tear a passage through the flinty ribs                     20
Of this hard world, my ragged prison walls,
And for they cannot, die in their own pride.
Thoughts tending to content flatter themselves
That they are not the first of Fortune's slaves,
Nor shall not be the last; like seely beggars,
Who, sitting in the stocks, refuge their shame
That many have, and others must sit there.
And in this thought they find a kind of ease,
Bearing their own misfortunes on the back
Of such as have before endured the like.                       30
Thus play I in one person many people,
And none contented. Sometimes am I king.
Then treasons make me wish myself a beggar;
And so I am. Then crushing penury
Persuades me I was better when a king.
Then am I kinged again; and by and by
Think that I am unkinged by Bolingbroke,
And straight am nothing. But whate'er I be,
Nor I, nor any man that but man is,
With nothing shall be pleased till he be eased                 40
With being nothing. (*The music plays*) Music do I hear.
Ha, ha; keep time! How sour sweet music is
When time is broke, and no proportion kept.
So is it in the music of men's lives;
And here have I the daintiness of ear
To check time broke in a disordered string,
But for the concord of my state and time,
Had not an ear to hear my true time broke.
I wasted time, and now doth time waste me;
For now hath time made me his numbering clock.                 50
My thoughts are minutes, and with sighs they jar

Their watches on unto mine eyes, the outward watch
Whereto my finger, like a dial's point,
Is pointing still in cleansing them from tears.
Now, sir, the sound that tells what hour it is
Are clamorous groans which strike upon my heart,
Which is the bell. So sighs, and tears, and groans
Show minutes, times, and hours. But my time
Runs posting on in Bolingbroke's proud joy,
60    While I stand fooling here, his jack of the clock.
This music mads me. Let it sound no more;
For though it have holp madmen to their wits,
In me it seems it will make wise men mad.
Yet blessing on his heart that gives it me;
For 'tis a sign of love, and love to Richard
Is a strange brooch in this all-hating world.
        *Enter a Groom of the stable*

GROOM
    Hail, royal prince!
RICHARD                    Thanks, noble peer.
    The cheapest of us is ten groats too dear.
    What art thou, and how comest thou hither
70    Where no man never comes but that sad dog
    That brings me food to make misfortune live?

GROOM
    I was a poor groom of thy stable, King,
    When thou wert king; who travelling towards York
    With much ado at length have gotten leave
    To look upon my sometimes royal master's face.
    O, how it earned my heart when I beheld
    In London streets, that coronation day,
    When Bolingbroke rode on roan Barbary,
    That horse that thou so often hast bestrid,
80    That horse that I so carefully have dressed!

RICHARD

Rode he on Barbary? Tell me, gentle friend,
How went he under him?

GROOM

So proudly as if he disdained the ground.

RICHARD

So proud that Bolingbroke was on his back!
That jade hath eat bread from my royal hand;
This hand hath made him proud with clapping him.
Would he not stumble, would he not fall down –
Since pride must have a fall – and break the neck
Of that proud man that did usurp his back?
Forgiveness, horse! Why do I rail on thee,                 90
Since thou, created to be awed by man,
Wast born to bear? I was not made a horse,
And yet I bear a burden like an ass,
Spurred, galled, and tired by jauncing Bolingbroke.
    *Enter Keeper to Richard with meat*

KEEPER (*to Groom*)

Fellow, give place. Here is no longer stay.

RICHARD (*to Groom*)

If thou love me, 'tis time thou wert away.

GROOM

What my tongue dares not, that my heart shall say.
                                                    *Exit*

KEEPER

My lord, will't please you to fall to?

RICHARD

Taste of it first, as thou art wont to do.

KEEPER

My lord, I dare not. Sir Piers of Exton,                   100
Who lately came from the King, commands the contrary.

RICHARD (*attacks the Keeper*)

The devil take Henry of Lancaster, and thee.

Patience is stale, and I am weary of it.

KEEPER

Help, help, help!

*The murderers, Exton and servants, rush in*

RICHARD

How now! What means death in this rude assault?
Villain, thy own hand yields thy death's instrument.

*He snatches a weapon from a servant and kills him*

Go thou, and fill another room in hell.

*He kills another servant. Here Exton strikes him down*

RICHARD

That hand shall burn in never-quenching fire
That staggers thus my person. Exton, thy fierce hand
110 Hath with the King's blood stained the King's own land.
Mount, mount, my soul. Thy seat is up on high,
Whilst my gross flesh sinks downward here to die.

*He dies*

EXTON

As full of valour as of royal blood.
Both have I spilled. O, would the deed were good!
For now the devil, that told me I did well,
Says that this deed is chronicled in hell.
This dead King to the living King I'll bear.
Take hence the rest, and give them burial here.

*Exeunt with the bodies*


V.6        *Flourish. Enter King Henry with the Duke of York,*
           *other lords, and attendants*

KING HENRY

Kind uncle York, the latest news we hear
Is that the rebels have consumed with fire
Our town of Ciceter in Gloucestershire.
But whether they be ta'en or slain we hear not.

*Enter Northumberland*

Welcome, my lord. What is the news?

NORTHUMBERLAND

First, to thy sacred state wish I all happiness.

The next news is, I have to London sent

The heads of Salisbury, Spencer, Blunt, and Kent.

The manner of their taking may appear

At large discoursèd in this paper here.                              10

KING HENRY

We thank thee, gentle Percy, for thy pains;

And to thy worth will add right worthy gains.

*Enter Lord Fitzwater*

FITZWATER

My lord, I have from Oxford sent to London

The heads of Brocas and Sir Bennet Seely,

Two of the dangerous consorted traitors

That sought at Oxford thy dire overthrow.

KING HENRY

Thy pains, Fitzwater, shall not be forgot.

Right noble is thy merit, well I wot.

*Enter Harry Percy with the Bishop of Carlisle,*
*guarded*

PERCY

The grand conspirator Abbot of Westminster

With clog of conscience and sour melancholy                          20

Hath yielded up his body to the grave;

But here is Carlisle living, to abide

Thy kingly doom and sentence of his pride.

KING HENRY

Carlisle, this is your doom:

Choose out some secret place, some reverent room

More than thou hast, and with it joy thy life.

So as thou livest in peace, die free from strife;

For though mine enemy thou hast ever been,

High sparks of honour in thee have I seen.
*Enter Exton with the coffin*

EXTON

30 Great King, within this coffin I present
Thy buried fear. Herein all breathless lies
The mightiest of thy greatest enemies,
Richard of Bordeaux, by me hither brought.

KING HENRY

Exton, I thank thee not; for thou hast wrought
A deed of slander with thy fatal hand
Upon my head and all this famous land.

EXTON

From your own mouth, my lord, did I this deed.

KING HENRY

They love not poison that do poison need;
Nor do I thee. Though I did wish him dead,
40 I hate the murderer, love him murderèd.
The guilt of conscience take thou for thy labour,
But neither my good word nor princely favour.
With Cain go wander thorough shades of night,
And never show thy head by day nor light.
*Exit Exton*

Lords, I protest, my soul is full of woe
That blood should sprinkle me to make me grow.
Come mourn with me for what I do lament,
And put on sullen black incontinent.
I'll make a voyage to the Holy Land
50 To wash this blood off from my guilty hand.
March sadly after. Grace my mournings here
In weeping after this untimely bier.          *Exeunt*

# An Account of the Text

*Richard II* was first printed in 1597, in the edition known as the first Quarto (Q1). It is described on the title page as *The Tragedy of King Richard the Second. As it hath been publicly acted by the Right Honourable the Lord Chamberlain his Servants*. The Lord Chamberlain's was the acting company to which Shakespeare belonged. The play seems to have been printed from his own manuscript, and with an unusually high standard of accuracy. As no manuscript has survived, modern editions must be based on the first Quarto. But it lacks one important episode – that portraying Richard's abdication (IV.1.154–319). This was omitted most probably for political reasons, perhaps out of tact, or because the printers feared prosecution, or because they had been instructed to omit it. It contains nothing obviously inflammatory, but was certainly considered dangerous at a time of anxiety about the succession. A little tinkering was done to bridge the gap but there was no real revision, and the fact that the Abbot's line 'A woeful pageant have we here beheld' (IV.1.320) was retained though the 'pageant' had disappeared is a good reason for believing that the cut was not theatrical.

   *Richard II* was popular, and the Quarto was reprinted twice in 1598 (Q2 and Q3). The abdication scene continued to be omitted. The fourth edition (Q4) appeared in 1608. By this time the succession problem had been resolved, and the printer was able to announce on the title page *The Tragedy of King Richard the Second: With new additions of the Parliament Scene, and the deposing of King Richard, as it hath been lately acted by the King's Majesty's Servants at the Globe. By William Shakespeare.* Unfortunately the text of the added passages contains many obvious mistakes, and was printed probably from an unauthorized source. The next edition appeared in 1615, and is a reprint of the previous one.

The other important text is the one in the collected edition of Shakespeare's plays, the first Folio (F), of 1623. The printers seem to have worked from a copy of Q3 with the substitution of a few leaves from Q5. There are two main reasons why this text is important. One is that the Quarto from which it was printed had been altered from a source that was obviously theatrical in origin. The natural assumption is that it had been checked against the theatre prompt book, which would be a manuscript or printed copy annotated and marked in accordance with theatre practice. It would, for example, indicate trumpet calls that Shakespeare had not noted in the manuscript, and might mark cuts. The stage directions in F are notably more precise and businesslike than those in the Quartos. They obviously reflect the stage practice of Shakespeare's company and are our main source of information about how the play was put on the stage in his time. They have been incorporated in the present edition. Other alterations were made, some of which may be considered improvements on Q1. We have no reason to suppose that F presents an authoritatively corrected text, and the present edition is conservative in adopting Folio readings where Quarto ones are acceptable. The collations, however, record plausible readings from F among the rejected emendations.

The other main reason for F's importance is that it includes a good text of the abdication episode omitted from the early Quartos. Modern editors therefore use F as their basic text for this passage, while adopting some readings from Q4. The present edition is closer to F than most modern ones.

Fifty-one lines of the play were omitted from F. They are: I.3.129–33; I.3.239–42; I.3.268–93; II.2.77; III.2.29–32, 49, 182; IV.1.52–9; V.3.98. Some of these omissions may be accidental, some may represent theatrical cutting.

In the present edition, spelling and punctuation have been modernized, speech-prefixes have been made consistent, and stage directions have been regularized and amplified where necessary. The collations that follow record departures from Q1 (F for the abdication episode); places where the present edition preserves original readings that other editors have often altered; and the more important modifications of the original stage directions. Quotations from early editions are given in the original spelling, but long 's' [ʃ] has been replaced by the modern form. 'Q' indicates a reading common to all the early Quartos (Q1–5). The more interesting textual points are discussed in the Commentary.

## COLLATIONS

### *ı Emendations*

The following list indicates readings in the present edition of *Richard II* which depart from the first edition (Q1) or, in the abdication episode (IV.1.154–319), from the first Folio (F). It does not list corrections of simple misprints. Alterations of punctuation are recorded when a decision affecting the sense has had to be made. When the emendation derives from a later Quarto or the Folio, this is indicated. Most of the other emendations were first made by eighteenth-century editors.

The Characters in the Play] *not in* Q, F

**I.1**

    3 Hereford] Q1 *often, but by no means regularly, spells* Herford

  15 presence. *Exit Attendant* Face] presence face

 118 my] F; *not in* Q

 122 subject, Mowbray. So] subject Mowbray so

 152 gentlemen] F; gentleman Q

162–3 When, Harry, when? | Obedience bids] When Harry? when obedience bids, | Obedience bids Q1; When *Harrie* when? Obedience bids, | Obedience bids Q2–5, F

**I.2**

 47 sit] F; set Q

**I.3**

 33 comest] Q5, F; comes

 172 then] F; *not in* Q

 180 you owe] F; y'owe Q

 193 far as] fare as Q; fare, as F (*see Commentary*)

222 night] Q4–5, F; nightes Q1–3
239 had it] had't

I.4

20 cousin, cousin] F; Coosens Coosin Q
52–3 *Enter Bushy* | Bushy, what news?] F; *Enter Bushie with*
*newes.* Q
65 ALL] *not in* Q, F (*which also omits* 'Amen')

II.1

18 fond] found Q1
48 as a moat] Q4–5, F; as moate Q1–3
102 encagèd] F (incaged); inraged Q
124 brother] Q2–5; brothers Q1, F
177 the] F; a Q
257 King's] Q3–5, F; King Q1
280 The son of Richard Earl of Arundel] *not in* Q, F
284 Coint] Coines Q; *Quoint* F

II.2

16 eye] F; eyes
147 BAGOT] *not in* Q (F *gives the line to Bushy*)

II.3

9 Cotswold] Cotshall Q; Cottshold F
36 Hereford, boy?] Q3; Herefords boy? Q1
163 Bristol] Bristow

III.2

31 not – heaven's offer we] not, heauens offer, we Q1
32 succour] succors
40 boldly] bouldy Q1
72 O'erthrows] F; Ouerthrowes Q

III.3

12–13 Would you have been so brief with him, he would |
Have been so brief with you to shorten you] F; would
you haue beene so briefe with him, | He would haue
bin so briefe to shorten you Q
31 lord] F; Lords Q
59–60 rain | My waters – on] raigne. | My water's on Q1–2;
raine | My water's on Q3–5; raine | My Waters on F
119 a prince and] (Sisson) princesse Q1–2; a Prince Q3–5;
a Prince, is F

140 Swellest thou, proud heart? I'll] F; Swellst thou (prowd heart) Ile

### III.4

*Speech-prefixes to 3, 6, 10, 11 (second part), 19 (first part), 21]* *Lady* Q; *La.* F

11 joy] griefe

21 weep, ... good.] Q2; weep; ... good? Q1

34 too] F; two

*Speech-prefixes to 40, 54 (first part), 67] Man.* Q; *Ser.* F

57 garden! We at] garden at

80 Camest] Q2; Canst

### IV.1

22 him] Q3 (my Q2); them

43 Fitzwater] F; Fitzwaters

54 As may] As it may

55 sun to sun] sinne to sinne

62 true.] true (true, Q2; true: F)

76 my] Q3; *not in* Q1 (the Q2)

83-4 gage. | That] gage, | That

154-319 *This passage is not in* Q1-3. *See An Account of the Text,* *p.109. In its place,* Q1 *has:* Bull. Let it be so, and loe on wednesday next, | We solemnly proclaime our Coronation, | Lords be ready all.

182 and] (Q4, 5) *not in* F

250 and] (Q4) a F

253 haught, insulting] (haught insulting Q4-5) haught-insulting F

254 Nor] (Q4) No, nor F

259 mockery king] (Q4) Mockerie, King F

318-19 proclaim | Our coronation. Lords, be ready, all.] Q1; set downe | Our Coronation: Lords, prepare your selues. F

332 I will] Ile

### V.1

20 this.] this: Q1 (*where the colon could be the equivalent of a modern fullstop*)

41 thee] Q2; the

88 off than, near,] (*unpunctuated,* Q) off, then neere, F

**V.2**

    11, 17 thee] F; the Q (*where, however, 'thee' is often spelt thus*)

**V.3**

      35 that I may] Q2; that May

      74 shrill-voiced] Q3; shril voice

    110 KING HENRY] Q2; *yorke*

  134–5 With all my heart | I pardon him] I pardon him with al my heart

**V.5**

    27 sit] Q3; set

**V.6**

     8 Salisbury, Spencer] F; Oxford, Salisbury Q

   43 thorough shades] through shades Q1; through the shade Q2–5, F

### 2 Rejected Emendations

The list printed below gives readings of the authoritative editions (Q1, and F1 for the abdication scene) which have been preserved in the present edition but which are often emended. The common emendations are given to the right of the square bracket. The aim has been to list alterations affecting the sense, especially those that are to be found in some of the editions still current. Most of them derive from the Folio, which until the early years of this century was generally considered the most authoritative early text. As the Folio has a special interest in spite of its generally inferior authority, some of its more interesting variants are noted even when they have been generally rejected. When a reading derives from an early edition (Q1–5, F) this is indicated. Most of the unattributed emendations were first made by eighteenth-century editors, many of them in an attempt to regularize the metre. The temptation to do this is strong, but Shakespeare may not have had the precise rhythmic sense that many of his editors assume in him.

**I.I**

    97 Fetch] Fetcht Q3–5, Fetch'd F

  186 up] downe F

  187 deep] foule F

**I.2**

    62 thy] my F

**I.3**

    15 As] And
    20 my succeeding] his succeeding F
    26 ask] demand of
    84 innocence] innocency
  193 far as] fare as (*see Commentary*)

**I.4**

    23 Ourself and Bushy] Ourself and Bushy, Bagot here, and Green
    59 the] his F

**II.1**

    70 raged] ragged; reined
  115 And thou – | KING RICHARD – a lunatic] And thou. | *King*. Ah lunatick Q3–5; And – | *Rich*. And thou, a lunaticke F
  254 noble] *omitted in* F *and by many editors*
278, 285 Brittaine] Britain; Brittany; Bretagne

**II.2**

    12 trembles. At something] (trembles, at something Q1) trembles, yet at something
    25 more is] more's F
    31 on thinking] in thinking
    88 The nobles they are fled. The commons they are cold] The nobles they are fled, the commons cold
  110 disorderly thrust] thrust disorderly
  112 T'one] (Q: Tone) Th'one F
  113 T'other] (Q: tother) th'other F
  118 Berkeley] Barkley Castle F
  128 that is] that's F
  137 Will the hateful commons] The hateful commons will

**II.3**

    65 thank's] thankes, F
    80 self-borne] self-born
    98 lord] the Lord F
  122 in] of Q2–5, F

150 never] ne'er (ne're Q3–5; neu'r F)
157 unto] to Q2–5, F

## II.4

8 are all] all are Q2–5, F

## III.2

30 neglected; else heaven] (Q1: neglected. Else heauen)
   neglected; else, if heaven
38 that] and
40 boldly] (bouldy Q1) bloudy Q2, bloody F
133–4 Would they make peace? Terrible hell | Make war upon
      their spotted souls for this.] Would they make peace?
      terrible Hell make warre | Vpon their spotted Soules
      for this Offence. F

## III.3

17 mistake the] mistake; the; mistake. The; mistake: the
100 pastor's] (pastors Q1) pasture's; pastures'
121 thus. The King returns] thus the King returns:
168 laid there] (laide; there Q1) laid – there
177 you,] you;
182 base-court. Come down – down] (Q1: base court come
    downe: downe) base court? Come down? Down
202 hands] hand F

## III.4

27 They will] They'le F
29 young] yon Q2
67 you the] you then the
80 this] these

## IV.1

13 mine] my F
49 And if] An if
89 he is] hee's F
91 never] ne're F
112 fourth of that name] of that Name the Fourth F
165 knee] limbes? Q4
182 thine] yours Q4
209 duteous oaths] duties rites Q4
214 are made] that sweare Q4
219 Henry] Harry Q4
275 that] the Q4

284 Is this the face which] Was ... that Q4
285 That] And Q4
288 an] a Q4
295 manner] manners Q4
       laments] lament
318–19 proclaim | Our coronation. Lords, be ready, all.] set
       downe | Our Coronation: Lords, prepare your selues.
       F

### V.1

25 thrown] stricken F
32 the correction] thy correction Q2
       correction, mildly] Correction mildly, F
34 the king] a King Q2, F
37 sometimes] sometime Q3, F
43 quite] quit F
44 tale] fall F
62 He] And he
64 urged another way,] urged, another way,; urged, another
       way; urged another way
66 men] friends F
71 Doubly divorced! Bad] (Doubly diuorst (bad) Q1;
       Doubly diuorc'd? (bad F
84 RICHARD] *North.* F

### V.2

18 the one] one F
28 gentle] *not in* F
52 Do these justs and triumphs hold?] Hold those Iusts &
       Triumphs? F
55 prevent not] prevent me not; prevent it not
74 *Some editors add the direction:* Enter a Servant. *See
       Commentary.*
78 by my life, by my troth] my life, my troth Q2, F; by
       my life, my troth
113 Spur, post] Spurre post F

### V.3

10 Which] While
20 Yet] But yet [*with relineation, lines ending* yet, hope,
       forth, means] (Harold Brooks, in Ure's Arden edition)
30 my roof] the roof

        40  Villain] *omitted* (Ure)
        45  What is the matter,] *omitted* (Ure)
        67  An] And F *and editors*
       105  still] shall F
       143  cousin,] Cosin too, Q6

**V.4**

         7  wishtly] wistly Q3, F

**V.5**

        56  which] that F
        70  never] euer Q5, F
       105  means] meanest

### *3 Stage Directions*

Stage directions in the present edition are based on those of Q1.
The original directions have been normalized and clarified. They
are often inadequate, failing for instance to indicate many obvious
entrances and exits. Additional directions have been made from
F, which is much more precise in its instructions to the performers,
and often indicates the practice of Shakespeare's company. Further
directions have been added where necessary to clarify the action.
All directions for speeches to be given aside or addressed to a
particular character are editorial. Below are listed some of the
other additions and alterations to Q's stage directions. When these
derive in whole or part from F, this is noted. Minor alterations
such as the addition of a character's name to *Exit*, the change of
*Exit* to *Exeunt*, the normalization of character names, and the
provision of exits and entrances where these are obviously
demanded by the context are not listed here.

**I.1**

         0  *Enter King Richard and John of Gaunt, with other nobles,*
            *including the Lord Marshal, and attendants*] *Enter King*
            *Richard, Iohn of Gaunt, with other Nobles and attendants.*
            Q, F
        15  *not in* Q, F
        69  *not in* Q, F
        78  *not in* Q, F

149 *not in* Q, F
165 *not in* Q, F
195 F; *not in* Q

**I.3**

6 *The trumpets sound and the King enters with his nobles,
including Gaunt, and Bushy, Bagot, and Green. When
they are set, enter Mowbray, Duke of Norfolk, in arms,
defendant; and a Herald*] *The trumpets sound and the
King enters with his nobles, when they are set, enter the
Duke of Norfolke in armes defendant.* Q; *Flourish. Enter
King, Gaunt, Bushy, Bagot, Greene, & others: Then
Mowbray in Armor, and Harrold.* F

25 *The trumpets sound. Enter Bolingbroke, Duke of Hereford,
appellant, in armour; and a Herald*] *The trumpets sound.
Enter Duke of Hereford appellant in armour.* Q; *Tucket.
Enter Hereford, and Harold.* F

54 *not in* Q, F

117 *A charge sounded. King Richard throws his warder into
the lists*] *not in* Q. *A charge sounded* F

122 *A long flourish. King Richard consults his nobles, then
addresses the combatants*] *not in* Q. *A long Flourish.* F

248 *Flourish. Exit King Richard with his train*] *not in* Q. *Exit.
Flourish.* F

**I.4**

0 *Enter the King with Bagot and Green at one door, and the
Lord Aumerle at another*] *Enter the King with Bushie, &c
at one dore, and the Lord Aumarle at another.* Q; *Enter
King, Aumerle, Greene, and Bagot.* F

52 *(see Commentary)*

**II.1**

0 *Enter John of Gaunt sick, with the Duke of York, the Earl
of Northumberland, attendants, and others*] *Enter Iohn of
Gaunt sicke, with the duke of Yorke, &c.* Q; *Enter Gaunt,
sicke with Yorke.* F

68 *Enter King Richard, Queen Isabel, Aumerle, Bushy,
Green, Bagot, Ross, and Willoughby*] F; *Enter king and
Queene, & c.* Q

223 *Flourish. Exeunt King Richard and Queen Isabel.*

*Northumberland, Willoughby, and Ross remain*] *Exeunt King and Queene: Manet North.* Q; *Flourish. Manet North. Willoughby, & Ross.* F

## II.3

82 *not in* Q, F

## III.1

o *Enter Bolingbroke, York, Northumberland, with Bushy and Green, prisoners*] *Enter Duke of Hereford, Yorke, Northumberland, Bushie and Greene prisoners.* Q; *Enter Bullingbrooke, Yorke, Northumberland, Rosse, Percie, Willoughby, with Bushie and Greene Prisoners.* F

## III.2

o *Drums; flourish and colours. Enter King Richard, Aumerle, the Bishop of Carlisle, and soldiers*] *Enter the King Aumerle, Carleil, &c.* Q; *Drums: Flourish, and Colours. Enter Richard, Aumerle, Carlile, and Souldiers.* F

## III.3

o *Enter with drum and colours Bolingbroke, York, Northumberland, attendants, and soldiers*] *Enter Bull. Yorke, North.* Q; *Enter with Drum and Colours, Bullingbrooke, Yorke, Northumberland, Attendants.* F

61 *The trumpets sound parley without, and answer within; then a flourish. King Richard appeareth on the walls with the Bishop of Carlisle, Aumerle, Scroop, and Salisbury*] *The trumpets sound, Richard appeareth on the walls.* Q; *Parle without, and answere within: then a Flourish. Enter on the Walls, Richard, Carlile, Aumerle, Scroop, Salisbury.* F

183 *not in* Q, F

186 *not in* Q, F

209 F; *not in* Q

## III.4

o *Enter the Queen with two Ladies, her attendants*] *Enter the Queene with her attendants* Q; *Enter the Queene, and two Ladies.* F

23 *Enter Gardeners, one the master, the other two his men*] *Enter Gardeners.* Q; *Enter a Gardiner, and two Seruants.* F

28 *not in* Q, F
72 *not in* Q, F
101 *Exit Queen with her Ladies*] *Exit* Q, F

**IV.1**

0 *Enter Bolingbroke with the Lords Aumerle, Northumberland,
Harry Percy, Fitzwater, Surrey, the Bishop of Carlisle, the
Abbot of Westminster, another Lord, Herald, and officer,
to Parliament*] *Enter Bullingbrooke with the Lords to
parliament.* Q; *Enter as to the Parliament, Bullingbrooke,
Aumerle, Northumberland, Percie, Fitz-Water, Surrey,
Carlile, Abbot of Westminster. Herauld, Officers, and
Bagot.* F

1 *Enter Bagot with officers*] *Enter Bagot.* Q; *not in* F
24 *not in* Q, F
34 *not in* Q, F
48 *not in* Q, F
55 *not in* Q, F
70 *not in* Q, F
83 *not in* Q, F
157 F; *not in* Q4
161 *Enter Richard and York*] F; *Enter king Richard.* Q4
267 *not in* F, Q4
274 *Enter attendant with a glass*] *Enter one with a Glasse.* F;
*not in* Q4
287 *not in* F, Q4
319 *Exeunt all except the Abbot of Westminster, the Bishop
of Carlisle, Aumerle*] *Exeunt. Manent West. Caleil,
Aumerle.* Q1; *Exeunt.* F

**V.1**

6 *Enter Richard and guard*] F; *Enter Ric.* Q
96 *not in* Q, F
98 *not in* Q, F

**V.2**

71 *He plucks it out of his bosom, and reads it*] Q; *Snatches
it* F
87 *not in* Q, F

**V.3**

 0  *Enter Bolingbroke, now King Henry, with Harry Percy
    and other lords*] *Enter the King with his nobles*. Q; *Enter
    Bullingbrooke, Percie, and other Lords*. F

37  *Aumerle locks the door. The Duke of York knocks at the
    door and crieth*] *The Duke of Yorke knokes at the doore
    and crieth*. Q; *not in* F

38  YORK *(within)*] *Yor*. Q; *Yorke within*. | *Yor*. F

44  *King Henry opens the door. Enter York*] *not in* Q; *Enter
    Yorke*. F

73  DUCHESS OF YORK *(within)*] *Du*. Q; *Dutchesse within*. |
    *Dut*. F

81  *Aumerle admits the Duchess. She kneels*] *not in* Q; *Enter
    Dutchesse*. F *(after line 85)*

96, 97  *not in* Q, F

135  *not in* Q, F

**V.3.145–V.4.0**

     *Exeunt* | *Enter Sir Piers of Exton and a Man*] *Exeunt.
     Manet sir Pierce Exton, &c*. Q; *Exeunt*. | *Enter Exton
     and Seruants*. F

**V.4**

11  *Exeunt*] *not in* Q; *Exit*. F

**V.5**

41  *The music plays*] Q; *Musick (at end of* 38*)* F

94  *Enter Keeper to Richard with meat*] *Enter one to Richard
    with meate*. Q; *Enter Keeper with a Dish*. F

102  *not in* Q, F

104  *The murderers, Exton and servants, rush in*] *The murderers
     rush in*. Q; *Enter Exton and Seruants*. F

106  *not in* Q, F

107  *He kills another servant. Here Exton strikes him down*]
     *Here Exton strikes him downe*. Q; *Exton strikes him
     downe*. F

112  *not in* Q, F

118  *Exeunt with the bodies*] *not in* Q; *Exit*. F

**V.6**

 0  *Flourish. Enter King Henry with the Duke of York, other
    lords, and attendants*] *Enter Bullingbrooke with the duke*

 *of Yorke.* Q; *Flourish. Enter Bullingbrooke, Yorke, with*
 *other Lords & attendants.* F
18 *Enter Harry Percy with the Bishop of Carlisle, guarded*]
 *Enter H Percie.* Q; *Enter Percy and Carlile.* F
44 *not in* Q, F

# Genealogical Table

King Edward III
1312–1327–1377

Edward
(The Black Prince)
1330–1376

King Richard II
1367–1377–1399–1400 =
Queen Isabel
1389–c. 1409
(his second wife)

Lionel,
Duke of Clarence
1338–1368

John of Gaunt,
Duke of Lancaster
1340–1399

Henry Bolingbroke,
Duke of Hereford,
King Henry IV
1367–1399–1413

King Henry V
1387–1413–1422

Edmund of Langley,
Duke of York
1341–1402 =
Duchess of York

Edward,
Earl of Rutland,
Duke of Aumerle
c. 1373–1415

Thomas of Woodstock,
Duke of Gloucester
1354–97 =
Duchess of Gloucester
1359 or 1366–1399

NOTE: King Edward III had seven sons, two of whom died in infancy. He also had five daughters. This table is designed mainly to show those of his descendants who are important in the play and in *Richard II*. The names of those who appear in the play are in italic. Italicized dates are those of reigns; other dates are those of births and deaths.

# Commentary

Q here refers to the first Quarto, 1597. Later Quartos are referred to as Q2, Q3, etc. F refers to the text of the play in the first Folio, of 1623.

Biblical quotations are from the Bishops' Bible (1568), the version likely to have been best known to Shakespeare. Quotations from Holinshed's *Chronicles* have been modernized from the second edition, of 1587; those from *Woodstock* are from Rossiter's edition. For details of these and other sources quoted in the Commentary, see the Introduction, pp. xxxv–xxxvi.

*Title*
The title page of Q calls the play *The Tragedy of King Richard the Second*. In F the play is *The Life and Death of King Richard the Second*.

I.I

> The matter of this scene is adapted and compressed from Holinshed, according to whom the first accusations between Mowbray and Bolingbroke were made at Shrewsbury in spring 1398, followed six weeks later by the formal 'appeal' at Windsor.
>
> A formal grouping is required, with the King centrally seated.
>
> o *King Richard*: He was known as Richard of Bordeaux, was born in 1367, succeeded to the throne in 1377, and died in 1400. The play covers the last two years of his reign. He had an army of 'livery men' who wore the white hart as his badge.

*John of Gaunt*: The fourth (third surviving) son of
Edward III; he lived from 1340 to 1399, and was Duke
of Lancaster.

*Gaunt*: Ghent, his birthplace.

*Lord Marshal*: Mowbray himself was the Earl Marshal
at the time, but Holinshed says that the Duke of Surrey
acted as his deputy on this occasion. Surrey appears
later in the play (IV.1), but there is no reason to think
that Shakespeare cared about the identity of the Lord
Marshal; he is important simply for his function.

1 *Old . . . time-honoured*: In 1398 John of Gaunt was fifty-
eight. Here and elsewhere Shakespeare contrasts the
comparative age of Richard's uncles with the King's
own *youth* (II.1.69).

2 *band*: An alternative form of 'bond'.

3 *Hereford*: In the play the name usually has two syllables. In the early editions it is frequently spelt 'Herford'.

4 *boisterous*: (Two syllables; Q has *boistrous*, a common
Elizabethan spelling) rough and violent.

*late*: Recent.

*appeal*: Accusation (of treason).

5 *our . . . us*: Richard uses the royal plural, in keeping
with the formality of the occasion.

*leisure*: That is, lack of leisure.

8 *sounded*: Inquired of.

9 *appeal*: Accuse.

*on ancient malice*: Because of long-standing personal
enmity.

12 *As near . . . argument*: This is an alexandrine. Most lines
in the play are pentameters, but short and long lines are
not uncommon. Editors have often attempted to regularize them, either by rearrangement or addition of extra
words, but some of them can be justified dramatically (a
short line may add emphasis). Others may represent an
attempt to avoid monotony, or be the result of negligence.
*As near as I could sift him*: So far as I could discover by
examining him.

*argument*: Subject.

13 *apparent*: Obvious.

15 *Exit Attendant*: This is not marked in Q; but it seems
the most satisfactory way of managing the stage
business.

*presence. Face to face*: Q reads *presence face to face*. It is
possible (though not likely) that the passage should be
interpreted 'Then call them to our presence face to face,
and – [they] frowning brow to brow – ourselves . . .'.

16 *ourselves*: We (royal plural) ourself.

18–19 *High-stomached . . . as fire*: These lines are sometimes
spoken aside.

18 *High-stomached*: Proud, haughty.

19 *deaf*: That is, to remonstrance; cf. *King John*, II.1.451:
'The sea enragèd is not half so deaf.'

*Bolingbroke*: Henry Plantagenet, Gaunt's son by his first
wife; he lived from 1367 to 1413. *Bolingbroke* (often
pronounced 'Bullingbrooke') was a nickname, from
his birthplace, in Lincolnshire.

*Mowbray*: Thomas Mowbray was born about 1366, and
died in 1399 at Venice (IV.1.97–100). It seems likely
that in 1397 he was responsible for the murder of
Richard's uncle, Gloucester, by Richard's command.
Mowbray in *Henry IV, Part II* is his eldest son.

22 *Each day still better other's happiness*: May each day be
happier than the previous one.

23–4 *Until . . . your crown*: In *Woodstock* (I.1.37–8) it is said
of the Black Prince that 'heaven forestalled his diadem
on earth | To place him with a royal crown in heaven'.
Cf. V.1.24–5.

23 *envying*: The accent is probably on the second syllable:
'heav'ns, envỳing'.

*hap*: Fortune.

26 *cause you come*: Cause about which you come.

30 *heaven be the record to my speech*: This might be regarded
as a parenthesis.

*record*: Witness.

32 *Tendering*: Watching over, being careful of.

34 *appellant*: In accusation.

36 *greeting*: Address.

38 *divine*: Immortal.

40 *Too good*: Too high in rank.

41–6 *Since the more ... may prove*: Here, as often, the verse
moves into rhymed couplets. This has often been
objected to, and in the theatre the play's rhyming
passages have sometimes been omitted or rewritten.
There is of course no justification for this. In general,
couplets signalize a higher degree of formality in the
action, or a stronger emphasis on what is being said than
on what is happening. Coleridge said of this passage:
'the rhymes ... well express the preconcertedness of
Bolingbroke's scheme, so beautifully contrasted with
the vehemence and sincere irritation of Mowbray'.

41 *crystal*: Clear (as crystal), bright.

43 *note*: Reproach, mark of disgrace (from the Latin *nota*,
a mark of censure).

46 *right-drawn*: Drawn in a just cause.

47 *Let not my cold words here accuse my ʒeal*: Do not let
my calm language cast doubt upon my ardour (or
'loyalty').

49 *eager*: Sharp.

51 *cooled*: By death.

54 *reverence of*: Respect for.

56 *post*: Hasten (continuing the riding metaphor of *curbs*,
*reins and spurs*, and, perhaps, *free*).

57 *These terms of treason*: Refers to *traitor* and *miscreant*
(39).

58–9 *his high blood's royalty,* | *And let him be no kinsman to
my liege*: Bolingbroke was Richard's first cousin.

59 *let him be*: Assuming that he were.

63 *tied*: Bound, obliged.

65 *inhabitable*: Not habitable, uninhabitable. Similar
expressions occur elsewhere, as in *Macbeth*, III.4.103:
'And dare me to the desert with thy sword.' A fight to
the death is implied.

67 *this*: Perhaps his sword; more probably, the affirmation
in the following line.

69 *gage*: Pledge. It was usually a glove or gauntlet,
but according to Holinshed hoods were used on the
occasion when Fitzwater accused Aumerle of causing

Gloucester's death (IV.1). However, the phrase *manual seal* (IV.1.25) in Shakespeare's version suggests that he thought of the gage as a glove.

72 *except*: Set aside (cf. 58).

74 *honour's pawn*: The gage or pledge of 69; the phrase recurs at IV.1.55 and 70.

77 *What I have spoke or thou canst worse devise*: The accusations that I have made, or any more heinous ones that you can think of.

78 *I take it up*: And thus accept the challenge.

79 *gently*: Perhaps 'conferring nobility' rather than 'with a light touch' or 'in friendly fashion'.

80 *answer thee*: Give you satisfaction.

80–81 *in any fair degree | Or chivalrous design of knightly trial*: To any fair measure or any form of combat allowed by the laws of chivalry.

82 *light*: Dismount, alight.

85–6 *inherit us . . . of*: Put us in possession of.

87 *Look what*: Whatever (a usage common in Shakespeare).

88 *nobles*: A noble was a gold coin, worth twenty groats, or 6s. 8d. in the currency of the time.

89 *lendings*: Money paid to Mowbray for distribution to the soldiers, perhaps as advances when circumstances would not permit them to be given regular payments. Holinshed has 'Thomas Mowbray Duke of Norfolk hath received eight thousand nobles to pay the soldiers that keep your town of Calais.'

90 *lewd employments*: Improper use.

93 *Or . . . or*: Either . . . or.

95 *eighteen years*: The phrase is from Holinshed. Its significance (which Shakespeare did not necessarily recognize) is that the commons, under Wat Tyler and others, had risen in 1381.

96 *Complotted*: Plotted in combination with others.
*contrivèd*: Could mean 'plotted' or 'devised' as well as 'brought about'.

97 *Fetch*: Derive. The metaphor is of drawing water from the *head* of a fountain, or a *spring*.

98–9 *maintain | Upon his bad life to make all this good*:

Bolingbroke seems to mean that he undertakes to prove
all this by taking Mowbray's *bad life*.

100 *he did plot the Duke of Gloucester's death*: Thomas of
Woodstock, Duke of Gloucester, died at Calais in 1397
while in the custody of Mowbray, then captain of Calais.
He was probably murdered by Mowbray or his agents
at Richard's instigation. This view was commonly held
in Shakespeare's time. Holinshed says 'The King sent
unto Thomas Mowbray . . . to make the Duke secretly
away', and reports that Mowbray 'caused his servants
to cast featherbeds upon him, and so smother him to
death, or otherwise to strangle him with towels (as some
write)'. Shakespeare leaves the matter open in this first
scene but in the next one Gloucester's widow and his
brother assert Richard's guilt. The Duke of York, too,
implies belief in it (II.2.100–102). In IV.1 Bolingbroke,
taking it for granted that Richard was the instigator,
inquires 'who performed | The bloody office' (4–5),
and Bagot seems to suggest that Aumerle, not Mowbray,
was responsible. This episode, too, is based on
Holinshed. The question is left unsettled. In portraying
the varying views, Shakespeare may have been concerned
to suggest the uncertainties in our interpretation of the
past; and the reopening of the question later in the play,
with Aumerle's vehement denials, helps Richard's cause
with the audience just before he makes big demands on
their sympathy, in the deposition scene.

101 *Suggest his soon-believing adversaries*: Incite Gloucester's
enemies, who were predisposed to believe Mowbray.
The enemies included Richard.

102 *consequently*: Subsequently.

104 *sacrificing Abel's*: The allusion is to the biblical story of
Abel, who sacrificed 'the firstlings of his sheep' (Genesis
4:4), and to his murder by his brother, Cain. His blood
cried from the ground (Genesis 4:10), and, unlike
Christ's, called for retribution (Hebrews 12:24). It is
echoed, ironically, in Bolingbroke's words to Piers of
Exton (V.6.43–4), when he has murdered Richard at
Bolingbroke's instigation.

105 *tongueless*: Dumb (though resonant).

106 *To me*: As his nephew – as Richard also is.

109 *pitch*: Highest point of a falcon's flight before it swoops on its prey.

113 *slander of his blood*: Disgrace to the blood royal, shared by both Richard and Bolingbroke.

115 *eyes and ears*: Replying to *face* and *ears* in Mowbray's speech.

118 *my sceptre's awe*: The reverence due to my sceptre.

119 *sacred*: A hint of the theme of the divine nature of kingship, emphasized elsewhere.

120 *partialize*: Make partial, bias.

122 *He is our subject, Mowbray. So . . .*: We might equally read: 'He is our subject. Mowbray, so . . .'

124–5 *as low as to thy heart | Through the false passage of thy throat thou liest*: This is a heightening of the common expression 'to lie in the throat', used menacingly.

126 *receipt*: Sum received when Mowbray was captain of Calais.

*Calais*: The early editions use the spelling 'Callice', which represents the Elizabethan pronunciation.

128 *by consent*: Holinshed does not record that Richard agreed that Mowbray should retain any of the money.

129 *For that*: Because.

130 *remainder of a dear account*: The balance of a heavy debt.

*dear*: Has a wide range of meaning, including 'important', 'of great value' and 'serious'. Heavy expenses were incurred in Mowbray's expedition to France to negotiate Richard's marriage.

131 *to fetch his queen*: In fact, Richard himself escorted his bride from France to England.

132 *For*: As for.

133–4 *to my own disgrace | Neglected my sworn duty in that case*: What his *sworn duty* was is obscure. He may mean that he should have killed Gloucester, but this is tantamount to an accusation against Richard. Alternatively his *sworn duty* may have been to guard Gloucester. Holinshed reports that he 'prolonged time for the

executing of the King's commandment, though the
King would have had it done with all expedition,
whereby the King conceived no small displeasure and
sware that it should cost the Earl his life if he quickly
obeyed not his commandment', and the point is
repeated later. So probably Mowbray is here claiming
to have saved Gloucester's life for a time, and perhaps
taking refuge in the fact that he did not personally kill
him.

137 *Once did I lay an ambush for your life*: In Holinshed,
too, Mowbray admits having 'laid an ambush to have
slain the Duke of Lancaster', and claims that he was
forgiven. No details are known.

140 *exactly*: 'Expressly' or 'completely'.

142 *appealed*: Alleged.

144 *recreant*: Could be an adjective – 'cowardly' – as well
as a noun.

145 *Which in myself I boldly will defend*: The truth of which
statement I personally shall boldly defend.

146 *interchangeably*: Reciprocally, in turn.
   *hurl*: Present, not future, tense; Mowbray throws down
   his gage. Bolingbroke must pick it up at some unspec-
   ified point, since at 161 his father tells him to throw it
   down.

148–9 *prove . . . in*: Probably in the sense 'demonstrate . . . by
shedding'.

149 *chambered*: Enclosed.

150 *In haste whereof*: To hasten which.

153 *purge this choler without letting blood*: Drain away anger
(*choler*, or bile) without the letting of blood (playing
on the idea of bloodshed).

154 *though no physician*: The notion of a king as his
country's physician was common.

156 *conclude*: Come to terms.

157 *doctors*: Learned men, astrologers.
   *this is no month to bleed*: Some seasons were supposed
   to be more favourable than others to the medical practice of blood-letting.

164 *We bid*: That is, 'since I, the King, bid'.

*boot*: Alternative, help for it.

167 *The one my duty owes*: My duty as a subject compels
me to put my life at your disposal.

167–8 *name,* | *Despite of death that lives upon my grave*: Name
that will live on my tomb despite death. The awkward
inversion of the natural word order is presumably a
result of the use of rhyme.

170 *impeached*: Accused.

*baffled*: Treated ignominiously, publicly disgraced. To
'baffle' a knight found guilty of cowardice is explained
in Hall's *Chronicle*: 'he was content that the Scots should
baffle him, which is a great reproach among the Scots,
and is used when a man is openly perjured, and then
they make of him an image painted reversed, with his
heels upward, with his name . . .'. Sometimes the knight
seems actually to have been hung up by his heels.
Mowbray is not using the word in its fullest literal
sense.

172–3 *his heart-blood* | *Which*: The heart-blood of him who.

173 *breathed this poison*: Uttered this venomous slander.

174 *his*: Bolingbroke's; King Richard repeats his demand.
*Lions make leopards tame*: The analogy between the king
and the lion (the king of beasts) is common. The lion
was part of the royal coat-of-arms, and the crest of the
Norfolks, worn by Mowbray, was a golden leopard.

175 *Yea, but not change his spots*: The modern proverb 'The
leopard cannot change his spots' goes back to the Bible
('May a man of Ind change his skin, and the cat of the
mountain her spots?', Jeremiah 13:23) and was probably proverbial by the time Shakespeare was writing.
*spots*: Also has the sense of 'stains (of shame)'. The
line thus connects with 166.
*Take but my shame*: Simply remove the disgrace.

177 *mortal times*: Human life.

182 *in one*: Inseparably.

184 *try*: Put to the test.

186 *throw up your gage*: Richard tells Bolingbroke to relin-
quish Mowbray's gage, which he is holding. *Throw up*
may indicate that Richard is situated at a higher level

than the disputants, perhaps on a throne, possibly (on
the Elizabethan stage) on the upper stage. F, however,
reads *throw downe*, which may represent a method of
staging different from that first imagined by Shakespeare.

188 *crest-fallen*: Humbled.

189 *beggar-fear*: Fear appropriate to a beggar.
*impeach my height*: Disgrace my rank.

190 *outdared*: Both 'excelled in' and 'overcome by' daring.
*dastard*: Coward.

191 *such feeble wrong*: The wrong of speaking so feebly.

192 *sound so base a parle*: The metaphor is, appropriately,
from the sounding of trumpets in combat to ask for a
truce.

192-5 *my teeth shall tear ... even in Mowbray's face*: The
image seems strained and far-fetched. But behind it
lies a story of a philosopher who bit off his tongue and
spat it in a tyrant's face. This story was reasonably
well known; also, neo-Senecan plays popular when
*Richard II* was written sometimes required even the
staging of such horrific incidents. In Thomas Kyd's
*The Spanish Tragedy* (written about 1587), for instance,
the chief character, Hieronimo, 'bites out his tongue',
provoking the comment 'See, Viceroy, he hath bitten
forth his tongue | Rather than to reveal what we
required' (IV.4.193-4). And in Shakespeare's own
*Titus Andronicus* the idea recurs when Titus, addressing
his daughter, Lavinia, whose tongue has been horribly
cut out, asks 'Or shall we bite our tongues, and in
dumb shows | Pass the remainder of our hateful days?'
(III.1.131-2).

193 *motive*: Instrument, organ (here, the tongue).

194 *in his high disgrace*: In disgrace of the tongue itself.
Shakespeare regularly uses 'his' for modern 'its'.

195 *Exit John of Gaunt*: The direction is in F, but not in Q.
There is no good reason why Gaunt should leave except
that he is to re-enter at the beginning of the following
scene. The Folio direction probably represents
Elizabethan stage practice, and perhaps Shakespeare
here fails to think in fully theatrical terms.

199 *Saint Lambert's Day*: 17 September. Shakespeare takes
the date from Holinshed, who however said: 'Here
writers disagree about the day that was appointed;
for some say it was upon a Monday in August; other
upon Saint Lambert's day, being the seventeenth of
September, other on the eleventh of September.'

202 *atone*: Reconcile.

203 *design the victor's chivalry*: Indicate the winner in a
combat of chivalry. The theory behind trial by combat
is that the justice of God will reveal itself by causing
the right man to win.

205 *home alarms*: Troubles at home (distinct from the Irish
rebellion referred to later (I.4.38)).

I.2

This scene marks the difference in time between the
first and third scenes, set in April and September.

0 *Duchess of Gloucester*: She was born in either 1359 or
1366, and died in 1399; but Shakespeare probably
thought of her as an older woman.

1 *the part I had in Woodstock's blood*: My blood-relation-
ship to Thomas of Woodstock, Duke of Gloucester
(Gaunt's brother).
*Woodstock's*: F has *Glousters*, which would be easier
for an audience unaware that they were the same
person.

4–5 *correction lieth in those hands | Which made the fault that
we cannot correct*: The power to punish the murder is
in the hands of the man (Richard) who committed the
crime that we cannot undo.

6 *Put we our quarrel*: Let us commit our cause.

7 *Who, when they*: Which, when it. It is not uncommon
in Shakespeare for 'heaven' to take a plural agreement.

11 *Edward*: Edward III.

12–13 *seven vials . . . seven fair branches*: Shakespeare preserves
throughout the speech the double metaphor com-
pounded of the medieval genealogical symbol of the
Tree of Jesse, and the figure of the vials of blood. A
typical Elizabethan genealogical table would represent
a tree, the founder of a family being at the foot or root

(and not, as in modern custom, at the head). Thus the sons are *branches springing from one root*.

15  *Some of those branches by the destinies cut*: The line recalls the epilogue of Marlowe's *Doctor Faustus*, written only a few years before *Richard II*: 'Cut is the branch that might have grown full straight.'

*The destinies*: The Fates – Clotho, Lachesis and Atropos.

21  *envy*: The word was stronger than it is now, and could mean 'malice' or 'hatred'.

23  *mettle*: Stuff, substance.

*self*: Same.

28  *model*: Copy, image.

29  *despair*: A sinful as well as pitiable state of mind.

30  *suffering*: Permitting.

31  *naked pathway to thy life*: 'Undefended way by which your murderers can reach your life'; or perhaps 'that the way to your life is undefended . . .'.

33  *mean*: Ordinary, common, not noble.

36  *venge*: An old form of 'avenge'.

37–8  *God's substitute,* | *His deputy*: A common way of thinking of the king.

46  *cousin*: The word was often used to mean no more than 'relative'. Hereford was the Duchess's nephew.

*fell*: Fierce, cruel (since she thinks of him as the agent in her husband's murder).

47  *sit*: Q reads *set*; F *sit*; but 'set' was a common spelling of 'sit'.

49  *if misfortune miss the first career*: If misfortune does not overcome (Mowbray) at the first encounter. To *career* a horse was to run it at full speed and then stop suddenly. In the following lines Mowbray is imagined overbalancing at the stop and being 'thrown'.

53  *caitiff recreant*: Wretched coward.

54  *sometimes*: Sometime ('wife of him who was your brother' or 'she who was your brother's wife').

58–9  *Grief boundeth where it falls,* | *Not with the empty hollowness, but weight*: The Duchess is apologizing for adding *one word more*. The image is of a bouncing (bounding) tennis ball; but her grief bounces with the force of its weight, not because of its hollow lightness.

66 *Pleshey*: Gloucester's country house, near Dunmow in Essex.

68 *lodgings*: Rooms.

*unfurnished walls*: Possibly 'walls unhung with tapestry' which was taken down when the rooms were out of use; or the phrase may just mean that the rooms are unfurnished.

69 *offices*: Servants' rooms.

**I.3**

The events represented in this scene took place at Coventry in September 1398. Holinshed describes an occasion of great splendour. The dukes came 'in great array, accompanied with the lords and gentlemen of their lineages. The King caused a sumptuous scaffold or theatre, and royal lists there to be erected and prepared.' Aumerle and the Marshal (Surrey) 'entered into the lists with a great company of men apparelled in silk sendal embroidered with silver, both richly and curiously, every man having a tipped staff to keep the field in order'. Bolingbroke entered to them, before the King arrived, accompanied by all the peers of the realm and 'above ten thousand men in armour, lest some fray or tumult might rise amongst his nobles'. Shakespeare makes Richard enter to his seat, which, according to Holinshed, was 'richly hanged and adorned', before the contestants, and then Mowbray before Bolingbroke, who, as appellant, should have entered the lists first. In Holinshed, the dukes arrived on elaborately costumed horses, dismounted, and sat on their ceremonial chairs, Bolingbroke's of green velvet, Mowbray's of crimson 'curtained about with white and red damask'. After they had received their lances (100–103) the chairs were removed, and the combatants were instructed to remount. At the sound of the trumpet they moved towards each other. Shakespeare simplifies the setting, though he mentions the chairs (120). It can hardly be supposed that horses were used, though they have

sometimes figured, more or less prominently, in nine-
teenth- and twentieth-century performances. In *Henry
IV, Part II* (IV.1.115–26) Mowbray's son describes the
events of this scene, attributing Richard's downfall to
his intervention in the combat.

0 *Duke of Aumerle*: Edward of York; he lived from about
1373 to 1415, and was York's eldest son. *Aumerle* is
Albemarle, a town in France. In fact he became the Duke
of York whose noble death at Agincourt is recounted
in Shakespeare's *Henry V* (IV.6); but Shakespeare may
not have realized this when writing *Richard II*. He is
present here in his function as High Constable. See also
Commentary to V.2.43.

2 *at all points*: Completely (that is, he is wearing all the
different pieces of his suit of armour).

3 *sprightfully*: Spiritedly.

5 *stay*: Wait.

6 *Bushy*: Sir John Bushy held a number of important
offices, and was Speaker of the House of Commons for
several years. He was Richard's chief agent in the House,
and is said always to have advanced before the King
with obeisances, to Richard's pleasure. He was beheaded
in 1399.

*Bagot*: Sir William Bagot, like Bushy, held various offices
of state. He escaped to Ireland after Bolingbroke landed,
and later was arrested and released. He died in 1407.

*Green*: Sir Henry Green, a Member of Parliament and
follower of King Richard, executed with Bushy at
Bristol.

*When they are set*: A separate flourish of trumpets should
sound for Mowbray's entrance.

*set*: The King and his nobles seat themselves in state.

9 *orderly*: According to the rules.

10 *swear him in the justice of his cause*: A knight entering
the lists was required to swear that his cause was just.
One of them was thus likely to commit perjury, and so
deserve defeat.

11 *say who thou art*: This was not a pure formality, as the
knight's visor would be down.

13 *quarrel*: Cause of complaint.

18 *defend*: Forbid.

20 *my succeeding issue*: F reads *his* ... Perhaps Mowbray would have been more likely to swear by the King's descendants than his own; but the latter is not impossible and has the generally superior authority of Q to support it.

28 *plated in habiliments*: Wearing plate-armour.

30 *Depose him*: Swear him, take his sworn statement.

42–5 *On pain of death, no person be so bold | Or daring-hardy as to touch the lists | Except the Marshal and such officers | Appointed to direct these fair designs*: According to Holinshed, a king-at-arms (that is, a chief herald) 'made open proclamation, prohibiting all men in the name of the King, and of the High Constable and Marshal, to enterprise or attempt to approach or touch any part of the lists upon pain of death, except such as were appointed to order or marshal the field'.

51 *several*: 'Various' or 'respective'.

55 *as*: In so far as.

58 *Lament we may, but not revenge thee dead*: Bolingbroke's defeat would indicate his guilt, so Richard would not be justified in seeking revenge.

59–60 *profane a tear | For me*: Misuse a tear in weeping for me.

66 *lusty*: Strong, vigorous.
   *cheerly*: In good cheer.

67 *as at English feasts*: This is an allusion to the English habit of ending banquets with elaborate sweet confections. The phrase seems to have been current; Bacon wrote: 'Let not this Parliament end, like a Dutch feast, in salt meats; but like an English feast, in sweet meats.'
   *regreet*: Greet, salute.

70 *regenerate*: Reborn.

73 *proof*: Power of resistance.

75 *waxen coat*: Coat of mail as if it were made of wax.

77 *haviour*: An old form of 'behaviour'.

81 *amazing*: Stupefying (the sense was much stronger than now).
   *casque*: Helmet.

84 *to thrive*: I rely on for success.

88 *freer*: More willing.

90 *uncontrolled enfranchisement*: Liberation from control.

93–6 *Most mighty liege ... breast*: Mowbray moves into couplets as he approaches the ritual of the combat.

95 *to jest*: To go to a sport or entertainment.

96 *Truth hath a quiet breast*: Related to the proverb 'Truth fears no trial'.

97 *Securely*: Confidently (*couchèd*).

100–103 *Harry of Hereford ... Duke of Norfolk*: 'The Lord Marshal viewed their spears to see that they were of equal length, and delivered the one spear himself to the Duke of Hereford, and sent the other unto the Duke of Norfolk by a knight' (Holinshed).

102 *Strong as a tower in hope*: A biblical phrase: 'for thou hast been my hope, and a strong tower for me against the enemy', Psalm 61:3.

117, 122 *A charge sounded ... A long flourish*: 'The Duke of Norfolk was not fully set forward when the King cast down his warder and the heralds cried "Ho Ho!" Then the King caused their spears to be taken from them, and commanded them to repair again to their chairs, where they remained two long hours while the King and his council deliberately consulted what order was best to be had in so weighty a cause' (Holinshed). It is not easy to say precisely what stage action Shakespeare imagined here. Probably Richard descends from his raised throne as he throws down his warder, or just after doing so. *Withdraw with us* (121) would be addressed to his councillors, and they would consult in a cluster while the trumpets sounded their *long flourish*. Richard could then return to his throne to deliver his decision.

117 *warder*: A truncheon or staff to give the signal for the beginning or ending of hostilities.

122 *While we return*: Until we tell.

125 *For that*: So that.

129–33 *And for we think ... sleep*: These lines were omitted from F, and though the passage does not make very

good sense without them, it is not surprising that
clarification was sought. The problem is that *peace* (132),
having been aroused, goes on to *fright fair peace* (137).
There may be some textual fault, but it is just as likely
that Shakespeare lost control of his metaphors.

131 *set on you*: Set you on.

142 *regreet*: Greet again (not merely 'greet', as in 67).

143 *stranger*: Foreign (this is not a comparative, but the noun
used adjectivally).

145 *That sun that warms you here shall shine on me*: The
biblical 'he maketh his sun to rise on the evil and on
the good' (Matthew 5:45) had acquired proverbial force.

148 *heavier doom*: Severer punishment.

150 *determinate*: Bring to an end.

151 *dateless limit*: Limitless period.
*dear*: Dire, grievous.

156 *A dearer merit*: A better reward.

159 *these forty years*: In fact Mowbray was thirty-three in
1398; but 'forty' was sometimes used as a round figure,
with no implication of exactness.

162 *Than an unstringèd viol or a harp*: *unstringèd* refers to
*harp* as well as *viol*. The viol is a stringed instrument
played with a bow.

163 *cunning*: 'Skilfully made' or 'requiring skill to play'.

167 *portcullised*: Fortified (a portcullis is a heavy metal
grating in a gateway).

170 *a nurse*: A nurse might have the responsibility of
teaching her charges to speak.

172 *speechless*: The word is subtly chosen. In death, speech
is impossible; so Mowbray's exile will be death to him.

174 *boots*: Serves.
*to be compassionate*: Either 'to be sorry for yourself' or
'to appeal for pity'.

175 *plaining*: Complaining.

181 *Our part therein*: That part of the duty you owe to God
that belongs to me, as God's deputy.

188 *advisèd*: Deliberated.

193 *so far as to mine enemy*: This is the first time in the scene
that either combatant has spoken to the other. These

words seem intended as Bolingbroke's preface to what
he is about to say, intimating that though he now deigns
to address Mowbray, he continues to hold him in enmity.
Some editors read 'fare' instead of *far* (Q spells *fare*),
interpreting 'Bolingbroke bids Norfolk make his way
( *fare*) through the world in a fashion appropriate to
an enemy.'

196 *sepulchre*: Accented on the second syllable.

202 *My name be blotted from the book of life*: This is a clear
echo of Revelation 3:5: 'He that overcometh shall be
thus clothed in white array, and I will not blot out his
name out of the book of life.' It is appropriate to the
solemnity of Mowbray's utterance.

205 *rue*: Transitive: 'the King shall rue what thou art'.

206–7 *no way can I stray;* | *Save back to England, all the world's
my way*: I cannot go astray now, since I can go anywhere
in the world except England.

208 *glasses of thine eyes*: Your eyes as mirrors (mirroring
his feelings).

209 *aspect*: Accented on the second syllable.

214 *wanton*: Luxuriant.

220 *bring their times about*: Accomplish the cycles of their
seasons.

222 *extinct with*: Extinguished by.

223 *My inch of taper will be burnt and done*: Shakespeare uses
the same image elsewhere. The best-known example is
*Macbeth*, V.5.23: 'Out, out, brief candle!' Here it links
with *oil-dried lamp* (221).

224 *blindfold death*: Death is blindfold because there are no
eyes in its traditional emblem, the skull, and also perhaps
by analogy with Atropos, the blindfold destiny who
cuts the threads of life (Milton's 'blind fury with the
abhorrèd shears', *Lycidas*, line 75). The image is capable
of other interpretations, and indeed may have had
multiple associations for Shakespeare. Death's being
blindfolded causes its impartiality. Dover Wilson ingen-
iously suggests that the image is of death wearing a
hood which resembles in shape the extinguisher of a
candle or *taper*. And it has also been suggested that

death simply *is* the blindfold that will prevent Gaunt
from seeing his son.

227 *sullen*: Gloomy, melancholy.

230 *his pilgrimage*: Its journey.

231 *current*: Valid.

234 *party-verdict*: One person's share of a joint verdict.

236 *Things sweet to taste prove in digestion sour*: This is a
     proverbial expression deriving from Revelation 10:10,
     where it is said of a book that it 'was in my mouth as
     sweet as honey; and as soon as I had eaten it, my belly
     was bitter'.

240 *To smooth*: In glossing over.

241 *partial slander*: The accusation of partiality.

243 *looked when*: Expected that.

249 *What presence must not know*: What we shall not be able
     to communicate in person. It may be that Aumerle
     should depart after this leave-taking, especially as he
     enters at the beginning of the next scene. It is also a
     little odd that he should take such formal leave of
     Bolingbroke, since he accompanies him *to the next
     highway* (I.4.4).

251–2 *My lord ... your side*: The Marshal's friendly attitude
     to Bolingbroke here is one of the signs that Shakespeare
     was not concerned to identify him with the Duke of
     Surrey, one of Richard's supporters.

257 *To breathe*: In breathing.
     *dolour*: There is a pun on 'dollar', in conjunction with
     *hoard* (253) and *prodigal* (256).

258–9 *grief ... grief*: Both 'grievance' and 'cause of sorrows'.

262 *travel*: 'Travel' and 'travail' were interchangeable in
     spelling and closely related in meaning. M. M. Mahood
     comments: 'When Gaunt bids him call his exile "a
     *trauaile* that thou takst for pleasure" and a "*foyle*
     wherein thou art to set, The pretious Iewell of thy
     home returne", Bolingbroke takes up *travel* in its
     harsher sense of "travail" and *foil* in the meaning "frus-
     tration, obstacle" to fashion the bitter wordplay of his
     reply' (*Shakespeare's Wordplay*, 1957, p. 78).

265 *sullen*: Melancholy (and 'dull in colour').

269 *remember*: Remind.
    *deal of world*: Distance.

271–4 *Must I not serve a long apprenticehood | To foreign
      passages, and in the end, | Having my freedom, boast of
      nothing else | But that I was a journeyman to grief*:
      Bolingbroke expects to serve a long apprenticeship in
      his foreign travels and experiences (*passages*), and when
      he gains his freedom, as an apprentice does, in the rank
      of *journeyman* (qualified artisan, with a hint of 'one
      who goes a journey'), and also his freedom from exile,
      he will still be subject to grief. The tense of the last
      sentence causes difficulty because the apprentice would
      normally become a journeyman on completion of his
      apprenticeship. It is as if *Having my freedom* meant simul-
      taneously 'having gained this amount of experience'
      and 'when, no longer in exile, I look back upon this
      period . . .'. The sense would be easy if we could inter-
      pret *was* as 'have become'.

275–8 *All places that the eye of heaven visits | Are to a wise
      man ports and happy havens. | Teach thy necessity to
      reason thus: | There is no virtue like necessity*: A source
      for this passage has been seen in Lyly's *Euphues* (1578),
      in which Lyly is translating Plutarch's *De Exilio*: 'Plato
      would never account him banished that had the sun,
      fire, air, water, and earth that he had before, where he
      felt the winter's blast and the summer's blaze, where
      the same sun and the same moon shined, whereby he
      noted that every place was a country to a wise man,
      and all parts a palace to a quiet mind.' 'A wise man
      makes every country his own' was proverbial; so was
      the phrase 'to make a virtue of necessity'.

279–80 *Think not the King did banish thee, | But thou the King*:
      Again Shakespeare seems to recall Lyly's *Euphues*:
      'When it was cast in Diogenes' teeth that the
      Synoponetes had banished him, Pontus, "Yea," said he,
      "I them of Diogenes."'

281 *faintly*: Faintheartedly.

284 *pestilence*: Plague.

286 *Look what*: Whatever.

289 *presence strewed*: The King's presence chamber, strewed with rushes.

291 *measure*: Stately dance.

292 *gnarling*: Snarling.

294–9 *O, who can hold ... fantastic summer's heat*: Again Shakespeare seems to recall Lyly's *Euphues*: 'he that is cold doth not cover himself with care, but with clothes; he that is washed in the rain drieth himself by the fire, not by his fancy; and thou which art banished oughtest not with tears to bewail thy hap, but with wisdom to heal thy hurt'. This is from the same passage as that quoted in the note to 275–8.

295 *Caucasus*: Regularly thought of as cold by the Elizabethans, as in Lyly's *Euphues*: 'If thou be as hot as the Mount Etna, feign thyself as cold as the hill Caucasus.'

296 *cloy*: Surfeit.

299 *fantastic*: Imagined.

300 *apprehension*: Conception.

302–3 *Fell sorrow's tooth doth never rankle more | Than when he bites, but lanceth not the sore*: Cruel sorrow, which bites (292), makes his most festering wounds when he bites but does not pierce the skin, as does a physician's lance (on a boil or abscess). Bolingbroke seems to imply that Gaunt's consolations blunt a sorrow which it would be better for him to accept at its worst.

304 *bring*: Accompany.

305 *stay*: Perhaps 'away from England' – he would not accept banishment; or perhaps 'linger' – he would leave immediately.

**I.4**

The main facts conveyed in this scene were available in Holinshed. The description of Bolingbroke's departure (23–36) may have been suggested by him: 'A wonder it was to see what number of people ran after him in every town and street where he came before he took the sea, lamenting and bewailing his departure, as who would say that when he departed the only shield, defence, and comfort of the commonwealth was vaded and gone.'

Shakespeare may also have derived a hint for Bolingbroke's *courtship to the common people* from Froissart's description of his return to London: 'and always as he rode he inclined his head to the people on every side'. The coolness of Aumerle to Bolingbroke is not in the sources; and the suggestion that Richard's farming of the realm was particularly to provide resources for his Irish campaign seems to be Shakespeare's.

o *Enter the King*: Q's stage direction reads *Enter the King with Bushie, &c at one dore, and the Lord Aumarle at another*. Probably Shakespeare originally intended Bushy to enter with the other favourites, but then decided to bring him on at 52. F has *Enter King, Aumerle, Greene, and Bagot*. See also notes to 23 and 52–3.

1 *We did observe*: Richard enters in the midst of a conversation. We learn at 24 that what he observed was Bolingbroke's *courtship to the common people*.

2 *high*: As the apparent irony in Aumerle's reply suggests, various shades of meaning, including 'high-ranking', 'proud' and perhaps 'haughty', may be felt.

6 *for me*: On my part.
   *except*: Except that.

8 *Awaked the sleeping rheum*: Made our eyes water.
   *rheum*: Watery discharge.

13 *that*: His heart's disdain.

13–15 *taught me craft | To counterfeit oppression of such grief | That words seemed buried in my sorrow's grave*: Taught me the skill (*craft*) to pretend to be so stricken with grief that words seemed buried in my sorrow as in a grave.

20 *cousin, cousin*: Richard, Bolingbroke and Aumerle were each other's cousins. Q reads *Coosens Coosin*; F, *cousin, cousin*. The Q reading (meaning 'cousin's cousin') may be right, Richard reminding Aumerle of his relationship with Bolingbroke.

23 *Ourself and Bushy*: In F this line reads '*Our selfe, and Bushy: heere Bagot and Greene*, which may be what Shakespeare first wrote. But Q's stage direction at the beginning of the scene includes Bushy among those who enter, though he is also required to enter at 52.

Probably Shakespeare originally intended him to enter
at the beginning of the scene, but then he or the actors
decided to use Bushy as the carrier of news. This may
have resulted in the need to alter this line, though the
version found in Q seems unsatisfactory. It sounds
clumsy; and the absence of the second part of the line
has the theatrical disadvantage of leaving Bagot and
Green unidentified on this, their first speaking appearance. A harmless fabrication which would seem nearest
to Shakespeare's intentions as well as providing a
regular verse line would be 'Ourself and Bushy; Bagot
here and Green', which is in fact the reading of the
(unauthoritative) Quarto of 1634.

29 *underbearing*: Enduring.

30 *banish their affects with him*: Take their affections (*affects*)
into banishment with him.

35 *As were our England in reversion his*: As if my England
were his in reversion (that is, would revert to him on
my death). Richard means it sarcastically but there is
a deeper irony.

38 *for*: As for.
    *the rebels which stand out in Ireland*: Holinshed records
    that 'the King being advertised that the wild Irish daily
    wasted and destroyed the towns and villages within the
    English pale, and had slain many of the soldiers which
    lay there in garrison for defence of that country, deter-
    mined to make eftsoons a voyage thither, and prepared
    all things necessary for his passage now against the
    spring ... and so in the month of April, as divers
    authors write, he set forward from Windsor and finally
    took shipping at Milford, and from thence with two
    hundred ships and a puissant power of men of arms
    and archers he sailed into Ireland'.
    *stand out*: Resist, hold out.

39 *Expedient manage must be made*: Speedy measures must
be taken.

43–4 *for our coffers with too great a court | And liberal largess
are grown somewhat light*: Richard was notorious for
extravagance.

43 *for*: Because.

45 *farm our royal realm*: Let my land by lease. The
   procedure is explained by a passage in *Woodstock*,
   IV.1.180–93: 'These gentlemen here, Sir Henry Greene,
   Sir Edward Bagot, Sir William Bushy, and Sir Thomas
   Scroope, all jointly here stand bound to pay your
   majesty, or your deputy, wherever you remain, seven
   thousand pounds a month for this your kingdom; for
   which your grace, by these writings, surrenders to their
   hands: all your crown lands, lordships: manors, rents:
   taxes, subsidies, fifteens, imposts; foreign customs,
   staples for wool, tin, lead and cloth: all forfeitures of
   goods or lands confiscate; and all other duties that do,
   shall, or may appertain to the king or crown's revenues;
   and for non-payment of the sum or sums aforesaid,
   your majesty to seize the lands and goods of the said
   gentlemen above named, and their bodies to be imprisoned at your grace's pleasure.'

48 *blank charters*: Holinshed records that, in order to placate
   the King after he had been displeased with the City of
   London, 'many blank charters were devised and
   brought into the city, which many of the substantial
   and wealthy citizens were fain to seal, to their great
   charge, as in the end appeared. And the like charters
   were sent abroad into all shires within the realm,
   whereby great grudge and murmuring arose among the
   people; for when they were so sealed, the King's officers
   wrote in the same what liked them, as well for charging
   the parties with payment of money as otherwise.' The
   author of *Woodstock* makes a good deal of this.

50 *subscribe them for*: Put them down for.

51 *them*: The sums of gold.

52 *presently*: Immediately.

52–3 *Enter Bushy | Bushy, what news*: This is F's alteration
   from Q, which reads *Enter Bushie with newes*. Probably
   the manuscript from which the play was printed gave
   the passage substantially as it appears here, but without
   the second *Bushy*, and with *what* abbreviated in such a
   way that it was mistaken for 'with' and thus was run

on with the stage direction. The confusion may be
connected with a late decision to use Bushy as the
bringer of news – see note to 23.

58 *Ely House*: This, the palace of the Bishops of Ely, was
at Holborn, near London. It was often rented to
noblemen.

59 *put*: This may be imperative, as interpreted here, or
subjunctive, in which case the sense would be 'Now if
God should put it . . .' and a lighter point after *immediately* would be required.

61 *lining*: Contents.

**II.I**

Richard's visit to the dying John of Gaunt is
Shakespeare's invention. The matter of the scene may
be indebted to Froissart, who relates that Gaunt was
displeased at his son's exile 'for so little a cause, and
also because of the evil governing of the realm by his
nephew King Richard; for he saw well that if he long
persevered and were suffered to continue, the realm
was likely to be utterly lost. With these imaginations
and other the Duke fell sick, whereon he died; whose
death was greatly sorrowed of all his friends and lovers.
The King, by that he showed, took no great care for
his death, but soon he was forgotten' (Lord Berners's
translation). Richard's seizure of Gaunt's belongings
comes from Holinshed, as does York's unfavourable
reaction. (See note to 201–7 below.) The final episode
is based on Holinshed's statement that 'divers of the
nobility, as well prelates as other and likewise many of
the magistrates and rulers of the cities, towns, and
commonalty here in England, perceiving daily how the
realm drew to utter ruin, not like to be recovered to
the former state of wealth whilst King Richard lived
and reigned, as they took it, devised with great delib-
eration and considerate advice to send and signify by
letters unto Duke Henry, whom they now called (as he
was indeed) Duke of Lancaster and Hereford, requiring
him with all convenient speed to convey himself into
England, promising him all their aid, power, and

assistance if he, expelling King Richard as a man not meet for the office he bare, would take upon him the sceptre, rule, and diadem of his native land and region'.

0 *Duke of York*: Edmund of Langley, 1341–1402, fifth (fourth surviving) son of Edward III. The House of York took its name from him.

*Earl of Northumberland*: Henry Percy, the first Earl, 1342–1408. He does not speak till 147, but as he there reports Gaunt's death his presence at the scene's opening seems likely.

2 *unstaid*: Unrestrained.

5–6 *they say the tongues of dying men | Enforce attention like deep harmony*: The notion that last words have an oracular quality was common, and Shakespeare makes much of it.

9 *listened*: Listened to, paid attention to.

10 *glose*: Speak flatteringly (like Richard's favourites).

12 *music at the close*: The cadence, or closing phrase of a piece of music.

13 *last taste of sweets*: The last taste of sweet things (before the taste disappears).

*sweetest last*: Perhaps 'sweetest in its most recent manifestation; or 'sweetest because it comes last'.

18 *the wise are fond*: Even the wise are fond. Q reads *found*, and the line may be corrupt.

19 *metres*: Verses, poems.

21 *fashions in proud Italy*: Italy was a traditional source of folly and wickedness. *Fashions* may refer to clothes or may extend to manners and behaviour. This passage is reminiscent of the lines in Scene 1 of Marlowe's *Edward II* in which Gaveston imagines how he will win the King's favour:

> Music and poetry is his delight;
> Therefore I'll have Italian masques by night,
> Sweet speeches, comedies, and pleasing shows … (53–5)

A similar accusation against King Richard and his favourites is made in *Woodstock*, II.3.88–93:

They sit in council to devise strange fashions,
And suit themselves in wild and antic habits
Such as this kingdom never yet beheld:
French hose, Italian cloaks, and Spanish hats,
Polonian shoes with peaks a hand full long,
Tied to their knees with chains of pearl and gold.

22 *still*: Always.

*tardy-apish*: Ready to ape fashions after they have become stale.

25 *there's no respect*: No one cares.

28 *will doth mutiny with wit's regard*: Desire conflicts with the claims of intelligence.

30–32 *breath ... new-inspired ... expiring*: Having been reminded of his shortage of breath, the fact that he will not breathe much longer, Gaunt imagines himself to be newly inspired (playing on the sense of 'given breath'), and so, expiring – that is, both 'breathing out' and 'dying' – foretells ... This type of serious word-play is particularly characteristic of Gaunt.

31 *Methinks I am a prophet new-inspired*: Cf. 5–6.

34–7 *For violent fires ... feeder*: These lines all have a prover-bial ring. Behind the first lies the proverb 'Nothing violent can be permanent', on which many writers played variations, as Shakespeare did in *Romeo and Juliet*, II.6.9: 'These violent delights have violent ends.' *He tires betimes that spurs too fast betimes* was an expres-sion comparable to 'More haste, less speed'.

35 *Small showers last long*: The four long syllables show Shakespeare matching the sound to the sense.

36 *betimes*: Soon, early.

38 *cormorant*: Glutton.

41 *This earth of majesty*: This land which is the proper seat of majesty.

*seat of Mars*: Home of Mars (the god of war).

45 *little world*: World in little. Cf. *Cymbeline*, III.1.12–13: 'Britain's a world | By itself'.

52 *Feared by*: Inspiring fear by.

55 *stubborn Jewry*: The land of the Jews, obstinate both in refusing Christianity and in resisting the crusaders.

59–60 *leased out ... Like to a tenement or pelting farm*: This may be a reference to *Woodstock*, IV.1.145–7, where Richard fears criticism because, he says, 'we ... to ease our wanton youth | Become a landlord to this warlike realm, | Rent out our kingdom like a pelting farm ...'.

60 *tenement*: Estate held by a tenant.
   *pelting*: Paltry.

61–3 *England ... with shame*: Shakespeare makes the Duke of Austria speak of England in similar terms in *King John*, II.1.21–30:

> to my home I will no more return
> Till Angiers and the right thou hast in France,
> Together with that pale, that white-faced shore,
> Whose foot spurns back the ocean's roaring tides
> And coops from other lands her islanders,
> Even till that England, hedged in with the main,
> That water-wallèd bulwark, still secure
> And confident from foreign purposes,
> Even till that utmost corner of the west
> Salute thee for her king.

*bound in ... bound in*: Surrounded by ... legally restrained by.

64 *blots*: The blank charters.

68 *Enter King Richard*: If, as F suggests, King Richard's exit (223) is marked by a flourish, trumpets should sound too for his entrance here.

*Queen Isabel*: At the time of the events of the play, King Richard's wife was Isabel, daughter of Charles VI of France, whom he had married in 1396, 'she being as then not past eight years of age' (Holinshed). Shakespeare does not give a name to Richard's Queen, and it is important to the scheme of the play that she should be presented as a woman who feels more than childlike love for her husband. Isabel was King Richard's second wife. The character in the play is closer to his first, Anne, to whom

he had been deeply devoted and with whose portrayal in *Woodstock* Shakespeare's Queen has much in common.
*Ross*: Lord Ross sat in Parliament from 1394. He died in 1414.
*Willoughby*: Lord Willoughby sat in Parliament from 1397, and died in 1409. King Richard made him Knight of the Garter, but he joined Bolingbroke. He later married the Duke of York's widow.

73 *composition*: State of both mind and body.

75 *grief hath kept a tedious fast*: Fasts were sometimes observed as an expression of grief.

77 *watched*: Stayed awake at night (worrying over England *sleeping* in sloth or ignorance of what is happening).

78 *Watching*: Sleeplessness.

80 *Is my strict fast*: I must go without.

83 *inherits*: 'Possesses' or 'will receive (at my death)'.

84 *nicely*: 'Subtly' and 'triflingly'.

85 *misery makes sport to mock itself*: It is misery (not sickness) which finds amusement in ridiculing itself.

86 *to kill my name in me*: By banishing his son.

88 *flatter with*: Try to please.

89 *flatter*: Perhaps in the sense of 'try to cheer up'.

93 *see thee ill*: The stress is on *thee*.

94 *Ill in myself to see, and in thee seeing ill*: Myself having poor power of sight, and seeing evil in you.

98 *Committest thy anointed body to the cure*: This line appears to be an alexandrine, but probably should be spoken as a pentameter by pronouncing 'commits' and eliding *thy* and *anointed*.

102 *verge*: Three senses are relevant: (1) compass; (2) the sphere of jurisdiction of the king's marshal, twelve miles round the royal residence; (3) a measure of land of from fifteen to thirty acres.

103 *waste*: The legal meaning of 'a tenant's destruction of his landlord's property' is relevant.

104–5 *had thy grandsire with a prophet's eye | Seen how his son's son should destroy his sons*: That is, had Edward III seen how his grandson, Richard, would destroy his (Edward's) sons – Gloucester and Gaunt.

107–8 *possessed . . . possessed*: Put in possession . . . possessed by a devil, mad.

109 *regent*: Ruler.

111 *for thy world enjoying but this land*: As this land is all the world that you rule.

114 *state of law is bondslave to the law*: Legal status is now that of one who is bound to obey the law (instead of above the law, as a king should be).

115 *– a lunatic*: Richard interrupts Gaunt's sentence, and turns it back on him. It would be up to the actor to make this clear, perhaps by pointing to Gaunt, or even by saying 'thou' simultaneously with him. F gives *thou* to Richard, not to Gaunt. Q3 reads *Ah lunatick . . .*, which is plausible but lacks authority.

122 *roundly*: 'Bluntly' or 'glibly'.

123 *unreverent*: Disrespectful.

124–5 *Edward . . . his father Edward*: The Black Prince, Richard's father; son of Edward III, who was also Gaunt's father.

126 *pelican*: An allusion to the common belief that the young pelican feeds on its mother's life-blood.

128 *Gloucester, plain well-meaning soul*: Possibly influenced by the portrait of Gloucester as 'plain Thomas' in *Woodstock*.

129 *fair befall*: May good befall.

130 *precedent*: Example, proof.

131 *thou respectest not*: You do not scruple to (the verb may be in the past tense – an elliptical form of 'respectedest').

133 *unkindness*: The word had a stronger sense to the Elizabethans than it has now: 'unnatural behaviour'.

135 *die not shame with thee*: May your ill-reputation live after you.

139 *sullens*: Sulks.

140 *become*: Are fit for.

143–5 *He loves you . . . so his*: York means that Gaunt loves Richard as much as he loves his son; but Richard embarrasses him by taking him to mean 'as much as Bolingbroke loves you'.

149 *stringless instrument*: The image recalls that used by
   Mowbray at I.3.161–2.

152 *death*: The state of being dead.

153 *The ripest fruit first falls*: Proverbial.

154 *our pilgrimage must be*: Our pilgrimage through life lies
   before us, and it too will come to an end.

156 *supplant*: Get rid of.
   *rug-headed*: Shaggy-headed. Edmund Spenser in *The
   Present State of Ireland* (1596) said of the Irish: 'They
   have another custom from the Scythians, that is the
   wearing of mantles and long glibs, which is a thick
   curled bush of hair hanging down over their eyes and
   monstrously disguising them.' (*Rug* is a shaggy material.)
   *kerns*: Light-armed Irish foot-soldiers.

157–8 *live like venom where no venom else | But only they have
   privilege to live*: This is an allusion to the legend that
   St Patrick banished snakes from Ireland.

159 *charge*: Expense.

164 *suffer*: Tolerate.

166 *Gaunt's rebukes*: The insults and shames offered to Gaunt
   (by Richard).

167–8 *the prevention of poor Bolingbroke | About his marriage*:
   This refers to an event not mentioned elsewhere in the
   play. It is explained by Holinshed, who writes that
   when Bolingbroke, during his exile in Paris, was about
   to marry the French king's cousin, Richard 'sent the
   Earl of Salisbury with all speed into France, both to
   surmise by untrue suggestion heinous offences against
   him, and also to require the French King that in no
   wise he would suffer his cousin to be matched in
   marriage with him that was so manifest an offender'.

168 *my own disgrace*: We do not know to what York refers.
   There may be significance in the fact that in *Woodstock*,
   III.2.4, Gloucester says to York and Lancaster that
   Richard has 'Disgraced our names and thrust us from
   his court'.

170 *bend one wrinkle*: 'Cause one frown to appear' or 'once
   frown (at you)'.

172–83 *Of whom thy father* ... *his kin*: This comparison
between Richard and his father may owe something to
one made by Gaunt in *Woodstock*, I.1.27–45:

> A heavy charge good Woodstock hast thou had
> To be protector to so wild a prince
> So far degenerate from his noble father
> Whom the trembling French the Black Prince called
> Not of a swart and melancholy brow
> (For sweet and lovely was his countenance)
> But that he made so many funeral days
> In mournful France: the warlike battles won
> At Crecy Field, Poitiers, Artoise and Maine
> Made all France groan under his conquering arm.
> But heaven forestalled his diadem on earth
> To place him with a royal crown in heaven.
> Rise may his dust to glory! Ere he'd 'a done
> A deed so base unto his enemy,
> Much less unto the brothers of his father,
> He'd first have lost his royal blood in drops,
> Dissolved the strings of his humanity
> And lost that livelyhood that was preserved
> To make his (unlike) son a wanton king.

173 *lion raged more fierce*: Either 'lion raged more fiercely'
or 'a more fierce (en-)raged lion'.

177 *Accomplished with the number of thy hours*: At your age.
*Accomplished with*: Furnished with.

185 *compare between*: Either York breaks down, leaving his
sentence incomplete, or this expression is complete in
itself, meaning 'draw comparisons between them'.

186 *Why, uncle, what's the matter*: Richard may be callously
detached or genuinely bewildered.

188 *withal*: None the less.

190 *royalties*: Rights granted to a subject by the king; royal
prerogatives.

192 *Harry*: Bolingbroke, Duke of Hereford. He is *true* in
having accepted exile.

195 *Take* ... *and take*: If you take ... you will take.

201–7 *If you do wrongfully seize Hereford's rights,* | *Call in the*
      *letters patents that he hath* | *By his attorneys general to*
      *sue* | *His livery, and deny his offered homage,* | *You pluck*
      *a thousand dangers on your head,* | *You lose a thousand*
      *well-disposèd hearts,* | *And prick my tender patience*:
      Holinshed has 'The death of this duke gave occasion
      of increasing more hatred in the people of this realm
      toward the King, for he seized into his hands all the
      goods that belonged to him, and also received all the
      rents and revenues of his lands which ought to have
      descended unto the Duke of Hereford by lawful inher-
      itance, in revoking his letters patents, which he had
      granted to him before, by virtue whereof he might make
      his attorneys general to sue livery for him of any
      manner of inheritances or possessions that might from
      thenceforth fall unto him, and that his homage might
      be respited with making reasonable fine; whereby it was
      evident that the King meant his utter undoing.

      'This hard dealing was much misliked of all the
      nobility, and cried out against of the meaner sort; but
      namely, the Duke of York was therewith sore moved
      . . .' The letters patent would have allowed Bolingbroke
      to institute suits to obtain his father's lands, which
      under feudal law would revert to Richard until it had
      been proved that the heir, Bolingbroke, was of age.
      When the lands were restored to the heir, he was
      required to make an act of homage to the king. Richard
      is said to refuse (*deny*) this, which was to be 'respited
      with making reasonable fine' (presumably because the
      exiled Bolingbroke could not pay homage in person).

203–4 *sue* | *His livery*: Institute suits for obtaining Gaunt's lands.

213–14 *But by bad courses may be understood* | *That their events*
      *can never fall out good*: Not a very elegant way of saying
      'You cannot expect bad courses of action to have good
      results.'

215   *the Earl of Wiltshire*: He was Richard's treasurer. He
      was executed at Bristol with Bushy and Green, but does
      not appear in the play.
      *straight*: Immediately.

216 *Ely House*: Where Richard now is.

217 *see*: See to.

    *Tomorrow next*: Tomorrow ('morrow' originally meant simply 'morning').

218 *trow*: Believe.

220–21 *York . . . he is just, and always loved us well*: This appreciation of York seems surprising considering his immediately preceding criticism of Richard. It is caused at least partly by Shakespeare's telescoping of events. In Holinshed, some time passes between Gaunt's death and Richard's decision to go to Ireland.

228 *great*: Big with sorrow.

229 *liberal*: Unrestrained.

231 *speaks thy words again to do thee harm*: Uses what you say in evidence against you.

232 *Tends that thou wouldst speak to*: Does what you would say refer (favourably) to.

243 *Merely*: Purely.

246–8 *The commons . . . lost their hearts*: This echoes *Woodstock*, V.3.94: 'thou well may'st doubt their loves that lost their hearts'.

246 *pilled*: Plundered.

250 *blanks*: Blank charters (see I.4.48).

    *benevolences*: Forced loans.

    *wot*: Know.

252 *Wars hath*: The singular form of the verb with a plural subject is not uncommon in Elizabethan English. It may possibly be a northern dialectal form especially appropriate to Northumberland. He uses it again at II.3.5.

252–4 *warred he hath not, | But basely yielded upon compromise | That which his noble ancestors achieved with blows*: This probably refers to the giving up of Brest to the Duke of Brittany in 1397, which was a cause of dispute between Richard and Gloucester.

254 *noble*: This was omitted by F, and many editors follow suit, explaining it as an accidental anticipation of the same word in 262. But Shakespeare may have written the alexandrine.

256  *in farm*: The 'farming' of the land is referred to at I.4.45.

257  *The King's grown bankrupt like a broken man*: Q reads
     *King*. *King's* is in all the early editions after Q2. But
     Shakespeare may have written 'King', intending
     Northumberland to complete Willoughby's sentence.

266  *strike*: Strike sail (perhaps also 'resist').
     *securely*: Carelessly, with excessive sense of security.

268  *unavoided*: Unavoidable.

269  *suffering*: Putting up with, doing nothing about.

270  *eyes*: Eye-sockets.

275  *are but thyself*: Share your feelings, are of one mind
     with you.

277-88  *Then thus . . . northern shore*: This is based on Holinshed:
     'there were certain ships rigged and made ready for
     him at a place in base Brittaine called Le Port Blanc,
     as we find in the chronicles of Brittaine, and when all
     his provision was made ready he took the sea together
     with the said Archbishop of Canterbury and his nephew
     Thomas Arundel, son and heir to the late Earl of
     Arundel beheaded at the Tower Hill, as you have heard.
     There were also with him Reginald Lord Cobham, Sir
     Thomas Erpingham, and Sir Thomas Ramston, knights,
     John Norbury, Robert Waterton, and Francis Coint,
     esquires. Few else were there, for (as some write) he
     had not past fifteen lances, as they termed them in those
     days, that is to say men-of-arms, furnished and
     appointed as the use then was. Yet other write that the
     Duke of Brittaine delivered unto him three thousand
     men of war to attend him, and that he had eight ships
     well furnished for the war, where Froissart yet speaketh
     but of three.'

278  *Brittaine*: Brittany, or Bretagne. No modernized form
     of Q's spelling seems wholly satisfactory.
     *intelligence*: Information, news.

280  *The son of Richard Earl of Arundel*: This line is not in
     any of the early editions, but was first added by Edmond
     Malone in 1790. Something like it seems necessary
     because Holinshed has 'the Earl of Arundel's son,
     named Thomas, which was kept in the Duke of Exeter's

house, escaped out of the realm'. Shakespeare is heavily dependent on Holinshed in this passage.

The Archbishop of Canterbury (282) was Richard Earl of Arundel's brother. He was *late* Archbishop because he had been banished in 1397, when his brother the earl was executed as one of the Lords Appellant. It is possible that the line was deliberately cut because Queen Elizabeth had had Philip Howard Earl of Arundel executed in 1595, and she did her best to deprive his young son of his inheritance as well as his title.

281 *broke*: Escaped.

283 *Sir Thomas Erpingham*: He appears as a character in *Henry V* (IV.1). He was one of Richard's active opponents.

*Sir John Ramston*: His real name was Thomas. He became Warden of the Tower when Richard was confined there.

284 *Coint*: This is Holinshed's form of the name. Q reads *Coines*; F, *Quoint*, which Ure takes to be a conscious correction of Q, perhaps based on consultation of the prompt book. But it might be simply a variant spelling.

285 *Duke of Brittaine*: John de Montford, who died in 1399 and whose widow, Joan of Navarre, became Bolingbroke's second wife.

286 *tall*: Large, fine.

287 *expedience*: Speed.

289–90 *they stay | The first departing of the King for Ireland*: Holinshed explains that Bolingbroke 'did not straight take land, but lay hovering aloof, and showed himself now in this place and now in that, to see what countenance was made by the people, whether they meant enviously to resist him, or friendly to receive him'.

292 *Imp out*: Repair (a metaphor from falconry).

293 *broking pawn*: The possession of the King's money-lenders.

294 *gilt*: Used punningly.

296 *in post*: In haste, travelling by relays of horses.

*Ravenspurgh*: A port on the Humber.

300 *Hold out my horse*: If my horse holds out.

**II.2**

The Queen's emotion both creates foreboding and suggests a more sympathetic view of the King. The events of the remainder of the scene are rearranged and developed from Holinshed.

3   *life-harming*: Cf. Ecclesiasticus 30:23: 'as for sorrow and heaviness, drive it far from thee; for heaviness hath slain many a man, and bringeth no profit'.

14  *Each substance of a grief hath twenty shadows*: For each real cause of grief there are twenty illusory ones. This anticipates the imagery used by Richard at IV.1.294–8.

18  *perspectives*: Pronounced with stresses on the first and third syllables. A perspective in this sense is a painting or drawing which from a normal point of view appears distorted, but which produces a clear image when looked at from a particular, and unusual, angle. There is a well-known example in the National Gallery in Holbein's portrait *The Ambassadors*, most of which is painted normally but which includes a weird object which when looked at awry is seen to be a skull. It is said to have been painted from the reflection of a skull in a curved mirror. Lines 16–17 are suggestive also of another kind of perspective, a multiplying glass cut into a number of facets, each one of which creates a distinct image. Queen Isabel's eyes, out of focus as the result of her tears, produce a similar effect.

20  *Distinguish form*: Show distinct forms.

21–4 *Looking awry upon your lord's departure,* | *Find shapes of grief more than himself to wail,* | *Which looked on as it is, is naught but shadows* | *Of what it is not*: Here the two types of perspective mentioned in the note to 18 become confused. Isabel, looking awry (which with the first type would produce a single, true image), sees a multiple image, as if she were looking at a multiplying glass. If, says Bushy, she looked at it from a normal angle (*as it is*), she would see that her cause of grief was all an illusion.

21  *Looking awry upon*: Considering mistakenly.

27  *weeps*: Weeps for.

29 *Persuades . . . it be*: This line has twelve syllables, but can be spoken with five main stresses: 'Per*suades* me *it* is *othe*rwise. Howe'er it *be*'.

31 *though on thinking on no thought I think*: Though I try to think about nothing.

32 *with heavy nothing*: Isabel returns to the thought of the *unborn sorrow*, which in a sense is *nothing*, expressed in 10–12.

33 *conceit*: Fancy.

34 *nothing less*: Anything but that.

34–40 *Conceit is still derived . . . 'tis nameless woe, I wot*: A fancied grief always (*still*) derives from a real one. Mine cannot be fancied, because it derives from an unreal one (the *nothing* at 12); or else the unreal one that afflicts me exists somewhere, and I own it as I might own an object that as yet is in someone else's keeping. But I cannot give a name to this thing whose identity I do not yet know; I think it must be 'Nameless Woe'.

46 *retired his power*: Withdrawn his army (from Ireland).

49 *repeals*: Recalls from exile.

50 *uplifted arms*: Brandished weapons.

53–4 *Northumberland . . . Willoughby*: These are all among the supporters of Bolingbroke mentioned by Holinshed.

53 *Henry*: This is printed as *H.* in Q; it may be that we should expand to 'Harry'.

57 *the rest, revolted faction, traitors*: The exact interpretation of this line is disputed. Some take 'rest revolted faction' together as 'rest of the revolted faction'. Others interpret 'and all the rest that are revolted, faction-traitors'. The present reading assumes that *revolted faction* is in apposition to *rest*.

58 *the Earl of Worcester*: He was Thomas Percy, the Earl of Northumberland's brother, and steward of the royal household. He becomes an important character in *Henry IV, Part I*. Holinshed says: 'Sir Thomas Percy, Earl of Worcester, lord steward of the King's house . . . brake his white staff, which is the representing sign and token of his office, and without delay

went to Duke Henry. When the King's servants of
household saw this – for it was done before them all –
they dispersed them-selves . . .'.

63 *heir*: Offspring.

64 *prodigy*: Monstrous birth (the *unborn sorrow ripe in
fortune's womb* (10)).

69 *cozening*: Cheating.

71 *Who*: Referring to death.

72 *lingers in extremity*: Prolongs to the utmost.

74 *signs of war about his agèd neck*: York is wearing the
piece of armour called a gorget. It could be worn with
civilian dress.

75 *careful business*: Anxious preoccupation.

76 *comfortable*: Comforting.

79 *crosses*: Troubles.

85 *try*: Put to the test (some of the *friends* are of course
on stage with York).

86 *your son was gone*: Aumerle was with the King in Ireland.

88 *The nobles they are fled. The commons they are cold*: This
is the reading of all the early editions. Some editors
emend to 'The nobles they are fled, the commons cold',
which may be correct, but long lines are not uncommon
in this play.

90 *sister*: Sister-in-law.

91 *presently*: Immediately.

92 *Hold: take my ring*: The signet ring will be proof that
he comes from York.

97 *An hour before I came the Duchess died*: Holinshed
mentions the Duchess's death, but does not say where
or when it happened, and attributes it to grief at
her son's death. In fact it appears to have occurred
in October 1399, later than the events of this
scene. Shakespeare places it here to increase the *tide
of woes*.

101 *So*: So long as, provided that.
    *untruth*: Disloyalty.

105 *Come, sister – cousin, I would say*: A. C. Sprague
comments: 'He is almost a comic character; a pitiful
one, by the same token, and very real. "Come, sister

...." his mind turning back, even as he speaks, to the past; to that final piece of news, which as yet he has scarcely taken in' (*Shakespearian Players and Performances*, 1953, p. 168).

108–9, *Gentlemen ... these affairs*; *Well, somewhat ... seven*:
116–21 The metre is irregular. Rearrangement is sometimes attempted, but a regular rhythm cannot be obtained from these words. The irregularity may reflect York's harassed state of mind. The present edition follows Q except that there 119–21 are printed as two lines, the first ending with *permit*. The rhyme demands rearrangement.

117 *dispose of*: Make arrangements for.

118 *Berkeley*: F reads *Barkley Castle*. 'Castle' may have been added in performance.

122–48 *The wind sits fair ... never*: The remainder of the scene is based on Holinshed's 'The Lord Treasurer, Bushy, Bagot, and Green, perceiving that the commons would cleave unto and take part with the Duke, slipped away, leaving the Lord Governor of the realm and the Lord Chancellor to make what shift they could for themselves. Bagot got him to Chester, and so escaped into Ireland. The other fled to the castle of Bristol, in hope there to be in safety.'

122–3 *The wind sits fair for news to go for Ireland, | But none returns*: The wind is favourable for news to go to Ireland, but not for it to come from there.

126–7 *our nearness to the King in love | Is near the hate of those love not the King*: The King's affection for us makes us hated by those who oppose the King.

127 *those love*: Those who love.

132 *If judgement lie in them*: If our fate depends on them ('the commons' or 'the commons' hearts').

133 *ever*: Constantly.

136 *office*: Service.

140 *No, I will to Ireland to his majesty*: According to Holinshed, Bagot 'got him to Chester, and so escaped into Ireland. The other [Bushy and Green] fled to the castle of Bristol'. Shakespeare follows this here. However, in II.3.164 Bagot, not Green, is rumoured to

be at Bristol with Bushy. In III.1 Bushy and Green are executed at Bristol. It looks as if Shakespeare was rather confused or careless. The discrepancies would probably not be noticed in performance.

141–2  *If heart's presages be not vain,* | *We three here part that ne'er shall meet again*: Thomas of Woodstock takes leave of his brothers in similar words (*Woodstock*, III.2.102–6):

> Adieu, good York and Gaunt, farewell for ever.
> I have a sad presage comes suddenly
> That I shall never see these brothers more:
> On earth, I fear, we never more shall meet.
> Of Edward the Third's seven sons we three are left ...

141  *presages*: The accent is on the second syllable.

143  *That's as York thrives to beat*: That's according to how far York succeeds in beating.

145  *numbering sands and drinking oceans dry*: Proverbial expressions for attempting the impossible.

II.3

In its fluidity of setting this scene is characteristic of the Elizabethan stage. It begins somewhere in Gloucestershire, on the way to Berkeley Castle where, according to Holinshed, Bolingbroke went from Doncaster, and where York had halted on his way to meet the King on his return from Ireland. At 53 the action localizes itself outside the castle. The material of the scene is created by Shakespeare from facts given by Holinshed.

4  *high wild hills*: Northumberland is referring to the Cotswolds. He, of course, comes from the north of England.

5  *Draws ... makes*: For the grammar, see Commentary to II.1.252.

7  *delectable*: Accented on the first and third syllables.

9  *Cotswold*: Q reads *Cotshall*, an old form of the name of the Gloucestershire hills. In *The Merry Wives of Windsor* it is spelt 'Cotsall', and in *Henry IV, Part II*,

'Cotsole'. Shakespeare's pronunciation was probably something like 'Cotsul'.

11  *beguiled*: Passed pleasantly.

12  *tediousness and process*: Tedious process.

16  *By this*: By this hope (of enjoying Bolingbroke's company).

20  *Harry Percy*: He lived from 1364 to 1403, when he was killed at the battle of Shrewsbury. He was known as Hotspur because of his daring in battle against the border clans. He is vividly characterized in *Henry IV, Part I*. There is no proof in *Richard II* that Shakespeare had yet conceived the idiosyncrasies of the character as he later portrayed it.

22  *whencesoever*: From somewhere or other; wherever he may be.

26–8  *he hath forsook . . . of the King*: As reported at II.2.58–61.

36  *Have you forgot the Duke of Hereford, boy*: A rebuke to Harry Percy for not greeting Bolingbroke. *Boy* is unhistorical, as in fact 'young' Percy was two years older than Bolingbroke. In *Henry IV, Part I*, Hotspur is of the same generation as Prince Hal – he was actually twenty-two years older.

38  *To my knowledge*: So far as I know; to the best of my knowledge.

43–4  *Which elder days shall ripen and confirm | To more approvèd service and desert*: Ironical, considering what happened later, portrayed by Shakespeare in *Henry IV, Part I*.

45–50  *I thank thee . . . thus seals it*: Hotspur recalls this conversation with disgust at Bolingbroke's teachery in *Henry IV, Part I*, I.3.236–51.

45  *gentle*: Noble, 'gentlemanly'.

47  *As in a soul remembering*: As having a heart which remembers.

49  *still*: Continually, all the time.

50  *my hand thus seals it*: They shake hands.

51–2  *what stir | Keeps*: 'What event detains' or 'what is [he] doing'.

56 *Enter Ross and Willoughby*: They actually joined
   Bolingbroke when he landed at Ravenspurgh, not at
   Berkeley.

61 *unfelt*: Intangible.
   *which*: Refers to *treasury*.

65 *Evermore thank's the exchequer*: 'Thank you' is always
   (or 'always will be') the exchequer . . . F has *Euermore
   thankes, th'Exchequer of the poor*, which many editors
   follow; but 'thank' as an expression of gratitude is an
   authenticated usage. *Thank* is the antecedent of *Which*
   in the following line.

66 *to years*: To years of discretion, into its own.

67 *Stands for*: Represents, does duty for.
   *Berkeley*: He was a baron, and sat in Parliament from
   1381 till 1417, when he died.

70 *my answer is to 'Lancaster'*: Berkeley has addressed him
   by his former title of 'Hereford'. He replies that he
   answers only to the title of 'Lancaster', which he has
   inherited from his father. It may be that he begins to
   reply with 'my answer is', and then interjects 'to
   "Lancaster"', meaning that this is the only title to which
   he will reply; or perhaps he says simply 'I reply only
   in the name of Lancaster.' Northumberland referred to
   him as 'Hereford' without rebuke at 36.

75 *raze one title of your honour out*: Q has *race*, a variant
   form. The title is imagined as an inscription, as at
   III.1.25 where Bolingbroke complains that his enemies
   have *Razed out my imprese*. There is probably also a
   pun on 'title', meaning 'any part of'.

79 *absent time*: Time of (King Richard's) absence.

80 *self-borne*: This may mean 'born of' or 'originating in'
   yourself, or 'carried for your own cause', or 'carried
   by yourself', or may be a quibble on these meanings:
   'begotten and carried on your own initiative and for
   your own ends'.

84 *duty*: The act of kneeling.
   *deceivable*: Deceptive.

86 *Tut, tut*: This extra-metrical exclamation has been
   suspected of being an actor's interpolation.

*grace me no grace, nor uncle me no uncle*: Shakespeare
uses a similar contemptuous refusal of courtesy in
*Romeo and Juliet*, III.5.152: 'Thank me no thankings,
nor proud me no prouds.'

87–8 *'grace' . . . profane*: Alluding to the religious connota-
tions of 'grace', which would have been felt more
strongly by Shakespeare's than by a modern audience.

88 *ungracious*: Wicked. The word was much stronger in
Shakespeare's time than it is at present.

90 *dust*: Grain of dust.

91 *But then more 'why'*: But even if that can be answered
there are more questions (and, perhaps, ones even more
indicative of astonishment) to be asked.

94 *ostentation*: Display.

98 *lord*: F reads *the Lord*, which may be correct; but the
irregular metre has strength.

98–101 *Were I but . . . thousand French*: There is no clear source
of this incident.

100 *the Black Prince*: King Richard's father.

102–3 *arm of mine, | Now prisoner to the palsy*: Palsy is a para-
lytic condition. This may be no more than a general
reference to York's advanced years, but it has been said
that there is historical warrant for the statement.

103 *chastise*: The accent is on the first syllable.

106–7 *condition . . . condition*: In its first use, the word refers
to Bolingbroke's personal qualities; in its second, to the
circumstances of the rebellion.

111 *braving*: Defiant, daring (adjectival rather than verbal).

113 *for*: 'In the character of', 'as'; or 'to assume the title
and rights of'.

115 *indifferent*: Impartial.

118–19 *condemned | A*: Condemned as a.

119 *royalties*: Rights granted to a subject by a king, as at
II.1.190.

120 *arms*: The sense 'coat-of-arms' is felt.

121 *unthrifts*: Spendthrifts, prodigals (such as the King's
favourites).

122–3 *If that my cousin King . . . Duke of Lancaster*: Cf. York's
argument to Richard on Bolingbroke's behalf, II.1.191–9.

122 *cousin King*: Cousin who is king; kingly cousin.

125 *thus*: As I have.

127 *rouse . . . wrongs . . . bay*: The metaphor is from hunting.
*rouse*: Startle from the lair.
*wrongs*: Presumably 'wrongdoers'; they are the quarry.
*bay*: Last stand.

128 *denied*: Refused the right.

128–9 *sue my livery . . . letters patents*: See Commentary to
II.1.203–4.

130 *distrained*: Seized, taken possession of by crown officers.

131 *and all*: And everything else.

132–5 *What would you . . . free descent*: Holinshed writes that
when Bolingbroke arrived at Doncaster he swore 'that
he would demand no more but the lands that were to
him descended by inheritance from his father and in
right of his wife'.

133 *challenge law*: Demand my rights.

135 *of free descent*: Free from flaw; direct.

137 *It stands your grace upon*: It is incumbent upon your
grace.

138 *his endowments*: The possessions with which he has
(involuntarily) endowed them.
*are*: Presumably this is accented; that is, 'it is true
that . . .'.

142 *kind*: Manner.

143 *Be his own carver*: The phrase seems to have been proverbial – 'help himself'. It gains point from the double
sense of carving with a table-knife and a sword.

144 *find out right with wrong*: Achieve your rights by doing
wrong.

150 *never*: Probably to be pronounced 'ne'er'.

153 *power*: Army.
*ill-left*: 'Left ill-equipped' or 'left in disorder'.

155 *attach*: Arrest.

158 *as neuter*: Neutral.

164 *Bagot*: At II.2.140 (see Commentary) he had declared
his intention of going to Ireland.

165 *caterpillars of the commonwealth*: Parasites on society.

166 *weed*: The word could be used of the removal of

harmful creatures as well as plants. It is part of the
recurrent image of England as a garden.

170 *Things past redress are now with me past care*: York
gives vent to his divided feelings in a semi-proverbial
expression.

**II.4**

This scene is based on Holinshed, who explains that
because of storms Richard was late in hearing that
Bolingbroke had landed in England, and that Richard
did not set out immediately on hearing the news, but
was persuaded to delay until his preparations were
complete.

0 *Earl of Salisbury*: John de Montacute (or Montagu),
1350–1400.

*Welsh Captain*: In Holinshed, the Welsh captain is
Owen Glendower, who figures prominently in *Henry
IV, Part I*. The fact that the Welsh Captain speaks of
omens and portents (8–15), as Glendower does in the
later play, gives some colour to the suggestion that
Shakespeare identified the two. But he seems to have
preferred not to give the captain a name. He is important rather for his representative quality than for any
personal characteristics. See Commentary to III.1.43.

1 *ten days*: According to Holinshed, the Welshmen waited
for fourteen days.

2 *hardly*: With difficulty.

3 *yet*: Still, so far.

5–6 *thou trusty Welshman.* | *The King reposeth all his confi-
dence in thee*: Holinshed records that Richard 'had also
no small affiance [confidence] in the Welshmen, and
Cheshire men'.

8 ff. *The bay trees . . .* : The expression of superstitious fear
in these lines is the main point of the scene. Glendower
in *Henry IV, Part I* (III.1) speaks similarly. Whether or
not the Welsh Captain is Glendower, Shakespeare may
have felt that such sentiments were specially appropriate in the mouth of a Welshman. According to
Holinshed the withering of the bay trees happened in
England, not Wales: 'In this year in a manner through-

out all the realm of England old bay trees withered, and afterwards, contrary to all men's thinking, grew green again, a strange sight, and supposed to import some unknown event.' This passage occurs first in the second (1587) edition of Holinshed, and the parallel is part of the evidence for Shakespeare's use of this edition. The bay tree was symbolical of victory and immortality; its withering was thus a particularly bad omen.

9 *meteors . . . fixèd stars*: Meteors, of course, are 'unfixed' stars.

10 *The pale-faced moon looks bloody on the earth*: *Looks* used of planets and stars implies influence as well as appearance. This line may mean that the normally pale-faced moon appears bloody to earthly watchers, or that it exerts a bloody influence.

11 *lean-looked*: Lean-looking.

*prophets*: Soothsayers (rather than religiously inspired men).

14 *to enjoy*: In hope of profiting.

19–21 *I see thy glory . . . west*: These lines anticipate Richard's imagery at III.3.178–83.

22 *Witnessing*: Betokening.

24 *crossly*: Adversely.

III.1

The basis of the scene is Holinshed's statement that 'the foresaid dukes with their power went towards Bristol where, at their coming, they showed themselves before the town and castle, being an huge multitude of people. There were enclosed within the castle the Lord William Scroop Earl of Wiltshire and Treasurer of England, Sir Henry Green, and Sir John Bushy, knights, who prepared to make resistance. But when it would not prevail they were taken and brought forth bound as prisoners into the camp before the Duke of Lancaster. On the morrow next ensuing they were arraigned before the Constable and Marshal and found guilty of treason for misgoverning the King and realm, and forthwith had their heads smit off.' Shakespeare omits

Wiltshire, who makes no appearance in the play, though
at II.2.135 he is said to be at Bristol, and at III.2.141–2
and III.4.53 he is mentioned as having been executed
along with Bushy and Green. It is possible that
Shakespeare wrongly identified him with Bagot – see
Commentary to III.2.122.

0 F directs Ross, Percy, and Willoughby also to enter.
They are not required by the action; but it may have
been the custom to bring them on to dress the stage.

3 *presently*: Immediately.
*part*: Leave.

4 *urging*: Stressing.

5–6 *to wash your blood | From off my hands*: To justify my
condemning you. The phrase inevitably recalls Pontius
Pilate's action, directly referred to by Richard at
IV.1.238–41.

9 *A happy gentleman in*: A gentleman fortunate in.
*blood and lineaments*: Birth and personal appearance.

10 *clean*: Utterly.

11–12 *You have in manner with your sinful hours | Made a
divorce betwixt his Queen and him*: This accusation does
not appear to be borne out by the relations between
Richard and his Queen in the rest of the play. It may
have been suggested by Holinshed's 'there reigned
abundantly the filthy sin of lechery, and fornication,
with abominable adultery, specially in the King ...'.
Shakespeare may also have been influenced by the
clearly homosexual relationship of Edward and
Gaveston in Marlowe's *Edward II*, though he does not
necessarily imply sexual opposition between the King's
favourites and the Queen. In *Woodstock* Richard
displays intense affection for Greene. Perhaps the principal point in *Richard II* is simply that the Queen stands
at this point in the play as a symbol of the virtue from
which Richard's favourites are diverting him.

11 *in manner*: As it were.

12 *divorce*: Used metaphorically.

13 *possession*: Joint rights.

20 *in*: Into (adding to them as well as mixing breath among

them. So in *Romeo and Juliet*, I.1.133: 'Adding to clouds
more clouds with his deep sighs').

22 *signories*: Estates, manors.

23 *Disparked*: Converted to other, less aristocratic, uses
land in which game had been kept.

24 *From my own windows torn my household coat*: Broken
the windows in which my coat-of-arms was emblazoned
('tear' could mean 'break').

25 *imprese*: Crest, heraldic device (this is the Italian plural
of the singular *impresa*).

27 *gentleman*: Nobleman.

36 *your house*: Langley.

37 *intreated*: Treated.

41 *at large*: In full (or 'in general terms').

43 *Glendower*: Owen Glendower is not mentioned elsewhere in this play (but see Commentary to II.4, opening
stage direction), though he is important in *Henry IV,
Part I*. Holinshed says that Glendower 'served King
Richard at Flint Castle when he [Richard] was taken
by Henry, Duke of Lancaster'. Probably Shakespeare's
main reason for the choice of name here was its obvious
Welshness, though he may have been thinking ahead
to the events of the reign of Henry IV.

III.2

The basis of this scene is Holinshed, who reports that
the King 'landed near the castle of Barkloughly in Wales
... and stayed a while in the same castle, being adver-
tised of the great forces which the Duke of Lancaster
had got together against him, wherewith he was marvel-
lously amazed, knowing certainly that those which were
thus in arms with the Duke of Lancaster against him
would rather die than give place, as well for the hatred
as fear which they had conceived at him'. He went to
Conway, 'but when he understood as he went thus
forward that all the castles even from the borders of
Scotland unto Bristol were delivered unto the Duke of
Lancaster, and that likewise the nobles and commons as
well of the south parts as the north were fully bent to
take part with the same Duke against him; and further,

hearing how his trusty councillors had lost their heads
at Bristol, he became so greatly discomforted that,
sorrowfully lamenting his miserable state, he utterly
despaired of his own safety and, calling his army
together, which was not small, licensed every man to
depart to his home'. Holinshed's later comment is interesting as an expression of the kind of sympathy which
Shakespeare too begins to evoke; he writes how remarkable it is that Bolingbroke should have been advanced
to the throne, 'and that King Richard should thus be left
desolate, void, and in despair of all hope and comfort,
in whom if there were any offence it ought rather to be
imputed to the frailty of wanton youth than to the malice
of his heart; but such is the deceivable judgement of
man which, not regarding things present with due
consideration, thinketh ever that things to come shall
have good success, with a pleasant and delightful end'.

0  *colours*: Banners.

*Bishop of Carlisle*: He was Thomas Merke, a friend and
follower of King Richard. The Pope appointed him
bishop in 1397, at Richard's request. He was arrested
in 1399 and pardoned in 1400, after which he became
a country vicar, and died in 1409. Holinshed reports
that he died 'shortly after' 1400.

1  *Barkloughly*: The name derives from Holinshed, where
it seems to be an error for a form of Harlech.

2  *brooks*: Enjoys.

6–7  *I . . . rebels*: The two words are contrasted.

6  *salute*: Greet. Richard bends to touch the ground.

8  *long-parted mother with*: Mother long parted from.

9  *fondly*: The word implies a mixture of affection and
slight folly. Shakespeare often uses the image of tears
and smiles at once, as in the description of Cordelia
hearing news of King Lear: 'You have seen | Sunshine
and rain at once; her smiles and tears | Were like a
better way' (*King Lear*, IV.3.17–19). See also V.2.32.

14  *spiders that suck up thy venom*: It was believed that spiders
were dangerously poisonous, and that they sucked their
poison from the earth.

15 *heavy-gaited*: Referring to the toad's clumsy movements.

*toads*: Like spiders, they were thought to be poisonous.

21 *double*: Forked.

23 *senseless*: Addressed to things which lack the sense of hearing.

24–5 *stones | Prove armèd soldiers*: This could be a reference to the myth of Cadmus, who sowed dragons' teeth which sprang up as soldiers. Gospel echoes are also possible: Luke 19:40: 'I tell you that if these would hold their peace then shall the stones cry immediately', and 3:8: 'God is able of these stones to raise up children unto Abraham.'

27 *Fear not*: Do not doubt that. Or perhaps *Fear not, my lord* should form a complete sentence.

29–32 *The means ... and redress*: These lines were omitted from F, perhaps because they are obscure. They could mean 'We must accept, not neglect, the means that the heavens offer; otherwise we run counter to heaven's wish – we refuse heaven's offer ...'. The sentiment is common, e.g. Prospero in *The Tempest*, I.2.181–4:

> my zenith doth depend upon
> A most auspicious star, whose influence
> If now I court not, but omit, my fortunes
> Will ever after droop.

34 *security*: Over-confidence.

36 *Discomfortable*: Disheartening. Shakespeare does not use the negative form elsewhere; it may have been suggested by Holinshed's statement that Richard became 'greatly discomforted'.

37–8 *when the searching eye of heaven is hid | Behind the globe, that lights the lower world*: Richard again compares himself with the sun; his absence in Ireland is like the nightly departure of the sun to light the other side of the world (*the lower world*). The notion that robberies are liable to take place at night is commonplace enough, but it may be worth comparing Falstaff's 'we that take

purses go by the moon and the seven stars, and not "by
Phoebus, he, that wandering knight so fair"' (*Henry
IV, Part I*, I.2.13–14). The syntax of Richard's lines is
obscure, and the sense difficult for the actor to convey,
but this is probably what Shakespeare wrote. A common
emendation alters *that* to 'and', which simplifies the
sentence and makes the meaning clearer.

41 *this terrestrial ball*: The earth.

42 *He*: The sun.
   *fires*: (Metaphorically) sets on fire.

46 *at themselves*: At the revelation of their own wickedness.

49 *the Antipodes*: The people living on the opposite side
   of the earth. Richard has only been as far as Ireland,
   but the metaphor is continued from 38.

54 *rude*: Rough, stormy.

55 *balm*: Consecrated oil.

57 *elected*: Chosen.

58 *pressed*: Conscripted.

59 *shrewd*: Harmful.

59–61 *crown . . . angel*: These were both coins, on the names
   of which Shakespeare often puns. Establishes the word-
   play which leads to the curious notion of wage-earning
   angels.

62 *still*: Always.

63 *power*: Army (though Salisbury takes it in the more
   abstract sense).

64 *nea'er*: Q prints *neare*, which in Elizabethan English
   could mean 'nearer'. 'Nearer' is required by the sense,
   and in speaking could be elided to form one syllable.

76–81 *But now . . . my pride*: Here the verse takes the form of
   the sestet of a sonnet.

76 *But now*: Just now.
   *twenty*: Perhaps the requirements of metre are responsible for the discrepancy with *twelve* (70).

79 *dead*: Death-like.

80 *fly*: This may be indicative – 'do fly'; imperative –
   'fly!'; or subjunctive – 'let [them] fly!'

90 *power*: Including the sense of 'army'.

*Scroop*: Sir Stephen Scroop was a famous warrior, and was among the few who remained faithful to King Richard after his arrest. He died in 1408.

91 *betide*: Subjunctive: 'may [they] betide . . .'

92 *care-tuned*: Tuned to the key of sorrow.

93 *Mine ear is open*: Dr Johnson comments: 'It seems to be the design of the poet to raise Richard to esteem in his fall, and consequently to interest the reader in his favour. He gives him only passive fortitude, the virtue of a confessor rather than of a king. In his prosperity we saw him imperious and oppressive, but in his distress he is wise, patient, and pious.'

95 *care*: Trouble.

99 *his fellow*: Bolingbroke's equal.

101 *They break their faith to God as well as us*: Because the King is God's deputy.

102 *Cry*: (Even if you) proclaim.

109 *his limits*: Its banks.

110 *fearful*: Filled with fear.

111 *steel*: Of arms and armour.

112 *Whitebeards*: Old men.

114 *speak big*: Imitate men's tones.
    *female*: Womanish.

115 *stiff unwieldy*: Perhaps because new, or because the boys are not strong enough to wear it properly.
    *arms*: Armour.

116 *beadsmen*: Almsmen, pensioners (with the duty of offering prayers or 'beads' on behalf on their benefactors).

117 *double-fatal yew*: Fatal both because the tree's berries are poisonous and because its wood is used to make bows.

118 *distaff-women*: Women normally occupied in spinning.
    *manage*: Wield.
    *bills*: Bill-hooks, halberds. These are *rusty* from long disuse.

119 *seat*: Throne.

122 *Where is Bagot*: He appears again in IV.1. It has been thought odd that Richard at 132, in referring to *Three*

*Judases*, and again at 141, when he names all but Bagot, should seem to know without being told that Bagot has survived. This may be the result of imperfect revision on Shakespeare's part. Ure comments: 'I suggest that Shakespeare, when he wrote l. 132, was already thinking ahead to ll. 141–2 and IV.1; he was planning to have one of the four men alive for IV.1, but forgot that Richard could not yet know, when he breaks out at l. 132, what Shakespeare was arranging to have him told at ll. 141–2: Shakespeare carelessly anticipated but did not grossly resurrect.' He may, however, have recalled that according to Holinshed Bagot 'escaped into Ireland', which probably means to join the King there. See Commentary to II.2.122.

125 *Measure*: Pass through.
    *peaceful*: Unopposed.

128 *Peace have they made with him indeed*: The quibble on 'making peace' is not uncommon, and Scroop's line should carry a sombre irony. Cf. *Macbeth*, IV.3. 178–9:

MACDUFF

   The tyrant has not battered at their peace?

ROSS

   No. They were well at peace when I did leave 'em.

129 *vipers, damned without redemption*: The viper was traditionally treacherous. Shakespeare may have been influenced by Matthew 23:33: 'Ye serpents, ye generation of vipers, how will ye escape the damnation of hell?' *without*: Beyond hope of.

131 *Snakes in my heart-blood warmed, that sting my heart*: The image was common. Shakespeare uses it again at V.3.57 (*A serpent that will sting thee to the heart*), and in *Henry VI, Part II*, III.1.343–4: 'I fear me you but warm the starvèd snake, | Who, cherished in your breasts, will sting your hearts.' There was a well-known fable about a farmer bitten by a snake which he found nearly dead from cold and warmed in his breast.

132 *Judases*: Richard elsewhere (for example, IV.1.170)
     compares himself to Christ; but 'Judas' was a common
     word for a traitor.

133 *Would they make peace? Terrible hell*: The line is metri-
     cally short. This may be intended to invite emphasis
     on Richard's outburst. *They* is emphatic. F reads:

> *Would they make peace? terrible Hell make warre*
> *Vpon their spotted Soules for this Offence.*

     This is probably an unauthentic attempt to regularize
     the metre.

134 *spotted*: Stained, sinful. There may also be a hint of the
     spotted skin of the viper.

135 *his property*: Its distinctive quality.

138 *hands*: For signing treaties, or shaking in amity, or lifting
     in submission.

138–40 *Those . . . ground*: The inflated expression gives weight
     to the statement of a fact which has been in suspense
     since 122.

140 *graved*: Buried.

141 AUMERLE: Richard's failure – or inability – to speak
     here may give a cue to the actor. As often in Shakes-
     peare, affliction does not find immediate expression.

150 *deposèd*: Richard already sees himself as deposed from
     the throne. The word may also carry the sense of
     'deposited'.

153–4 *that small model of the barren earth | Which serves as*
     *paste and cover to our bones*: Probably a reference to the
     flesh as microcosm, corresponding on a small scale to
     the earth. But *model* might also mean 'mould' or 'some-
     thing that envelops closely'. According to this inter-
     pretation, Richard says that all we finally possess is the
     earth that surrounds our body.

154 *paste*: Pastry (alluding to the pastry cover, sometimes
     called a coffin, in which meat was baked).

156 *stories of the death of kings*: The most famous collec-
     tion of such stories was *The Mirror for Magistrates* (1559
     etc.) but there were others. The lines that follow recall

Shakespeare's *Richard III*, V.3, in which the ghosts of his dead enemies appear to Richard.

158 *ghosts they have deposed*: Ghosts of those whom they have deprived of life.

162 *antic*: Buffoon, jester. Dr Johnson commented 'Here is an allusion to the *antick* or *fool* of old farces, whose chief part is to deride and disturb the graver and more splendid personages'; the image is continued in *little scene* (164). Death was frequently portrayed as a skeleton grinning at the futile pretensions of mankind.

163 *Scoffing his state*: Scoffing at his (the king's) splendour.

164 *scene*. The image of life as a play enacted upon the stage of the world was common.

165 *monarchize*: Play a king's part. This is the first known use of the word.

*kill with looks*: An image of kingly power, able to order execution with a glance.

166 *self and vain conceit*: Vain conceit of himself. *Self* is adjectival.

167–8 *As if this flesh which walls about our life | Were brass impregnable*: This may be influenced by Job 6:12: 'Is my strength the strength of stones? or is my flesh of brass?' But brass was a common symbol of imperishability. In the story of Friar Bacon and Friar Bungay, well known to Shakespeare and his audience through Robert Greene's play, one of Friar Bacon's aims is to surround Britain with a wall of brass; and Marlowe's Doctor Faustus says 'I'll have them wall all Germany with brass' (I.90).

168 *humoured thus*: (1) 'Death having thus amused himself'; (2) 'death having thus indulged the king'; (3) 'while the king is in this humour (mood)'. All three meanings may well be present.

169–70 *pin | Bores through his castle wall*: The image changes, and becomes that of an attack on a besieged castle.

171 *Cover your heads*: Replace your hats. Richard tells his subjects not to treat him with the reverence due to kingship. He is stressing his humanity.

175–6 *I live ... need friends*: The short lines invite the actor

to use pauses for emphasis. There is no need to assume
textual corruption.

176 *Subjected*: The King is a 'subject' – to human needs.

179 *presently*: Promptly.

*prevent the ways to wail*: An odd expression: *prevent* is
used in the now obsolete sense 'avoid by prompt action';
*the ways to wail* seems to mean 'paths to grief'. The
desire for alliteration probably played its part in
the choice of words.

183 *to fight*: In fighting; if you fight.

184–5 *fight and die is death destroying death,* | *Where fearing*
*dying pays death servile breath*: To die fighting is to
destroy death's power by means of death, whereas
to live in fear of death is to pay it underserved homage.

186 *of*: From (or perhaps, since at 192 Richard inquires
about York's whereabouts, 'about').

187 *make a body of a limb*: Make a single troop as effective
as an entire army.

189 *change*: Exchange.

*our day of doom*: Day that decides our fate.

190 *overblown*: Blown over, passed away.

194 *complexion*: General appearance.

196–7 *eye* | *My*: Eye that my. Q has a colon following *eye*.
An alternative reading is that 196 is a separate sentence.

198 *by small and small*: Little by little.

199 *To lengthen out the worst*: Lengthening, stretching out
the worst news. The metaphor is of the rack.

202 *gentlemen*: Men of rank.

*gentlemen in arms*: Perhaps both 'gentlemen-in-arms',
that is 'gentlemen bearing coats-of-arms', and
'gentlemen are up in arms'.

203 *Upon his party*: On his side.

204 *Beshrew*: Confound (a mild oath).

204–5 *forth* | *Of*: Out of, away from.

207–8 *By heaven . . . comfort any more*: Dr Johnson comments
'This sentiment is drawn from nature. Nothing is more
offensive to a mind convinced that his distress is without
a remedy, and preparing to submit quietly to irresistible
calamity, than these petty and conjectured comforts

which unskilful officiousness thinks it virtue to administer.'

212 *ear*: Plough, till.

*the land*: Used metaphorically for Bolingbroke's cause.

213 *none*: No hope (of growing, or prospering).

214 *counsel is but vain*: Advice (to the contrary) will be ineffectual.

215 *double wrong*: In thinking to deceive me and in increasing my grief by again leading me into false hope. The notion of the *double* or forked *tongue* of a snake may be present.

III.3

This scene takes place outside the walls of Flint Castle, on the estuary of the River Dee. It is based on Holinshed, though Shakespeare has omitted an episode in which King Richard, having arrived in Wales, is kidnapped and forcibly taken to Flint.

The staging of this scene presents problems. The first episode takes place outside the castle (20, 26). Bolingbroke sends Northumberland towards the castle in order to deliver his message (32). In the meantime he and those with him will *march* | *Upon the grassy carpet of this plain* (49–50), and he gives the command to do so. Some stylization of movement seems inevitable. Perhaps on the Elizabethan stage Bolingbroke and his men would have conversed at the front of one side of the platform, and marched across to the other. Richard's entry at 61 must be on an upper level and therefore at the back of the stage. For the staging of the rest of the scene, see Commentary to 61, stage direction, and 183, stage direction.

0 *colours*: Banners.

1 *So that by this intelligence*: The scene begins in the middle of a conversation. Presumably Bolingbroke enters with a written message that he has been reading. *intelligence*: Information.

6 *hid his head*: Taken shelter.

13 *so brief . . . to*: So brief as to.

14 *taking . . . the head*: (1) Acting without restraint; (2) omitting the title.

15 *Mistake*: Misunderstand.

17 *mistake the heavens are*: (1) 'Fail to remember that the heavens are'; (2) 'transgress against the heavens which ...' (though this does not sit well with Bolingbroke's response). Some editors break the sentence after *mistake*.

25 *lies*: Resides, dwells.

31 *Noble lord*: Probably Northumberland.

32 *rude ribs*: Rough walls.

33 *breath of parley*: Call (of a trumpet) inviting opponents to conference.

34 *his*: Its. This is the normal form; but the *ears* may be the King's as well as the castle's. Coleridge commented: 'I have no doubt that Shakespeare purposely used the personal pronoun, "his", to shew, that although Bolingbroke was only speaking of the castle, his thoughts dwelt on the king.'

35 *Henry Bolingbroke*: Coleridge commented: 'almost the only instance in which a name forms the whole line; Shakespeare meant it to convey Bolingbroke's opinion of his own importance'.

40 *banishment repealed*: The revoking of my banishment.

42 *advantage of my power*: Superiority of my forces.

43 *summer's dust*: Historically it was August 1399.

45 *The which ... Bolingbroke*: Coleridge's comment may afford a hint to the actor: 'At this point Bolingbroke seems to have been checked by the eye of York ... He passes suddenly from insolence to humility, owing to the silent reproof he received from his uncle.' But Bolingbroke could be hypocritical rather than humble. Coleridge suggests that 'York again checks him' at the end of 57.

46 *is such*: Is that such.

48 *stooping duty*: Submissive kneeling.

52 *tattered*: 'Having pointed projections' or 'dilapidated' (in contrast with *Our fair appointments*). The word does not necessarily imply that the castle is easily to be taken, though *ruined ears* (34) might support such an interpretation.

53–61 *fair appointments . . . on the walls*: Holinshed reports that Northumberland 'mustered his army before the King's presence, which undoubtedly made a passing fair show', and that the King 'was walking aloft on the brayes [outworks] of the walls to behold the coming of the Duke afar off'. His companions here seem to derive from a later stage in Holinshed's account, corresponding to Shakespeare's line 186: 'The King accompanied with the Bishop of Carlisle, the Earl of Salisbury, and Sir Stephen Scroop, knight, who bare the sword before him, and a few other, came forth into the outer ward and sat down in a place prepared for him.'

53 *appointments may be well perused*: Equipment may be well observed. The silence of the drums will make this a peaceable show of strength.

56 *fire and water*: In the form of lightning and rain or cloud.

56–7 *shock | At meeting tears the cloudy cheeks of heaven*: Bolingbroke alludes to the belief that thunder was caused by a clash between the opposed elements of fire and water in the form of lightning and rain.

57 *cheeks of heaven*: This may allude to the puffing cheeks of cherubs often represented in maps.

58 *fire . . . yielding water*: In the traditional 'chain of being' fire was dominant among the elements, so water would 'yield' to it. Similarly Richard is seen at 63 as the sun, dominant among planets, at 68 as the king, dominant among men, and at 69 as the eagle, dominant among birds. Bolingbroke is not obviously yielding to Richard. He may be claiming that while Richard rages, Bolingbroke will drop tears of sorrow on the ground. There may also be the implication that this is the more fruitful thing to do.

59–60 *I rain | My waters – on the earth, and not on him*: This is a difficult passage. Q prints:

*I raigne.*
*My water's on the earth, and not on him.*

If the second of these lines is intended to be a separate sentence, it may mean 'My (beneficent) water falls on the earth, not on Richard.' This would also mean that a strong pun would be felt at 59 ('rain', 'reign'). On the other hand the full stop after *raigne* in Q may be accidental – it comes at the end of a page. If so, Bolingbroke must mean 'Let him rage in anger while I scatter my blessings on the earth, though not on Richard.'

61 *King Richard appeareth*: King Richard's appearance on the walls is an impressive moment. When he speaks, at 72, he explains why he has not spoken before. This strongly suggests that his entry should be made in silence, to be commented on by Bolingbroke and York only when he has taken up his position. Formality of staging seems essential. Probably Northumberland and the other lords should be with the trumpeters, as Bolingbroke has instructed them to speak on his behalf, and King Richard's amazement (72) should be addressed directly to them. Bolingbroke and York should stand somewhat aside (91).

*The trumpets sound parley without, and answer within*: This presumably means that the stage trumpets (those *without*) sound and are answered by the backstage ones (those *within*), imagined to be inside the castle.

*the walls*: The upper level of the stage.

63 *blushing, discontented sun*: This passage may be referring to the proverb 'A red morning foretells a stormy day'. The rising sun is *discontented* because the day is to be one of bad weather.

65 *he*: The sun.

*envious*: In Shakespeare's time this word had the stronger sense of 'hostile', 'harmful', rather than simply 'jealous'.

68 *Yet*: 'Still' as well as 'nevertheless'.

68–9 *eye, | As bright as is the eagle's*: The eagle, king of birds, was believed to be able to look into the sun, chief of the heavenly bodies, without coming to harm.

69 *lightens forth*: Sends down as lightning, flashes out.

71  *stain*: Cf. 66.

    *show*: Sight.

72ff. *We*: Richard repeatedly uses the royal plural.

72–3 *stood | To watch*: Stood in expectation of seeing.

76  *awful duty*: Duty of showing awe or reverence.

77  *hand*: Signature.

79–81 *hand . . . he*: The hand is representative of the person.

81  *profane*: Commit sacrilege.

83  *torn their souls*: Sinned by turning their allegiance from Richard to Bolingbroke. The jingle with *turning* is deliberate.

85  *my*: Here and later in the speech Richard lapses from the plural form as he speaks of himself as an individual rather than a king.

88–9 *Your children . . . | That lift your*: The children . . . of you who lift your.

89  *vassal*: Subject.

91  *yon methinks he stands*: King Richard has not so far addressed Bolingbroke since he returned from exile, and now does not deign to address him directly.

93–4 *open | The purple testament*: Open the blood-coloured will (– in which war is bequeathed – preparatory to putting it into operation).

95  *ere the crown he looks for live in peace*: Before the English crown, which Bolingbroke hopes for (or 'expects'), may be worn in peace.

95–6 *crown . . . crowns*: Crown (of kingship) . . . heads.

97  *the flower of England's face*: Three senses are felt: England is likened to a flower; so is the human face; and *the flower* suggests brave young men.

100 *pastor's*: Shepherd's (Richard's). Many editors read 'pasture's' or 'pastures'.

102 *civil and uncivil arms*: *Civil*, used in civil war; *uncivil*, barbarous.

103 *thrice-noble*: By descent from Edward III; by descent from John of Gaunt; and on his own account, as the following lines make plain.

106 *your royal grandsire*: King Edward III.

108 *head*: Source (as of a spring).

112 *scope*: Aim.

113 *lineal royalties*: Hereditary rights of royalty.

114 *Enfranchisement*: Freedom from banishment (and restoration of rights).

115 *thy royal party*: Your majesty's part.

116 *commend*: Hand over.

117 *barbèd*: Armoured with barbs (coverings for the breasts and flanks of war-horses).

121–2 *returns | His*: Replies that his.

128 *look so poorly*: Seem so abject.
    *speak so fair*: Speak so courteously.

136 *sooth*: Blandishment, flattery.

140 *Swellest thou, proud heart? I'll*: Q has *Swellst thou (prowd heart) Ile*, which might suggest the meaning 'If thou swellest, I'll ...', but the interrogative form seems more actable. Presumably the King's excited state of mind has a physical effect; the actor would naturally put his hand to his heart.

140–41 *scope ... scope*: Room, space ... permission, opportunity (and cf. 112).

143–54 *What must the King ... obscure grave*: This passage may have been suggested by Hall's *Chronicle*, where it is said that Richard 'with a lamentable voice and a sorrowful countenance delivered his sceptre and crown to the Duke of Lancaster, requiring every person severally by their names to grant and assent that he might live a private and a solitary life, with the sweetness whereof he would be so well pleased that it should be a pain and punishment to him to go abroad'.

143 *the King ... he*: Richard begins by referring to himself in the third person, as if conscious of the division between the man and the office.

146 *A*: In.

147 *a set of beads*: A rosary.

149 *gay apparel*: Richard was known for his extravagance in dress. Holinshed records that 'he was in his time exceeding sumptuous in apparel, insomuch as he had one coat which he caused to be made for him of gold

and stone, valued at 30,000 marks'. See also Commentary to II.1.21.

*almsman*: Beggar who prayed for those who gave him alms.

*gown*: Suggests one who wore the uniform of a particular institution.

150 *figured*: Decorated.
   *dish of wood*: Alms-dish.

151 *palmer*: Pilgrim.

152 *carvèd saints*: Wooden figures of saints such as might be in a monk's cell.

154 *obscure*: Accented on the first syllable.

155 *I'll be buried in the King's highway*: There is obvious irony in the suggestion that the King will be buried, not in a sanctified place, but under his own highway.

156 *trade*: Traffic (quibbling with *tread*, at 158).

159 *buried once*: Once I am buried.

162 *Our sighs and they*: Like wind and rain.
   *lodge*: Beat down.

163 *revolting*: Rebelling.

164 *play the wantons*: Play a game, amuse ourselves.

165 *make some pretty match*: Play a clever game.

166 *still*: Continually.

167 *fretted us*: Worn out for us.

168–9 *there lies | Two kinsmen digged their graves with weeping eyes*: The rhyme helps to give this the quality of an imaginary epitaph.

171 *idly*: Foolishly.

173–4 *Will his majesty | Give Richard leave to live till Richard die*: A trick question, showing Richard's distrust.

175 *make a leg*: Make an obeisance, a bend of the knee. Addressing Northumberland, Richard seems ironically to be saying that if Northumberland gives assent, Bolingbroke is sure to say yes.

176 *base-court*: Lower or outer court of the castle, occupied by servants.

177 *may it please you to come down*: This may mean 'if it please you to come down', or may be an independent question.

178 *glistering Phaethon*: Phaethon (three syllables) was the mythical son of Apollo, the sun-god. He borrowed his father's sun-chariot but was too weak to control it and drove dangerously close to the earth. Zeus prevented the destruction of the earth by killing Phaethon with a thunderbolt. The story was a common image of rash failure. It is especially appropriate to Richard in this play because of his frequent association with the sun (which was his own badge). 'Phaethon' is the Greek for 'shining' (or 'glistering').

179 *Wanting the manage of*: Lacking the power to control.
*manage*: A technical term in horsemanship.
*unruly jades*: Compared with the rebellious nobles.
*jades*: A contemptuous term for horses.

181 *do them grace*: Favour them.

182 *base-court . . . court*: Richard plays on the ideas of 'court-yard' and the king's 'court', and also puns on 'base'.

183 *night-owls shriek where mounting larks should sing*: Instead of the lark's song we hear the cries of owls, foreboding evil.
*Exeunt from above*: Probably on the Elizabethan stage the King and his followers left the upper stage and descended out of view of the audience. On the modern stage a stairway is sometimes used so that he is in view throughout.

185 *fondly*: Foolishly.

187 *Stand all apart*: Probably he instructs his men to stand at a respectful distance from Richard.

188 *He kneels down*: This is one of the rare directions for action in Q.

188–207 *He kneels down . . . force will have us do*: Holinshed has: 'Forthwith as the Duke got sight of the King he showed a reverend duty, as became him in bowing his knee, and coming forward did so likewise the second and third time, till the King took him by the hand and lift [*sic*] him up, saying "Dear cousin, ye are welcome." The Duke humbly thanking him said "My sovereign lord and king, the cause of my coming at this present is, your honour saved, to have again restitution of my

person, my lands and heritage, through your favourable
licence." The King hereunto answered "Dear cousin,
I am ready to accomplish your will, so that ye may
enjoy all that is yours without exception.""

192  *Me rather had*: I had rather.

193  *courtesy*: Combining the modern, general meaning with
the sense of an obeisance.

195  *Thus high at least*: Richard touches his head to indicate
the crown.

202  *hands*: F's *hand* may well be correct.

203  *want their remedies*: Lack the capacity to cure the misfortunes with which they show sympathy.

204–5  *I am too young to be your father* | *Though you are old
enough to be my heir*: Historically both Richard and
Bolingbroke were thirty-three.

**III.4**

This scene has no historical basis. It is apparently set
in the Duke of York's garden (see II.2.116–17 and
III.4.70). In Q the stage direction refers to the Queen
*with her attendants*, who are not distinguished in the
speech-prefixes. F has *and two Ladies*. Shakespeare may
have thought of more than two ladies, one perhaps
suggesting each type of diversion; but the Folio probably reflects the stage practice of Shakespeare's time.
The division of speeches in the present edition is arbitrary, and may be varied at will by a producer.

1  *here in this garden*: This phrase sets the scene econom-
ically.

3  *bowls*: This was a common Elizabethan game. Bowling
greens were often found in gardens.

4  *rubs*: A *rub* in bowls was a technical term for anything
which impeded the course of the bowl. It was often
used metaphorically of a difficulty – 'Ay, there's the
rub' (*Hamlet*, III.1.65).

5  *runs against the bias*: In bowls, *bias* is a weight inserted
in the side of the bowl to make it run in a certain way.
The Queen feels that her fortune is going against its
natural inclination.

7–8  *can keep no measure . . . no measure keeps*: Cannot dance (*measure*, dance step) . . . knows no bounds.

13  *wanting*: Lacking, absent.

14  *remember*: Remind.

15  *being altogether had*: Since I possess it completely.

18  *boots*: Helps.

22–3  *And I could sing would weeping do me good,  | And never borrow any tear of thee*: The Queen probably means that she herself has already wept so much that if this could have done her any good all would now be well, and she would feel like singing.

23  *Enter Gardeners . . . his men*: Q has *Enter Gardeners*, F *Enter a Gardiner, and two Seruants*. The Gardener's first speech makes it clear that there are two under-gardeners. The fact that the Gardener has two men under him may make it less surprising that he should speak as formally as he does. The gardens of great Elizabethan estates were internationally famous, and their Head Gardeners had heavy responsibility. Admittedly Shakespeare's Gardener is not a pure administrator – he is going to *root away  | The noisome weeds* (37–8) – but he is a man of authority. More to the purpose, dramatically he is a symbolic rather than naturalistic character, and it is more important for the actor to concentrate attention on what he says than to entertain by his manner of saying it.

26  *My wretchedness unto a row of pins*: I will wager my misery against something very trivial that . . .

27  *They will*: The metre seems to demand elision: 'They'll'.

28  *Against a change*: When a change is about to happen.

29  *young*: Q1 has *yong*; Q2–5, *yon*; F, *yond*. Q1 has superior authority and this looks like a simple case of progressive textual corruption. A. W. Pollard comments: 'it is the word "yong" that suggested the comparison of the fruit to "vnruly children" in the next line' (*King Richard II: A New Quarto*, 1916, p. 56).
     *apricocks*: Apricots.

31  *Stoop*: Punning on the bending of the boughs and of the back of an old man.

    *prodigal*: Punning on 'excessive' and 'prodigal' or 'unruly' children; *weight* thus has both literal and metaphorical force.

32 *bending*: With the weight of the fruit.

35 *lofty*: 'Tall' and 'overweening'.

36 *even*: Equal.

38 *noisome*: Harmful.

40, 54, 67 FIRST MAN; SECOND MAN: Neither Q nor F differentiates between the two men. The present arrangement is arbitrary.

40 *compass of a pale*: Small area – in contrast to the kingdom.

    *pale*: Fence (and 'national boundary').

42 *firm*: Stable.

43 *sea-wallèd*: Cf. II.1.46–7.

46 *knots*: Flower-beds laid out in intricate designs.

47 *caterpillars*: Echoing Bolingbroke's word for the traitors, II.3.165.

48 *suffered*: Permitted.

49 *fall of leaf*: Autumn.

57 *at time of year*: In season.

58 *skin*: Introduced to stress the metaphor.

59 *overproud in*: Excessively swollen with.

65 *crown*: The king's, and the crown of a tree.

67 *What . . . deposed*: Editors have sometimes padded out the short line, but the rhythmical irregularity emphasizes the exclamation.

68 *Depressed*: Brought low.

69 *'Tis doubt*: There is a risk.

72 *pressed to death*: An allusion to *la peine forte et dure*, a punishment of pressing to death inflicted by English law on those accused of felony or petty treason who refused to plead either guilty or not guilty: who, that is, like the Queen here, stood silent.

73 *old Adam's likeness*: Adam was the first gardener.

75 *suggested*: Tempted.

79 *Divine*: Predict.

82 *To breathe*: In speaking.

84–9 *Their fortunes both are weighed . . . King Richard down*:

The Gardener's imagery anticipates the symbol of the buckets in IV.1.183–8.

84 *weighed*: Balanced against each other.

86 *vanities*: 'Follies'; or specifically, 'Richard's favourites' (opposed to the *peers* at 88).
    *light*: 'In the balance', and also 'of little value'.

89 *odds*: Advantage, superiority.

90 *Post*: Hasten.

93 *Doth not thy embassage belong to me*: Does your message not concern me.

95 *serve me*: Serve (your message) on me.

96 *Thy sorrow*: The sorrow that you report.

98 *What*: Perhaps 'why' rather than an exclamation.

104 *fall*: Let fall.

105 *rue, sour herb of grace*: The herb 'rue' was known as 'herb of grace' because 'rue' means 'repentance', which comes by the grace of God. Here it is associated especially with pity.

106 *for ruth*: As a symbol of pity.

**IV.1**

The place is Westminster Hall; Richard himself had caused it to be splendidly rebuilt. The material of the scene derives from Holinshed, but Shakespeare compresses the time-scheme and rearranges the order of events. He begins with accusations against Aumerle by Bagot, Fitzwater, and others. According to Holinshed, Bagot made his accusation on Thursday, 16 October 1399, and Fitzwater two days later. Bolingbroke's proposal (87) that Mowbray be recalled from exile was made on 27 October. After Carlisle has reported Mowbray's death, York enters with news of Richard's abdication. His brief speech reports the events of 30 September, when the commissioners who had witnessed the abdication reported to Parliament. Bolingbroke's acceptance of the throne is resisted by Carlisle, who speaks in defence of Richard. According to Holinshed, the Bishop made such a speech on 22 October, and it was directed, not against the deposition, but against the proposal that Richard 'might have judgement decreed against him so as the realm were not troubled by him'. Shakespeare then turns to the account of the abdication, which happened in the Tower of London on 29 September. In Holinshed, Richard signs an instrument of abdication, represented in the play by his great speech of renunciation (200–221). The scene's closing episode shows the beginning of the Abbot of Westminster's plot against King Henry. In Holinshed, this was planned at the Abbot's house some three months later.

0 *Fitzwater*: Walter, Baron Fitzwalter, 1368–1406 or 1407. *Fitzwater* is the form of the name in Holinshed, representing the old pronunciation.

*Surrey*: The son of Richard's half-brother, Sir Thomas Holland, he lived from 1374 to 1400, when he was executed. He is the Earl of Kent referred to in V.6.8, he and Aumerle both having been deprived of their dukedoms for their parts in the conspiracy against Bolingbroke – see Commentary to V.2.41. See also the note on the Lord Marshal, I.1, opening stage direction.

*Abbot of Westminster*: The Abbot at the time of the events shown in the play was William of Colchester.

*to Parliament*: This (as in Q) and F's *as to the Parliament* suggest a processional entry.

2 *speak thy mind*: Probably this is felt as a single, transitive verb – 'tell'.

4 *wrought it with the King*: 'Persuaded Richard to have Gloucester killed' or 'collaborated with him in the plan to have him killed'.

*wrought it*: 'Worked' it, brought it about.

5 *timeless*: Untimely.

6 *Aumerle*: Holinshed has: 'there was no man in the realm to whom King Richard was so much beholden as to the Duke of Aumerle; for he was the man that, to fulfil his mind, had set him in hand with all that was done against the said duke'.

10–17 *In that dead time when Gloucester's death was plotted . . . Bolingbroke's return to England*: This is historically inaccurate, as Gloucester was killed before Bolingbroke's banishment.

10 *dead time*: Past (with all the overtones of 'dead').

11 *of length*: Long.

12 *restful*: Quiet (untroubled by Gloucester's plots).

13 *Calais*: Where Gloucester was killed.

15–19 *I heard . . . cousin's death*: Holinshed says that in Bagot's bill, read to the Parliament of 16 October 1399, it was stated 'that Bagot had heard the Duke of Aumerle say that he had rather than twenty thousand pounds that the Duke of Hereford were dead, not for any fear he had of him, but for the trouble and mischief that he was like to procure within the realm'.

17 *Than Bolingbroke's return*: That is, than that Bolingbroke should return – an elliptical construction.

18 *withal*: As well.

21 *fair stars*: Noble birth. Dr Johnson comments: 'The *birth* is supposed to be influenced by the *stars*, therefore our author with his usual licence takes *stars* for *birth*.'

22 *On equal terms*: Aumerle, being of higher rank than Bagot, could refuse to fight him.

24 *attainder*: Accusation.

25 *gage . . . manual seal*: See Commentary to I.1.69.
*manual seal*: Or 'sign manual'.

28 *being*: It (the blood) is.

29 *temper*: Quality (especially the bright surface of a well-tempered sword).

31–2 *Excepting one . . . moved me so*: Though he despises Bagot as his inferior, Aumerle has challenged him. Now he says that, for his own greater honour, he wishes his accuser were the noblest of all present except Bolingbroke, whom he would prefer to fight.

31 *best*: Highest in rank.

32 *moved*: Angered.

33–90 *If that thy valour . . . his trial*: Holinshed's account of the examination of Bagot includes the statement that 'The Lord Fitzwater herewith rose up and said to the King that where the Duke of Aumerle excuseth himself of the Duke of Gloucester's death, "I say" quoth he "that he was the very cause of his death," and so he appealed him of treason, offering by throwing down his hood as a gage to prove it with his body. There were twenty other lords also that threw down their hoods as pledges to prove the like matter against the Duke of Aumerle.'

33 *thy valour*: Possibly ironical: 'thy valorous self'.

*stand on*: Insist on, raise difficulties about (as in 'stand on ceremony').

*sympathy*: Correspondence (in rank). Fitzwater sneeringly asserts his equality with Aumerle.

34 *in gage*: In pledge.

40 *rapier*: This could be either a long or a short sword, used for thrusting. It was in use in Shakespeare's time, but not in Richard II's. Dr Johnson sternly comments: 'The edge of a sword had served his purpose as well as the point of a rapier, and he had then escaped the impropriety of giving the English nobles a weapon which was not seen in England till two centuries afterwards.'

45 *appeal*: Accusation.

*all*: Entirely.

47–8 *to the extremest point | Of mortal breathing*: To the death.

49 *And if*: Perhaps *An if*, if.

50 *more*: Again.

52–9 *I task the earth ... such as you*: F omits these lines, perhaps simply to economize on actors, perhaps because the number of challenges seemed excessive.

52 *task the earth to the like*: Charge the earth in similar fashion (perhaps by throwing down another gage).

53 *lies*: Accusations of lying.

54 *hollowed*: Shouted loudly, 'hollered'.

55 *From sun to sun*: From sunrise to sunset. This was the prescribed time-limit for single combat. Q reads *sinne to sinne*, which could conceivably be defended.

56 *Engage it*: Take up the gage, accept the challenge.

57 *Who sets me else*: Who else challenges me, puts up stakes against me? *Sets* and *throw* are both dicing metaphors.

62 *in presence*: Present.

65 *boy*: A strong insult here; the word was used of a menial servant.

66 *That lie*: Both the accusation of lying, and the lie that the accusation is. These lines are full of quibbles on the word.

67 *it shall render*: My sword will give back in return (for the accusation).

72 *How fondly dost thou spur a forward horse*: Related to the proverb 'Do not spur a free horse'.
*fondly*: Foolishly, unnecessarily.
*forward*: Willing.

74 *in a wilderness*: That is, even in a wilderness, where they would fight uninterrupted to the bitter end. Cf. I.1.64–6.

76 *There is my bond of faith*: There is my gage (or *honour's pawn*, 70). Either he throws down a second gage or points to the one he threw at 34.

77 *tie thee to my strong correction*: Engage you to undergo severe punishment at my hands.

78 *in this new world*: Under the new order, with a new king.

79 *appeal*: Accusation.

80 *Norfolk*: Mowbray.

83–4 *Some honest Christian trust me with a gage. | That Norfolk lies*: Q and F have a comma after *gage*. Aumerle is asking to borrow a gage, either because he has thrown down both his gloves (at 25 and 57) or because Shakespeare is now thinking of the gages as hoods not gloves (see Commentary to I.1.69). It may be that he asks specially to be trusted with a gage with which to prove *That Norfolk lies*. If so he receives it after *lies*. Otherwise he receives it after *gage* and then says 'Now I throw down this to prove that . . .'.

85 *repealed*: Called back (from banishment).
*to try his honour*: This may modify *repealed* ('called back in order to put his honour to the test') or *throw* ('I throw this down . . . as a test of his honour').

86–9 *These differences . . . signories*: Holinshed: 'The King licensed the Duke of Norfolk to return, that he might arraign his appeal.' Holinshed also reports that 'This

year Thomas Mowbray, Duke of Norfolk, died in exile
at Venice, whose death might have been worthily
bewailed of all the realm if he had not been consenting
to the death of the Duke of Gloucester.'

86 *rest under gage*: Remain as challenges.

89 *he is*: This is printed as *hee's* in F, and elision seems
necessary; but the line is long in any case.

90 *we*: Bolingbroke begins to use the royal plural.
*his trial*: Either 'Aumerle's testing of Mowbray's
honour', or 'Mowbray's proving of his honour in
opposition to Aumerle' – in either case, in trial by
combat.

91 *never*: So Q; *ne're* in F, which may indicate the correct
pronunciation.

93 *field*: Of battle.

96 *toiled*: Exhausted.
*retired himself*: Withdrew.

103–4 *bosom | Of good old Abraham*: A biblical – and prover-
bial – way of saying 'heavenly rest'.

108 *plume-plucked*: Humbled (possibly in reference to the
fable attributed to Aesop about the crow that dressed
itself in stolen feathers and was shamed when other
birds took them away).

112 *fourth of that name*: The metre seems defective, and F's
version – *of that Name the Fourth* – is attractive.

113–35 *In God's name ... Hereford's King*: Holinshed reports
that Carlisle 'boldly showed forth his opinion
concerning that demand' (that Richard, having abdi-
cated, should be tried), 'affirming that there was none
amongst them worthy or meet to give judgement upon
so noble a prince as King Richard was, whom they had
taken for their sovereign and liege lord by the space of
two-and-twenty years and more. "And I assure you,"
said he, "there is not so rank a traitor nor so arrant a
thief nor yet so cruel a murderer apprehended or
detained in prison for his offence but he shall be brought
before the justice to hear his judgement; and will ye
proceed to the judgement of an anointed king, hearing
neither his answer nor excuse? I say that the Duke of

Lancaster, whom ye call king, hath more trespassed to King Richard and his realm than King Richard hath done either to him or us.'"

115–16 *Worst in this royal presence may I speak,* | *Yet best beseeming me to speak the truth*: Though in the presence of royalty it is as the lowest in rank that I speak, still it is fitting that I even more than anyone else should speak the truth (as I am a bishop). It is interesting that the Bishop modifies *royal* to *noble* two lines later, perhaps as he is about to deny Bolingbroke's regality.

119 *noblesse*: Nobility.

120 *Learn him forbearance*: Teach him to refrain.

*foul a wrong*: As presuming to sit in judgement on his king.

123 *but*: Except when.

124 *apparent*: Obvious.

125 *figure*: Image.

126 *elect*: Chosen.

129 *forfend it God*: May God forbid.

130 *souls refined*: Civilized, or Christianized, people.

134 *My Lord of Hereford*: The Bishop uses the least of Bolingbroke's titles.

136–49 *let me prophesy . . . woe*: The Bishop's prophecy recalls John of Gaunt's (II.1.33–68), though this is spoken in favour of Richard, whereas that criticized him. The two thus reflect a central problem of the play: that England, which has suffered under Richard's irresponsible reign, will suffer too if his right to the Crown is usurped. Carlisle looks forward to the state of affairs to be portrayed in *Henry IV, Parts I* and *II*. His sentiments reflect those of the 'Homily against Disobedience and Wilful Rebellion', which was familiar through being regularly read aloud in church.

141 *kin with kin, and kind with kind, confound*: Destroy kinsmen and fellow-countrymen by their own actions. The killing of each other by members of the same family, and especially of son by father or father by son, is a common symbol in Shakespeare for the worst kind of disorder such as is brought about by civil war.

144 *field of Golgotha and dead men's skulls*: Golgotha, or
Calvary, where Jesus Christ was crucified, means 'the
place of skulls'. Carlisle anticipates Richard's comparisons of himself with Christ (169–71, 238–41). In the
Bishops' Bible, Golgotha is called 'a place of a skull'
(Mark 15:22, etc.), and the Prayer Book Gospel for
Good Friday includes John 19:17: 'and went forth into
a place which is called the place of dead men's skulls;
but in Hebrew Golgotha'.

145 *this house against this house*: Carlisle foresees the Wars
of the Roses, with an echo of biblical phraseology as
in Mark 3:25: 'And if a house be divided against itself
that house cannot continue.'

149 *cry against you woe*: *woe* probably has adverbial rather
than exclamatory force.

150–53 *Well . . . day of trial*: Holinshed: 'As soon as the Bishop
had ended this tale he was attached by the Earl Marshal
and committed to ward in the abbey of Saint Albans.'

151 *Of*: On a charge of.

154–319 *May it please you . . . Lords, be ready, all*: This
passage is not in Q1–3. See An Account of the Text,
p. 109.

154 *commons' suit*: Holinshed: 'On Wednesday [22 October
1399] following, request was made by the commons
that sith King Richard had resigned and was lawfully
deposed from his royal dignity, he might have judgement decreed against him, so as the realm were not
troubled by him, and that the causes of his deposing
might be published through the realm for satisfying of
the people; which demand was granted.'

156 *surrender*: (His throne); abdicate.

157 *conduct*: Escort.

159 *sureties*: Men who will be responsible for your appearance.

*your days of answer*: The time when you must appear
to stand trial.

161 *looked for*: Expected.

*Enter Richard and York*: From this point onwards F ceases
to use 'King' for Richard in speech-prefixes and stage

directions. Q continues to do so till the end of V.i.

163 *shook*: Shaken (a common Elizabethan form).

167 *Yet I well remember*: Holinshed: 'Which renunciation to the deposed king was a redoubling of his grief, insomuch as thereby it came to his mind how in former times he was acknowledged and taken for their liege lord and sovereign, who now – whether in contempt or in malice, God knoweth – to his face forsware him to be their king.'

168 *favours*: 'Faces' and 'friendly acts'.

170 *Judas did to Christ*: Matthew 26:49: 'And forthwith when he came to Jesus, he said "Hail, master"; and kissed him.'

171 *Found truth . . . none*: An alexandrine.

173 *clerk*: Altar-server (who makes the responses – *Amen* being the most frequent – at the end of each prayer read by the priest).

176 *service*: Punning on the ecclesiastical and the general sense.

180 *Give me the crown*: Presumably it has been carried in by Richard's attendants.

183 *Now is this golden crown like a deep well*: In stage practice it is most effective if the crown is held upside-down between Richard and Bolingbroke. The notion of Fortune's buckets is not uncommon in medieval and Elizabethan literature. There was a proverbial expression 'Like two buckets of a well, if one go up the other must go down.'

184 *owes*: Owns, has.

*filling one another*: Because when the full bucket is raised it causes the other to descend and be filled in turn.

194–6 *Your cares . . . new care won*: These lines include elaborate wordplay on *care*. First it means 'grief', then 'responsibility', then 'diligence', then 'anxiety'. We may paraphrase: 'The cause of my grief is my loss of responsibility, brought about by my former lack of diligence; the cause of your trouble is the access of responsibility achieved by your recent pains.'

198 *'tend*: Are attendant upon.

200 *Ay, no. No, ay*: Both 'Yes, no. No, yes' and 'I, no. No
 I'. M. M. Mahood comments: 'besides suggesting in one
 meaning (Aye, no; no, aye) his tormenting indecision,
 and in another (Aye – no; no I) the overwrought mind
 that finds an outlet in punning, [it] also represents in the
 meaning "I know no I" Richard's pathetic play-acting,
 his attempt to conjure with a magic he no longer believes.
 Can he exist if he no longer bears his right name of
 King? The mirror shows him the question is rhetorical
 but he dashes it to the ground, only to have Bolingbroke
 expose the self-deception of this histrionic gesture: "The
 shadow . . ."' (*Shakespeare's Wordplay*, 1957, p. 87).
 *nothing*: And '*no* thing'.

201 *no no, for I resign to thee*: I cannot say 'no', because in
 fact I *do* resign in your favour.

202 *undo*: (1) 'Undress', as he removes the emblems of
 kingship; (2) 'unmake'; and (3) 'ruin'.

203 *heavy weight*: The crown; *heavy* also meaning 'sad'.

206 *balm*: Consecrated oil (with which he had been anointed
 at his coronation).

209 *release all duteous oaths*: Release my subjects from all
 the oaths of allegiance to me that they have sworn.

211 *revenues*: Accented on the second syllable.

214 *are made*: (That) are made.

215 *Make me*: (God) make me.
 *with nothing grieved*: There is a deliberate paradox here.
 Richard asks to be grieved by having nothing, but also
 to be grieved by nothing. The ambiguity is highly
 expressive of the delicate balance of Richard's state of
 mind, wishing to be relieved of his care yet reluctant
 to give up his Crown.

221–2 *that you read | These accusations*: In Holinshed, Richard
 himself 'read the scroll of resignation', though 'for the
 articles which before ye have heard were drawn and
 engrossed up . . . the reading of those articles at that
 season was deferred'. Shakespeare chooses not to
 remind us of Richard's sins.

221 *read*: Aloud, as an admission of guilt.

227 *ravel out*: Unravel; expose.

229 *record*: Accented on the second syllable.

231 *read a lecture*: Read aloud, as a warning.

232 *heinous article*: Holinshed reports that Parliament considered the thirty-three articles 'heinous to the ears of all men'.

*article*: Item.

234 *oath*: Bolingbroke's oath of loyalty.

237 *bait*: Torment.

238 *with*: Like.

*with Pilate*: Bolingbroke had implicitly compared himself to Pilate at III.1.5–6. The image occurs in Holinshed where, in the Flint Castle episode, the Archbishop of Canterbury promises that Richard shall not be hurt, 'but he prophesied not as a prelate, but as a Pilate'.

240 *delivered*: This may create a quibble on *Pilate* as 'pilot'. Christ was 'delivered' to Pilate and by him back to the Jews.

*sour*: Bitter.

245 *sort*: Pack, gang (contemptuous). Perhaps there is a pun on *salt*.

248–9 *soul's ... body*: In this antithesis, frequent in the play, Richard asserts his right to the Crown while renouncing its attributes.

249 *pompous*: Magnificent, splendid.

251 *state*: Stateliness.

253 *haught*: Haughty.

256 *'tis usurped*: Possibly an allusion to the Lancastrian rumour that Richard was illegitimate. Or he may mean that now he is unkinged, he has no identity. Either he admits that he himself usurps a name to which he has no right, or he claims that others usurp his name from him.

260 *sun of Bolingbroke*: Now the image of the sun is transferred from Richard to Bolingbroke.

261 *water-drops*: Tears.

263 *An if*: If.

*sterling*: Valid currency. The image is continued in *bankrupt* (266).

264 *straight*: Immediately.

266 *his*: Its.

267 *some*: Could mean 'some one'.

269 *torments*: A form of 'tormentest'.

280 *Was this face* ... : It is difficult not to associate these lines with Marlowe's *Doctor Faustus*, 13.90: 'Was this the face that launched a thousand ships ...', and Shakespeare's audience, too, may well have noticed the resemblance. Marlowe's play was written a few years before Shakespeare's.

281–2 *under his household roof | Did keep ten thousand men*: Holinshed, summarizing Richard's character, says that 'there resorted daily to his court above ten thousand persons that had meat and drink there allowed them'.

283 *wink*: Close their eyes.

284 *Is this the face which*: This is the reading of F, the most authoritative text for this section of the play. But Q4 repeats *Was ... that*, as at 280–81 and 282–3. We cannot say for certain which is right, and an actor would be justified in following Q4 if he preferred to do so.

284–5 *faced ... outfaced*: Countenanced ... discountenanced, superseded.

285 *That*: Q4 has *And*. The situation is the same as that referred to in the note to 284. An actor might prefer 'And'.

288 *an*: Q4's reading, *a*, is also possible. See the note to 284.

291–3 *shadow of your sorrow ... | 'The shadow of my sorrow'*: Bolingbroke speaks contemptuously: 'the (mere) shadow cast by your sorrow', the action provoked by it, or *external manner of laments* (295), has destroyed the shadow of your face simply by passing across it, as one shadow obliterates another. Richard takes up the phrase with a suggestion of greater reality: 'the shadowing forth, or embodiment, of my sorrow'.

295 *these external manner*: An archaic construction comparable with 'all manner of', or the modern colloquial 'these kind of ...'. Q4's *manners*, followed by many editors, is probably a sophistication.

296  *to*: Compared to.

298  *substance*: Opposed to *shadow*; cf. II.2.14: *Each substance of a grief hath twenty shadows*.

299  *thy . . . that*: Of you . . . who.

307  *to*: As.

312  *Then give me leave to go*: Richard's request seems anti-climactic. It may represent a calculated deflation of Bolingbroke, Richard having led him to expect a more taxing request.

314  *sights*: The sight of each one of you.

316  '*convey*': The word was slang for 'steal', and Richard picks it up in this sense.

317  *nimbly*: Also associated with thieving. Cf. *The Winter's Tale*, IV.4.667–8: 'a nimble hand is necessary for a cutpurse'.

320  *pageant*: Spectacle. (The line would have been inappropriate when the deposition scene was omitted.)

321–33  *The woe's to come . . . merry day*: Holinshed reports on 'the conspiracy which was contrived by the Abbot of Westminster as chief instrument thereof'. The Abbot 'highly feasted these lords his special friends' and they devised the plot referred to at V.2.52, 96–9, and V.3.14–19.

328  *bury mine intents*: Conceal my plans.

332  *supper*: The sentence is sometimes made to end here, but probably *Come* is subjunctive: 'If you will come . . .'.

V.I

The material of this scene is not derived from Holinshed (except for 51–2). In portraying a final meeting between Richard and his Queen, Shakespeare may have been influenced by Samuel Daniel's *Civil Wars*, though his treatment is different; see Commentary to 40–50.

0  *attendants*: Presumably the Ladies of III.4.

2  *Julius Caesar's ill-erected Tower*: The Tower of London. There was an old tradition that it had originally been built by Julius Caesar.

   *ill-erected*: Built for evil purposes or with evil results. The Queen is thinking especially of its present use, for imprisoning Richard.

3 *flint*: Flinty, merciless.

6 *guard*: Perhaps implying more than one man.

8 *rose*: In *Henry IV*, *Part I*, I.3.173, Hotspur calls Richard 'that sweet lovely rose'.

11 *the model where old Troy did stand*: She addresses Richard, and finds that in his present condition he is to his former self as the ruins of Troy were to the city in its greatness.

*model*: Ground plan.

*old Troy*: London was known as '*Troia novans*', or 'new Troy', because of a legend that after the Trojan war Aeneas led a party of Trojans to Britain and that his great-grandson, Brut, founded London and called it Troia-Nova.

12 *map*: Image, outline of former glory.

15 *triumph is become an alehouse guest*: Triumph is entertained in the *alehouse* Bolingbroke, opposed to the more beautiful and stately *inn*.

18 *state*: Stateliness, splendour.

22 *Hie*: Go, hasten.

24–5 *Our holy lives must win a new world's crown | Which our profane hours here have thrown down*: By leading holy lives we must win in heaven the crown that our worldly lives here have cast away.

25 *thrown*: Probably to be pronounced 'throwen'. F's *stricken* could be correct.

29–31 *The lion dying thrusteth forth his paw | And wounds the earth, if nothing else, with rage | To be o'erpowered*: The comparison between a monarch and lion is commonplace, but Shakespeare may have been influenced here by Marlowe's *Edward II*, 21.11–14, where Edward says of himself:

> But when the imperial lion's flesh is gored,
> He rends and tears it with his wrathful paw,
> And, highly scorning that the lowly earth
> Should drink his blood, mounts up to the air . . .

32 *correction, mildly kiss*: F has *Correction mildly, kiss*, which
   is as plausible a reading.
37 *sometimes*: Sometime, former.
38 *even*: Probably to be pronounced 'e'en'.
40–50 *In winter's tedious nights . . . a rightful king*: These lines
   seem to show the verbal influence of Daniel's *Civil
   Wars*, III, stanza 65. Richard soliloquizes on the
   difference between himself in prison and a peasant:

> Thou sitt'st at home safe by thy quiet fire,
> And hearest of others' harms, but feelest none;
> And there thou tellest of kings and who aspire,
> Who fall, who rise, who triumphs, who do moan.
> Perhaps thou talkest of me, and dost inquire
> Of my restraint, why I live here alone.
> O, know 'tis others' sin, not my desert,
> And I could wish I were but as thou art.

42 *betid*: Past.
43 *quite*: (Or 'quit') requite, cap.
44 *lamentable tale of me*: The phrase resembles one used
   by Sidney in *Astrophil and Stella* (1591), in which
   the lover complains that his beloved wept to hear a
   sad tale of love but does not pity his real plight. So
   he says:

> Then think, my dear, that you in me do read
> Of lover's suit some sad tragedy.
> I am not I; pity the tale of me.

46 *For why*: Because (that is, 'weeping because').
   *senseless*: Inanimate, without feeling.
   *sympathize*: Respond to.
48 *weep the fire out*: There is an allusion to the 'weeping'
   of resin from burning wood, as in *The Tempest*,
   III.1.18–19, when Miranda says to Ferdinand 'When
   this burns, | 'Twill weep for having wearied you.'
49 *some*: Of the brands.
52 *Pomfret*: Pontefract, in Yorkshire. Holinshed: 'For

shortly after his resignation he was conveyed to the
castle of Leeds in Kent, and from thence to Pomfret.'

53  *there is order ta'en*: Arrangements have been made.

55–9  *Northumberland, thou ladder ... into corruption*: These
lines are recalled by King Henry in *Henry IV, Part II*,
III.1.61–75:

> But which of you was by –
> You, cousin Nevil, as I may remember –
> When Richard, with his eye brimful of tears,
> Then checked and rated by Northumberland,
> Did speak these words, now proved a prophecy?
> 'Northumberland, thou ladder by the which
> My cousin Bolingbroke ascends my throne' –
> Though then, God knows, I had no such intent
> But that necessity so bowed the state
> That I and greatness were compelled to kiss –
> 'The time shall come' – thus did he follow it –
> 'The time will come that foul sin, gathering head,
> Shall break into corruption' – so went on,
> Foretelling this same time's condition
> And the division of our amity.

58–9  *foul sin, gathering head, | Shall break into corruption*:
Like an ulcer or boil.

61  *helping him to all*: As you have helped him to get it all.

68  *worthy*: Deserved.

69  *and there an end*: A common tag meaning 'and let that
be the end of it.

70  *part ... part*: Part (from your Queen) ... depart.

74  *unkiss the oath*: Unseal with a kiss the marriage vow
that had been ratified by a kiss.

75  *And yet not so*: 'Yet let us not kiss, since it was with a
kiss that the vow was made' *or* 'yet the oath cannot
be kissed away, as it was made with a kiss'.

77  *pines the clime*: Afflicts the land.

78  *pomp*: Splendour. Holinshed describes the great splendour of the wedding.

79  *She came adornèd hither like sweet May*: The scene moves

into couplets for the grave, stylized parting of Richard and his Queen.

80 *Hallowmas*: All Saints' Day, 1 November; because of the change in calendar, it corresponded in Shakespeare's time to our 12 November, so was closer to the shortest day.

*shortest of day*: The winter solstice.

84 *That were . . . policy*: F, followed by most editors, gives this line to Northumberland, but this breaks the rhythm of the speeches and has no special authority.

*little policy*: Hardly politic, poor statesmanship.

86–96 *So two together weeping . . . take I thy heart*: These lines bring together many of the words in the play's vocabulary of grief – *weeping, woe, sighs, groans, moans, sorrow,* and *grief.*

86 *So*: Tantamount to 'No; for if so . . .'.

88 *Better far off than, near, be ne'er the nea'er*: It is better to be far apart than, being near to each other, be no closer to being together. Dr Johnson comments: 'To be *never the nigher*, or as it is commonly spoken in the midland counties, *ne'er the ne'er*, is, *to make no advance towards the good desired*.' The final word is a comparative form which has become contracted.

92 *piece the way out*: Make the journey seem longer.

96 *mine*: My heart. The conceit that lovers exchanged hearts was commonplace.

97 *Give me mine own again*: In a second kiss.

97–8 *'Twere no good part | To take on me to keep and kill thy heart*: It would not be a good action for me to undertake to look after your heart and then to kill it (as my grief would kill me and therefore also it).

101 *make woe wanton*: Play verbal games with grief. The characters show consciousness of the dramatist's word-play, as Gaunt and Richard had at II.1.84–8.

*fond*: Loving yet also pointless.

V.2

The first part (to 40) is probably indebted to Daniel's *Civil Wars*, II, stanzas 66–70, which describe the triumphal entry of Bolingbroke into London, with

the humbled Richard behind him. Holinshed too has a
description of Bolingbroke's triumphal progress and
reception. The remainder of the scene is based on
Holinshed (see Commentary to 52–118).

0 *the Duchess*: Historically, York's wife at this time was
Aumerle's stepmother. Aumerle's mother, Isabella of
Castile, had died in 1394. Shakespeare was mainly inter-
ested in providing a wife for York and a mother for
Aumerle.

2 *story*: The Duchess's words recall Richard's prophecy
that the Queen, by telling *the lamentable tale of me*,
would *send the hearers weeping to their beds* (V.1.44–5).

3 *cousins*: Richard and Bolingbroke.

5–6 *Where rude . . . Richard's head*: This episode is recalled
by the Archbishop of York in *Henry IV, Part II*,
I.3.103–7, speaking of Richard:

> Thou that threwest dust upon his goodly head,
> When through proud London he came sighing on
> After the admirèd heels of Bolingbroke,
> Criest now 'O earth, yield us that king again,
> And take thou this!'

5 *rude*: Stronger in Shakespeare's time than now: 'brutal'.
*windows' tops*: Upper windows.

6 *King Richard*: The Duchess still refers to Richard as
the king.

9 *his aspiring rider seemed to know*: Seemed to know how
aspiring its rider was.

15–16 *that all the walls | With painted imagery*: This refers to
the painted cloths common in Elizabethan houses, on
which figures were portrayed with sentences issuing
from their mouths, as in a strip cartoon. York imagines
that the walls were covered with such cloths.

16 *at once*: All together.

19 *lower*: Bowing lower, deferentially addressing the
crowd.

21 *still*: Continually, all the time.

24 *well graced*: 'Graceful' and 'popular'.

25 *idly*: Listlessly, indifferently.

27 *Even*: Probably to be pronounced 'e'en'.

28 *gentle*: This word is omitted in F. Since it is extra-
metrical and comes again at 31, its presence in Q may
be accidental.

33 *badges*: Outward signs (*tears* of grief, *smiles* of patience).

36 *barbarism itself*: Even savages.

38 *bound our calm contents*: Submit ourselves in calm
content.

41 *Aumerle that was*: Holinshed: 'it was finally enacted that
such as were appellants in the last Parliament against
the Duke of Gloucester and other, should in this wise
following be ordered: the Dukes of Aumerle, Surrey,
and Exeter there present were judged to lose their names
of Dukes, together with the honours, titles, and digni-
ties thereunto belonging'.

42 *that*: That title.

43 *Rutland*: Aumerle had been made Earl of Rutland in
1390, and after the Duke of Gloucester's arrest was
given the dukedom of Aumerle.

44 *in Parliament*: See Commentary to 52–118.

46–7 *the violets now | That strew the green lap of the new-come
spring*: Those who are in favour in the new court.

52–118 *What news from Oxford? . . . Away, be gone*: Holinshed
reports that the Abbot of Westminster and his confederates 'devised that they should take upon them a solemn
justs to be enterprised between him [the Earl of
Huntingdon] and twenty on his part, and the Earl
of Salisbury and twenty with him at Oxford, to the
which triumph King Henry should be desired, and when
he should be most busily marking the martial pastime
he suddenly should be slain and destroyed, and so by
that means King Richard, who as yet lived, might be
restored to liberty and have his former estate and
dignity.' When Huntingdon arrived at Oxford, 'he found
all his mates and confederates there, well appointed for
their purpose, except the Earl of Rutland, by whose folly
their practised conspiracy was brought to light and
disclosed to King Henry. For this Earl of Rutland

departing before from Westminster to see his father the
Duke of York as he sat at dinner had his counterpane
of the indenture of the confederacy in his bosom.

'The father espying it would needs see what it was;
and though the son humbly denied to show it, the father
being more earnest to see it by force took it out of his
bosom, and, perceiving the contents thereof, in a great
rage caused his horses to be saddled out of hand and,
spitefully reproving his son of treason for whom he
was become surety and mainpernor for his good a-
bearing in open Parliament, he incontinently mounted
on horseback to ride towards Windsor to the King to
declare unto him the malicious intent of his complices.'
(The remainder of the episode is represented in
V.3.23–145.)

52 *Do these justs and triumphs hold*: F reads *Hold those Iusts
& Triumphs?* This improves the metre; but the line may
be deliberately irregular in preparation for the short
ones that follow.

*Do ... hold*: Will (they) be held.

*justs and triumphs*: Tournaments and processional shows.

55 *If God prevent not, I purpose so*: With sinister overtones.

56 *seal*: The wax seal, usually red, hanging from the document.

*without*: Outside.

57 *lookest*: The metre demands elision.

66 *'gainst*: In preparation for.

67 *Bound to himself*: York points out that if, as his wife
suggests, Aumerle had borrowed money on a bond, the
document would be in his creditor's possession, not his
own.

74 *Ho, who is within there*: Many editors add '*Enter a
Servant*' after *there*. This is unnecessary. York calls impa-
tiently, and is not answered until 84.

79 *I will appeach the villain*: York's vehemence against his
son may be explained partly by the fact that he has
entered into surety for Aumerle's loyalty (44–5).
Aumerle has thus let him down personally, as well as
endangered him.

*appeach*: Inform against, denounce.

85–7 *York's man*: The reactions of the silent servant are a likely source of comedy in the staging of this episode.

85 *Strike him, Aumerle! Poor boy, thou art amazed*: Presumably the Duchess instructs her son to strike the servant so as to obstruct York's preparations for departure. But he is too *amazed* ('bewildered') to do so.

87 *York's man gives him the boots and goes out*: The servant's exit is not marked in the early editions. He could remain on stage as a bewildered, perhaps amused, observer of the quarrel between his master and mistress.

90 *Have we more sons*: Historically the answer was yes; York had another son, Richard, who is the Earl of Cambridge in *Henry V*.

91 *my teeming-date*: The time during which I may have children.

95 *fond*: Foolish.

98 *interchangeably set down their hands*: Signed reciprocally (so that each had a record of the other's oath).

99 *He shall be none*: He shall not be one of them.

100 *that*: What they do.

103 *groaned*: In childbirth.

104 *Thou wouldst*: Probably to be pronounced 'thou'dst'.

113 *Spur, past ... to the King*: Holinshed: 'Rutland, seeing in what danger he stood, took his horse and rode another way to Windsor in post, so that he got thither before his father.'
     *post*: Hasten.

117–18 *never will I rise up from the ground* | *Till Bolingbroke have pardoned thee*: She fulfils this threat.

**V.3**

The first part of the scene looks forward to the plays about Prince Hal, and may have been written for this purpose. Legends about the young prince's dissolute behaviour were common. For the remainder of the scene, see Commentary to 23–145.

1 *unthrifty*: Prodigal, profligate.
  *son*: Prince Hal, later Henry V; historically he was only thirteen years old at this time.

3 *plague*: Calamity (as prophesied by Richard, III.3.85–90, and Carlisle, IV.1.137–47).

*hang over*: Because plague was believed to come from the clouds.

9 *watch*: Night-watchmen, civic guard.

*passengers*: Wayfarers, travellers.

10 *Which*: The construction seems clumsy. Many editors emend to 'While'.

*wanton*: Probably the noun, meaning 'spoiled child'.

11 *Takes on the*: Takes as a.

15 *gallant*: (Accented on the second syllable) fine young gentleman (ironically).

16 *would*: Would go.

*stews*: 'Brothels' or 'disreputable area'.

18 *with that*: With the glove as a favour.

20 *both*: Both his *dissolute* and his *desperate* characteristics.

22 *happily*: 'Perhaps' and 'happily'.

*amazed*: (This is Q's word) distraught.

23–145 *Where is the King? ... God make thee new*: Here Shakespeare resumes the episode begun at V.2.52 (see Commentary). Holinshed's narration continues: 'The Earl of Rutland, seeing in what danger he stood, took his horse and rode another way to Windsor in post, so that he got thither before his father, and when he was alighted at the castle gate he caused the gates to be shut, saying that he must needs deliver the keys to the King. When he came before the King's presence he kneeled down on his knees, beseeching him of mercy and forgiveness, and, declaring the whole matter unto him in order as everything had passed, obtained pardon. Therewith came his father, and, being let in, delivered the indenture which he had taken from his son unto the King, who, thereby perceiving his son's words to be true, changed his purpose for his going to Oxenford and dispatched messengers forth to signify unto the Earl of Northumberland his High Constable, and to the Earl of Westmorland his High Marshal, and to other his assured friends, of all the doubtful danger and perilous jeopardy.' The conspirators rose in open rebellion and were defeated at Cirencester.

25  *God save your grace*: Aumerle kneels, probably here,
    and remains kneeling until 37.

26  *To have*: That I may have.

30  *My tongue cleave to my roof within my mouth*: Cf. Psalm
    137:6: 'let my tongue cleave to the roof of my mouth'.

33  *on the first*: *Intended*, not *committed*.

34  *after-love*: Gratitude and future loyalty.

35  *turn the key*: Of one of the doors on the stage.

38–46  *My liege ... near is danger*: There are metrical irregu-
    larities in these lines – 41 and 45 are alexandrines, and
    38, 40 and 46 are short lines – but this is not uncommon
    in the play.

40  *safe*: Harmless (probably he draws his sword).

42  *secure*: Over-confident.

43  *Shall I for love speak treason to thy face*: Must I because
    of my love and loyalty speak treason (call you fool-
    hardy) to your face?

49  *my haste forbids me show*: Through lack of breath.

50  *thy promise passed*: The promise you have passed (or
    'given').

52  *hand*: Handwriting.

56  *Forget*: Forget your promise.

60  *sheer*: Pure.

63  *converts to bad*: Changes to bad (in Aumerle).

65  *digressing*: (Continuing the metaphor of the stream)
    transgressing.

66  *be his vice's bawd*: Serve his wickedness.

67  *An*: If. Q2 and later editions, as well as modern editors,
    read 'And'. But Q1 is the authoritative text, 'and' was
    in any case a common form of 'an' meaning 'if', and
    the sense is at least as good if we read *An* – York says
    'if he consumes my honourable reputation in his
    shameful one, then my virtue ...'.

69  *his dishonour dies*: That is, he dies himself.

79  *'The Beggar and the King'*: A reference to the title of
    an old ballad about King Cophetua and a beggar-maid.
    King Henry suggests that the *scene* has changed from
    that of a serious play to a frivolity.

84–5  *This festered joint cut off, the rest rest sound;* | *This let*

       *alone will all the rest confound*: If this diseased limb
       (Aumerle) is amputated, the others will remain healthy;
       otherwise it will contaminate and destroy all the others.

87 *Love loving not itself, none other can*: Probably the
       Duchess means 'If York does not love himself (in his
       son), he can love no other', that is, his advice to
       Bolingbroke cannot be trusted. But the line could be a
       more private plea, addressed either to York or uttered
       as a generalization: 'If York does not love his own son,
       who else can be expected to do so?'

88 *make*: Do.

89 *Shall thy old dugs once more a traitor rear*: Are you, old
       as you are, going to rear this traitor anew (by redeeming
       him from death)?

92 *walk upon my knees*: A traditional form of penance.

96 *Unto*: In support of.

97 *true*: Loyal.

101 *from our breast*: From the heart.

102 *would be denied*: Wishes to be refused.

105 *still kneel*: Will kneel perpetually (*shall* in F and some
       editions).

112 *An if*: If, supposing that.

116 *short as sweet*: The saying 'short and sweet' was current
       in Shakespeare's time.

118 *'Pardonne-moi'*: Excuse me; forgive me for refusing
       you. *Moi* rhymes with *destroy*.

121 *sets the word itself against the word*: Makes the word
       contradict itself.

123 *chopping*: A contemptuous word, perhaps meaning
       'affected', or perhaps 'chopping and changing' with
       reference to the wordplay that has just been heard.

124 *to speak. Set thy tongue there*: To show pity. Let your
       tongue express it.

125 *in thy piteous heart plant thou thine ear*: (An exception-
       ally strained image) let there be no division between
       your ear and your piteous heart.

126 *pierce*: Pronounced to rhyme with *rehearse*, as in *Love's
       Labour's Lost*, IV.2.82: 'Master Person – quasi Pierce-
       one'.

127  *rehearse*: Pronounce, repeat.

129  *suit*: As in a card game – *in hand* – as well as 'plea'.

131  *happy vantage of*: Fortunate gain from.

133  *Twice saying pardon doth not pardon twain*: Either the Duchess assures the King that to say 'pardon' again will not pardon someone else as well, or else *twain* means 'divide in two', in which case she must mean 'to say "pardon" again will not weaken the pardon (as a second negative weakens the first)'.

136  *But*: But as for.

   *trusty*: Used ironically.

   *brother-in-law*: John Holland, Duke of Exeter and Earl of Huntingdon, Richard II's half-brother on his mother's side. He had married Bolingbroke's sister, Elizabeth, and was deprived of his dukedom at the same time as Aumerle (see Commentary to V.2.41). He is referred to at II.1.281, but the reference here is not likely to mean much to the audience.

   *the Abbot*: Of Westminster, who appears at the end of IV.1.

137  *consorted crew*: Conspiring gang (there were about a dozen altogether; see V.2.96–9).

138  *straight*: Immediately.

139  *powers*: Forces.

145  *old*: Unregenerate. She refers to his character thus far, which she wishes to be changed. In fact Aumerle did 'prove true'. He died heroically at the battle of Agincourt. Shakespeare describes his death in *Henry V*, IV.6.3–32.

   *old . . . I pray God make thee new*: The biblical 'Therefore if any man be in Christ he is a new creature; old things are passed away; behold, all things are become new' (2 Corinthians 5:17) had passed into proverbial use.

**V.4**

This scene is based on Holinshed: 'One writer which seemeth to have great knowledge of King Richard's doings saith that King Henry, sitting on a day at his table, sore sighing, said "Have I no faithful friend which will deliver me of him, whose life will be my death,

and whose death will be the preservation of my life?"
This saying was much noted of them which were
present, and especially of one called Sir Piers of Exton.
This knight incontinently departed from the court with
eight strong persons in his company, and came to
Pomfret . . .' Shakespeare's indebtedness to this episode
resumes at V.5.98.

o *Enter Sir Piers of Exton and a Man*: Q has no scene
   divisions, and its stage direction here is *Manet sir Pierce
   Exton, &c.* Exton may have been among the nobles on
   stage at the beginning of the previous scene, but it seems
   unlikely that he would remain throughout the inter-
   view with York and his family: see V.3.27: *Withdraw
   yourselves, and leave us here alone.*
   *Sir Piers of Exton*: Nothing is known of him except that
   he is said to have been the murderer of King Richard.
   *Man*: Servant. (Q has *Man* as the speech-prefix; F has
   *Enter Exton and Seruants*. Only one servant is necessary, but there may be others.)

2 *will*: Who will.

5 *urged it*: Insisted on it.

7 *wishtly*: The context makes it clear that this word means
   'intently' or 'significantly', but the exact form and
   meaning of the word are doubtful. It may be a variant
   form of 'wistly' (as it is printed in Q3–5 and F),
   meaning 'intently', or of 'whistly', meaning 'silently',
   or of the later dialectical 'wisht', meaning 'melancholy'.

11 *rid*: Get rid of.

**V.5**

   Most of the first part is invented. Later Shakespeare
   uses Holinshed; see Commentary to 98.

3 *for because*: Because.

5 *hammer it out*: Puzzle it out.

8 *generation*: Progeny, offspring.
   *still-breeding thoughts*: Thoughts which will continually
   produce other thoughts.

9 *this little world*: The prison; also perhaps his *little world*
   of man – itself a prison.

10 *In humours like the people of this world*: In their tempera-

ments like the people of this real world.

13 *scruples*: Doubts.

13–14 *do set the word itself* | *Against the word*: Set one passage of Scripture against another, contradictory one (the expression is also used at V.3.121).

14–17 *'Come, little ones'*; | *And then again,* | *'It is as hard to come as for a camel* | *To thread the postern of a small needle's eye'*: The texts referred to here come together in Matthew 19:14, 24, Mark 10:14, 25, and Luke 18:16, 25. The second presents difficulties of interpretation of which Shakespeare may have been aware. *Camel* may mean 'cable-rope' rather than the animal; and *needle* the entrance for pedestrians in a large city-gate. Shakespeare's *thread* and *postern* seem to hint at both possibilities.

17 *needle*: Pronounced 'neele' or 'neeld'.

20 *ribs*: Framework of the castle, as the ribs are of a man's chest.

21 *ragged*: Rugged.

25 *seely*: Simple-minded.

26–7 *refuge their shame* | *That*: Take shelter from their shame in the thought that.

33 *treasons*: The thought of them.

40–41 *With nothing shall be pleased till he be eased* | *With being nothing*: The first *nothing* may be part of a double negative: 'shall be pleased by anything till he has been granted the "ease" of death'; or it may mean the opposite: 'shall be pleased by having nothing (or losing everything) till . . .'.

41 *Music do I hear*: This may be either a statement or a question.

42 *Ha, ha*: An exclamation as he catches out the musician in a rhythmical error; not a laugh.

43 *time is broke, and no proportion kept*: The rhythm is faulty, and the correct note values are not observed.

46 *check*: Rebuke.

46–8 *disordered string . . . true time broke*: E. W. Naylor (*Shakespeare and Music*, 1931, p. 32) explains: 'The "disorder'd string" is himself, who has been playing

his part "out of time" ("disorder'd" simply means "out
of its place" – i.e. as we now say, "a bar wrong"), and
this has resulted in breaking the "concord" – i.e. the
harmony of the various parts which compose the state.'

46  *string*: Stringed instrument.

47  *my*: Emphatic.

48  *my true time broke*: The discord in my own affairs.

49  *waste*: Including the sense of 'cause to waste away'.

50  *numbering clock*: One on which the hours are numbered,
not an hourglass.

51–4  *My thoughts are minutes, and with sighs they jar | Their
watches on unto mine eyes, the outward watch | Whereto
my finger, like a dial's point, | Is pointing still in cleansing
them from tears*: This is a difficult passage. It may be
paraphrased: 'each of my sad thoughts is like a minute,
and the sighs that they cause impel the intervals of time
forward to my eyes, which are the point on the outer
edge of the watch to which my finger, like a hand on
a dial, continually points in wiping tears from them'.

58  *times*: Quarters and halves.

59  *posting*: Hastening.

60  *jack of the clock*: A small figure of a man which struck
the bell of a clock every quarter or every hour. The
general meaning is that for Bolingbroke time now passes
with joyful rapidity, while Richard languishes in prison,
counting the hours away.

62  *though it have holp madmen to their wits*: The idea that
music could help to restore sanity was accepted in
Shakespeare's day. He makes notable use of it in *King
Lear*, IV.7.25ff.

*have holp*: May have helped.

66  *strange brooch*: Rare jewel.

67–8  *royal . . . noble . . . groats*: These were all coins. A royal
was ten shillings, a noble six-and-eightpence, and a
groat fourpence. The difference between a royal and a
noble was thus ten groats. Richard is *The cheapest* of
those present; to call him royal is to price him ten groats
too high. A similar witticism is recorded of Queen
Elizabeth. An eighteenth-century anecdote about a

clergyman called John Blower runs: "Tis said that he never preached but one sermon in his life, which was before Queen Elizabeth; and that as he was going about to caress the Queen, he first said "My royal Queen", and a little after "My noble Queen". Upon which says the Queen "What, am I ten groats worse than I was?" At which words being baulked (for he was a man of modesty) he could not be prevailed with to preach any more, but he said he would always read the Homilies for the future; which accordingly he did' (from Thomas Hearne's 'A letter containing an Account of some Antiquities between Windsor and Oxford' in his edition of *The Itinerary of John Leland the Antiquary*, 1711).

67 *peer*: 'Lord' and 'equal'.

70 *sad dog*: Dismal fellow.

75 *sometimes*: Once.

76 *earned*: Grieved.

78 *roan*: Of mixed colour.

*Barbary*: An exceptionally good breed of horse, here also used as the name of a particular one.

80 *dressed*: Tended, groomed.

85 *jade*: Worthless horse.

*eat*: (Pronounced 'et') eaten.

86 *clapping*: Patting.

88 *pride must have a fall*: The proverb is biblical (Proverbs 16:18: 'Pride goeth before destruction; and an high mind before the fall').

94 *galled*: Made sore.

*jauncing*: Moving up and down (with the horse's motion).

*meat*: Food.

95 *Fellow, give place. Here is no longer stay*: The change to couplets heightens the tension.

98 *My lord, will't please you to fall to*: Here Shakespeare resumes the episode from Holinshed quoted in the preliminary note to V.4. Sir Piers, arrived at Pomfret, commanded 'the esquire that was accustomed to sew [serve] and take the assay before King Richard to do so no more, saying "Let him eat now, for he shall not

long eat." King Richard sat down to dinner and was served without courtesy or assay; whereupon much marvelling at the sudden change he demanded of the esquire why he did not his duty. "Sir," said he, "I am otherwise commanded by Sir Piers of Exton, which is newly come from King Henry." When King Richard heard that word he took the carving knife in his hand and strake the esquire on the head, saying "The devil take Henry of Lancaster and thee together." And with that word Sir Piers entered the chamber, well armed, with eight tall men likewise armed, every of them having a bill in his hand.

'King Richard, perceiving this, put the table from him, and, stepping to the foremost man, wrung the bill out of his hands and so valiantly defended himself that he slew four of those that thus came to assail him. Sir Piers being half dismayed herewith leapt into the chair where King Richard was wont to sit, while the other four persons fought with him and chased him about the chamber. And in conclusion, as King Richard traversed his ground from one side of the chamber to another, and coming by the chair where Sir Piers stood he was felled with a stroke of a poleaxe which Sir Piers gave him upon the head, and therewith rid him out of life, without giving him respite once to call to God for mercy of his past offences. It is said that Sir Piers of Exton, after he had thus slain him, wept right bitterly as one stricken with the prick of a guilty conscience for murdering him whom he had so long time obeyed as king.'

99 *Taste of it first, as thou art wont to do*: It was a customary precaution for the king's food to be tasted before he ate it.

105 *What means death in this rude assault*: This line has been variously explained. It may mean 'what does death mean by assaulting me so violently?' or *means* may be equivalent to 'meanest': 'What do you mean, death, by . . . ?' or 'What – do you [the murderers] mean death . . . ?' Or the line may be taken along with the next as an expression of the paradox that though death

apparently means to kill him, yet he is able to wrest a weapon from one of his attackers and kill him with it.

107 *room*: Place.

109 *staggers*: Causes to stagger.

*my person*: A last assertion of royalty.

111–12 *Mount, mount . . . to die*: C. E. Montague writes of F. R. Benson that, having uttered these lines 'much as any other man might utter them under the first shock of the imminence of death, he half rises from the ground with a brightened face and repeats the two last words with a sudden return of animation and interest, the eager spirit leaping up, with a last flicker before it goes quite out, to seize on this new "idea of" the death of the body'.

**v.6**

The material of the final scene is compressed from Holinshed. See Commentary to 30.

3 *Ciceter*: The town now known as Cirencester, spelt here as in the early editions. The name is still often pronounced like this, or as 'Cicester'.

7–8 *The next news is, I have to London sent | The heads of Salisbury, Spencer, Blunt, and Kent*: The reason is given in Holinshed: 'the heads of the chief conspirators were set on poles over London Bridge, to the terror of others'. The baldness of the couplet is not altogether happy. Dover Wilson says of it and the following one: 'Is not this the very accent of Quince himself? The immortal lines

The actors are at hand and by their show
You shall know all that you are like to know,

go on like rhyming stilts, and to the identical jog-trot in metre' (New Cambridge edition, Introduction, p. lxx).

8 *Salisbury, Spencer, Blunt*: Q has *Oxford, Salisbury, Blunt. Oxford* is historically wrong; he was not implicated in the plot against Henry. This may well have been Shakespeare's error, though it is sometimes blamed on the printer. But the fact that the statement is corrected

in F, which may transmit an alteration made or approved
by Shakespeare, justifies the emendation.

10 *At large discoursèd*: Related in full.

14 *Brocas and Sir Bennet Seely*: This is based on Holinshed:
'Many other that were privy to this conspiracy were
taken and put to death, some at Oxford, as Sir Thomas
Blunt, Sir Bennet Cilie, knight ... but Sir Leonard
Brokas and [others] ... were drawn, hanged, and
beheaded at London.'

15 *consorted*: Conspiring.

18 *wot*: Know.

19–21 *The grand conspirator ... to the grave*: Holinshed has:
'the Abbot of Westminster, in whose house the
conspiracy was begun, as is said, going between his
monastery and mansion, for thought fell into a sudden
palsy, and shortly after, without speech, ended his life'.

20 *clog*: Burden.

*sour*: Bitter.

*melancholy*: Thought of as a physical substance, black
bile, causing disease when present in excess.

22–9 *But here is Carlisle ... have I seen*: Holinshed has: 'The
Bishop of Carlisle was impeached, and condemned of
the same conspiracy; but the King of his merciful
clemency pardoned him of that offence, although he
died shortly after, more through fear than force of sickness, as some have written.'

23 *doom*: Judgement.

25 *reverent room*: Place of religious retirement (*reverent*,
worthy of respect).

26 *More than thou hast*: Perhaps 'bigger than you have',
that is, your prison cell.

*joy*: 'Enjoy', or 'add joy to'. Probably Bolingbroke is
(whether ironically or not) proposing to Carlisle the
pleasures of monastic retirement.

30 *Great King, within this coffin I present*: Shakespeare takes
up again Holinshed's episode of the murder of Richard:
'After he was thus dead, his body was embalmed and
cered and covered with lead, all save the face, to the
intent that all men might see him and perceive that he

was departed this life; for as the corpse was conveyed from Pomfret to London, in all the towns and places where those that had the conveyance of it did stay with it all night, they caused dirge to be sung in the evening, and mass of Requiem in the morning; and as well after the one service as the other, his face, discovered, was showed to all that coveted to behold it.' Holinshed records King Henry's presence at the solemn obsequies at St Paul's and Westminster.

38 *They love not poison that do poison need*: Recalling the proverbial expression 'A king loves the treason but hates the traitor'.

43 *With Cain*: Like Cain (who killed his own brother). Cf. I.1.104.

48 *incontinent*: Immediately.

49 *I'll make a voyage to the Holy Land*: Henry's intention of undertaking a crusade in expiation of his sin is several times referred to in *Henry IV, Parts I* and *II*.

51 *Grace*: Honour with your presence.

# Penguin Shakespeare

---

**CYMBELINE**
WILLIAM SHAKESPEARE

The King of Britain, enraged by his daughter's disobedience in
marrying against his wishes, banishes his new son-in-law. Having fled
to Rome, the exiled husband makes a foolish wager with a villain he
encounters there – gambling on the fidelity of his abandoned wife.
Combining courtly menace and horror, comedy and melodrama,
*Cymbeline* is a moving depiction of two young lovers driven apart by
deceit and self-doubt.

This book includes a general introduction to Shakespeare's life and the
Elizabethan theatre, a separate introduction to *Cymbeline*, a chronology
of his works, suggestions for further reading, an essay discussing
performance options on both stage and screen, and a commentary.

Edited with an introduction by John Pitcher

General Editor: Stanley Wells

---

# PENGUIN SHAKESPEARE

**JULIUS CAESAR**
WILLIAM SHAKESPEARE

When it seems that Julius Caesar may assume supreme power, a plot to destroy him is hatched by those determined to preserve the threatened republic. But the different motives of the conspirators soon become apparent when high principles clash with malice and political realism. As the nation plunges into bloody civil war, this taut drama explores the violent consequences of betrayal and murder.

This book includes a general introduction to Shakespeare's life and the Elizabethan theatre, a separate introduction to *Julius Caesar*, a chronology of his works, suggestions for further reading, an essay discussing performance options on both stage and screen, and a commentary.

Edited by Norman Sanders

With an introduction by Martin Wiggins

General editor: Stanley Wells

# PENGUIN SHAKESPEARE

**MACBETH**
WILLIAM SHAKESPEARE

Promised a golden future as ruler of Scotland by three sinister witches, Macbeth murders the king to ensure his ambitions come true. But he soon learns the meaning of terror – killing once, he must kill again and again, and the dead return to haunt him. A story of war, witchcraft and bloodshed, *Macbeth* also depicts the relationship between husbands and wives, and the risks they are prepared to take to achieve their desires.

This book includes a general introduction to Shakespeare's life and the Elizabethan theatre, a separate introduction to *Macbeth*, a chronology of his works, suggestions for further reading, an essay discussing performance options on both stage and screen, and a commentary.

Edited by George Hunter

With an introduction by Carol Rutter

General Editor: Stanley Wells

# PENGUIN SHAKESPEARE

**THE MERCHANT OF VENICE**
WILLIAM SHAKESPEARE

A noble but impoverished Venetian asks a friend, Antonio, for a loan to
impress an heiress. His friend agrees, but is forced to borrow the sum
from a cynical Jewish moneylender, Shylock, and signs a chilling
contract to honour the debt with a pound of his own flesh. A complex
and controversial comedy, *The Merchant of Venice* explores prejudice
and the true nature of justice.

This book includes a general introduction to Shakespeare's life and the
Elizabethan theatre, a separate introduction to *The Merchant of Venice*,
a chronology of his works, suggestions for further reading, an essay
discussing performance options on both stage and screen, and a
commentary.

Edited by W. Moelwyn Merchant

With an introduction by Peter Holland

General Editor: Stanley Wells

# Penguin Shakespeare

**OTHELLO**
WILLIAM SHAKESPEARE

A popular soldier and newly married man, Othello seems to be in an enviable position. And yet, when his supposed friend sows doubts in his mind about his wife's fidelity, he is gradually consumed by suspicion. In this powerful tragedy, innocence is corrupted and trust is eroded as every relationship is drawn into a tangled web of jealousies.

This book includes a general introduction to Shakespeare's life and the Elizabethan theatre, a separate introduction to *Othello*, a chronology of his works, suggestions for further reading, an essay discussing performance options on both stage and screen, and a commentary.

Edited by Kenneth Muir

With an introduction by Tom McAlindon

General Editor: Stanley Wells

# PENGUIN SHAKESPEARE

**ROMEO AND JULIET**
WILLIAM SHAKESPEARE

A young man and woman meet by chance and fall instantly in love. But their families are bitter enemies, and in order to be together the two lovers must be prepared to risk everything. Set in a city torn apart by feuds and gang warfare, *Romeo and Juliet* is a dazzling combination of passion and hatred, bawdy comedy and high tragedy.

This book includes a general introduction to Shakespeare's life and the Elizabethan theatre, a separate introduction to *Romeo and Juliet*, a chronology of his works, suggestions for further reading, an essay discussing performance options on both stage and screen, and a commentary.

Edited by T. J. B. Spencer

With an introduction by Adrian Poole

General Editor: Stanley Wells

# PENGUIN SHAKESPEARE

---

**TIMON OF ATHENS**
WILLIAM SHAKESPEARE

After squandering his wealth with prodigal generosity, a rich Athenian
gentleman finds himself deep in debt. Unshaken by the prospect of
bankruptcy, he is certain that the friends he has helped so often will
come to his aid. But when they learn his wealth is gone, he quickly
finds that their promises fall away to nothing in this tragic exploration
of power, greed, and loyalty betrayed.

This book includes a general introduction to Shakespeare's life and the
Elizabethan theatre, a separate introduction to *Timon of Athens*, a
chronology of his works, suggestions for further reading, an essay
discussing performance options on both stage and screen, and a
commentary.

Edited by G. R. Hibbard

With an introduction by Nicholas Walton

General Editor: Stanley Wells

# Penguin Shakespeare

---

**TWELFTH NIGHT**
WILLIAM SHAKESPEARE

Separated from her twin brother Sebastian after a shipwreck, Viola disguises herself as a boy to serve the Duke of Illyria. Wooing a countess on his behalf, she is stunned to find herself the object of his beloved's affections. With the arrival of Viola's brother, and a trick played upon the countess's steward, confusion reigns in this romantic comedy of mistaken identity.

This book includes a general introduction to Shakespeare's life and the Elizabethan theatre, a separate introduction to *Twelfth Night*, a chronology of his works, suggestions for further reading, an essay discussing performance options on both stage and screen, and a commentary.

Edited by M. M. Mahood

With an introduction by Michael Dobson

General Editor: Stanley Wells

# PENGUIN SHAKESPEARE

**THE WINTER'S TALE**
WILLIAM SHAKESPEARE

The jealous King of Sicily becomes convinced that his wife is carrying the child of his best friend. Imprisoned and put on trial, the Queen collapses when the King refuses to accept the divine confirmation of her innocence. The child is abandoned to die on the coast of Bohemia. But when she is found and raised by a shepherd, it seems redemption may be possible.

This book includes a general introduction to Shakespeare's life and the Elizabethan theatre, a separate introduction to *The Winter's Tale*, a chronology of his works, suggestions for further reading, an essay discussing performance options on both stage and screen by Paul Edmondson, and a commentary.

Edited by Ernest Schanzer

With an introduction by Russ McDonald

General Editor: Stanley Wells

# PENGUIN SHAKESPEARE

*All's Well That Ends Well*
*Antony and Cleopatra*
*As You Like It*
*The Comedy of Errors*
*Coriolanus*
*Cymbeline*
*Hamlet*
*Henry IV, Part I*
*Henry IV, Part II*
*Henry V*
*Henry VI, Part I*
*Henry VI, Part II*
*Henry VI, Part III*
*Henry VIII*
*Julius Caesar*
*King John*
*King Lear*
*Love's Labour's Lost*
*Macbeth*
*Measure for Measure*
*The Merchant of Venice*

*The Merry Wives of
    Windsor*
*A Midsummer Night's
    Dream*
*Much Ado About Nothing*
*Othello*
*Pericles*
*Richard II*
*Richard III*
*Romeo and Juliet*
*The Sonnets and A Lover's
    Complaint*
*The Taming of the Shrew*
*The Tempest*
*Timon of Athens*
*Titus Andronicus*
*Troilus and Cressida*
*Twelfth Night*
*The Two Gentlemen of
    Verona*
*The Two Noble Kinsmen*
*The Winter's Tale*